The Changing Language of Modern English Drama 1945–2005

The Changing Language of Modern English Drama 1945–2005

Kate Dorney

Victoria & Albert Museum, London, UK

First published 2009 by
PALGRAVE MACMILLAN

Palgrave Macmillan in the UK is an imprint of Macmillan Publishers Limited, registered in England, company number 785998, of Houndmills, Basingstoke, Hampshire RG21 6XS.

Palgrave Macmillan in the US is a division of St Martin's Press LLC, 175 Fifth Avenue, New York, NY 10010.

Palgrave Macmillan is the global academic imprint of the above companies and has companies and representatives throughout the world.

Palgrave® and Macmillan® are registered trademarks in the United States, the United Kingdom, Europe and other countries.

ISBN-13: 978–0–230–01329–2 hardback

This book is printed on paper suitable for recycling and made from fully managed and sustained forest sources. Logging, pulping and manufacturing processes are expected to conform to the environmental regulations of the country of origin.

A catalogue record for this book is available from the British Library.

A catalog record for this book is available from the Library of Congress.

10 9 8 7 6 5 4 3 2 1
18 17 16 15 14 13 12 11 10 09

Printed and bound in Great Britain by
CPI Antony Rowe, Chippenham and Eastbourne

For Richard and Frances

Contents

Acknowledgements

This book would not have been written without the continued encouragement of my friends and family, particularly Frances Gray and Ros Merkin. I also owe a huge debt of gratitude to all colleagues past and present at the universities of Sheffield and Liverpool John Moores and at the British Library and the Victoria & Albert Museum. I also benefited enormously from the insights of the members of the Poetics and Linguistics Association and the historiography working group of the Theatre and Performance Research Association.

Introduction

This book aims to provide an account of language and drama between 1945 and 2005 which synthesises linguistic and dramatic knowledge in order to illuminate the ways in which attitudes to language have affected the practice and criticism of theatre. Examining contemporary developments in linguistics and folk-linguistics alongside plays, criticism and theatre writing from 1945 to 2005 the book seeks to account for the discourses within which language in drama is debated and described as well as analysing and interpreting the language used in relation to immediate social, cultural and theatrical contexts.[1]

The post-war period represents a concerted and sizeable body of commentary about language in the theatre, encompassing disapproval on a range of linguistic sore points, from Noel Coward's use of slang, the *ennui* of Absurdism, through to the verbal (as well as physical) shocks delivered by 'in-yer-face' theatre and the experiments in verbatim drama, via many other expressions of concern about 'deviant' language usage. This period also marks a number of decisive events in Britain's social, political and cultural history: the end of the Second World War; the introduction of subsidy and then wholly subsidised theatres; the abolition of stage censorship; the move towards a free-market capitalism which suppressed oppositional theatre in the mainstream by simply cutting subsidy, through to the commercialisation and the 'renaissance' of British theatre in the nineties and noughties. In terms of the linguistic study of verbal interaction, this period sees, among other things, the quest to describe language-in-use, rather than studying an idealised version, immeasurably advanced by the development of portable tape recorders (for recording samples of 'real' speech) and the gathering of a corpus of spoken language. It sees the end of formal grammar teaching in England and Wales in the 1960s and its reintroduction in the 1990s and the territorial disputes which ensued. It also sees the development of methods and theories which challenged the 'deficit' models of language and the conduit metaphor of communication in the work of Basil Bernstein and William Labov in the 1950s and 1960s through to James and Lesley Milroy, Tony Crowley and Deborah Cameron in the 1980s and Critical Discourse Analysis and discourse stylistics in the 1990s. Most significantly, the post-war period is one in which non-standard language takes centre stage in British theatre, although by the end of the 1990s it has been absorbed into the norm, anxiety giving way to acceptance and language minding moving onto other facets of language use.

'Minding language/minding about language'

Describing language about language is tricky: all language users can claim a degree of expertise in its use and proprietary feelings about its development and use by others. In the case of the English language, there is a vast body of literature devoted to the topic, ranging from manuals of usage, laments for a lost golden age and impassioned pleas to ride to the rescue of a language in imminent danger from the Barbarian hordes. The phrase I have chosen to describe these activities is 'minding language': a reference to the multiple meanings of 'minding' which acknowledges the sense of 'guarding', as well as to 'objecting to'. Among the usages the *OED* gives for 'mind' are:

> to 'record'; 'admonish, exhort'; 'speak of'; '*imper.* imply advice or warning'; 'attend to, concern oneself with, care for'; 'value'; 'take care; be careful'; 'concern oneself with'; and 'give heed to; notice' and 'to be wary concerning, be on one's guard against, look out for'; along with formulations such as 'do you mind!' which encapsulates the indignation which often fuels objections to 'marked' language.
>
> (*Oxford English Dictionary*)

Following on from this, 'minding' is the activity which results from recording, taking care of, concerning oneself with, taking notice of, objecting to and guarding language in various ways (e.g., by objecting to split infinitives, bemoaning the standards of spelling among secondary school children, and/or deploring 'txt' language). In this respect my work has been heavily informed by Deborah Cameron's *Verbal Hygiene* (1995), discussed at length in the first two chapters of the present work. I have chosen to use 'language minding' rather than 'verbal hygiene' because I wanted to avoid the connotations of 'cleaning up' language inherent in the phrase. This is not always the main preoccupation of the writers, critics and audience members discussed in this book: in drama, the debate is as often about 'dirtying' language so it reflects reality in a more satisfactory way. Indeed, in many cases, the writers and (some) commentators discussed here are from the 'lost generation' of formal grammar teaching (1965–1990) (as I am), and as such, lack the older generations' concern with split-infinitives, dangling participles and 'ungrammatical' speech.

Language minding: Three elements

The chief concern for the language minders examined here is that language and language use are in a terminal state of decay and decline. This concern has three parts to it. The first is that language is no longer elevated enough to allow 'true expression'. Second, language is insufficiently expressive, having descended into a series of meaningless platitudes and clichés (as, for example, George Steiner argues in *Language and Silence* (1969), *After Babel* (1976) and *Extra-Territorial* (1972)). Third, language use has become too informal, leading to sloppy speech and sloppy thinking (as, for example, Henry Newbolt suggests in *The Teaching of English in England* (1926), George Orwell argues in 'Politics and the English Language' (1946) and John Honey asserts in *The Language Trap* and *Does Accent Matter?*). Most language minding is a mixture of some, or all, of the three elements, and all three elements are examined at length in this work, both in the two chapters which form the theoretical framework and in the chapters which examine these minding strategies at work in the theatre in the period 1945–2005. These anxieties are as old as language itself, and are not exclusive to drama, but, as discussed later in this Introduction, dramatic language occupies a singular role because of its unstable position between speech and writing. Post-war British drama blurs the boundary between speech and writing even further in its attempts to truly represent 'life-like' speech and provokes a specific variety of language minding because of this. The rise of non-Standard English accents in previously (Received Pronunciation) RP-only enclaves (broadcasters, actors, MPs and government ministers) is reflected in the drama of this period, much to the consternation of language minders in and outside the theatre. The language minders discussed here range from theatre critics, theatre workers and academics to writers such as George Orwell, George Steiner, Richard Hoggart, Raymond Williams and F.R. Leavis.

Language minders: Two camps

Post-war dramatic language minders fall into roughly two camps: those who like their language 'standard', in some or all senses of the word, and those who desire a more 'reliable' representation of verbal interaction, or a more 'authentic' realisation of how the 'other half' – that is, the non-standard – live and speak. By 'standard' I mean written and spoken in the Standard English dialect, with or without an RP accent (on the whole 'with', up until the late 1950s), and displaying the expected degree of fluency that characterised most theatrical dialogue from the Greeks more or less to the present day. 'Authentic' is a more troublesome and nebulous concept, but should generally be taken to mean language that more closely reflects the way people actually talk to each other in real life. Theoretically, this means it can be written and spoken in any accent, using any dialect (including Standard English and Received Pronunciation); in practice, it is often only recognised as 'authentic' by its deviation from the standard outlined above. Throughout this book I use the term 'life-like' to describe this form, as 'authentic' is too closely connected to the idea of 'true', which in turn is a misleading way of characterising fictional language, let alone naturally occurring speech. In very simple terms then, certain reviewers, critics, actors and playwrights (and members of their audiences) minded very much when the monopoly of language on stage moved from the well-polished riposte, the passionate but articulate declaration of love, hatred and religious devotion (embodied as fully by New Wave hero Jimmy Porter as by Portia), and even witty repartee, to encompass the phatic communion of Beckett's double acts, Wesker's National Servicemen, David Storey's rugby players and Ravenhill's shoppers and fuckers. The book examines the attitudes evinced by these minders and seeks to situate their objections and anxieties within a larger framework encompassing linguistic scholarship as well as the socio-cultural contexts of British theatre at the time.

These objections and anxieties are culled from critical books about drama during this period (both contemporary and retrospective) and from reviews and articles published at the time of first performance. In *British Realist Theatre* (1995) Stephen Lacey summarises the value of contemporary reviews as follows: 'reviews suggest something of the dominant assumptions about what passes as a play in a given period, about what is considered good/bad/serious/original' (Lacey 1995, 6). For my purposes, reviews not only give a picture of what passes for a play in a particular period, they also provide a glimpse of the dominant assumptions about language in general, and by extension, about language in drama. The reviews and contemporary comment have been drawn from collected reviews of the period, based on the assumption that reviews enshrined in books further distill the essence of the dominant assumptions about language and drama at the time, as well as from the production files in the V&A's Theatre and Performance archives and *Theatre Record*, which are far more comprehensive in scope. The collected reviews of Hobson, Tynan, Morley and Billington have been illuminating – as often for the times when language goes unmentioned in plays where the language seems worthy of comment, as when comment is passed – even if they are infrequently quoted. In particular, John Elsom's *Post-war British Theatre Criticism* (1981) has been invaluable, providing a record of which plays were considered to be 'in their different ways, important in their contribution to the development of British theatre' more than 20 years ago, as well as the contemporary reactions of the critics at the time (Elsom 1981). Additionally, I draw on interviews with a range of theatre practitioners and audience members, some conducted by me, and others archived at the V&A and the British Library.

In aiming to provide an alternative way of interpreting language in the theatre of this period I have drawn on a range of linguistic scholarship. The study of language and ideology, language and philosophy, stylistics and discourse analysis, and many other aspects of applied linguistics have informed this work and I am conscious of having 'subverted' the original goals of many of the studies used here. As Ronald Carter notes:

> The context in which language use is studied should be a *real* one, according to discourse analysts. By real is meant that the examples studied should be genuine samples of actual data collected by or provided for the analyst rather than made up by analysts in the artificial environment of their own armchairs with normally only their intuitions to verify whether the example is real or not.
>
> (Carter 1997, xiii)

'Made up in their own armchairs' is, of course, a pretty accurate description of how much dramatic dialogue is arrived at. What I hope to demonstrate here is that studying the way in which these 'made-up' examples of natural speech developed and evolved in post-war British theatre is another way of reflecting wider preoccupations with language as a social marker, as an educational and cultural instrument and as a revolutionary tool. Thus far, linguistic research into dramatic dialogue has been done primarily in the field of stylistics. The focus tends to be on showing how closely dramatic language mirrors natural speech (and as such, is a useful tool for teaching people about how natural speech works), or for showing how certain types of drama work by revealing the power structures implicit in the speech of the characters. Susan Mandala's *Twentieth Century Drama Dialogue as Ordinary Talk* (2007) and Keith Sanger's *The Language of Drama* (2001) are examples of the former; Paul Simpson's 'Politeness Phenomena in Ionesco's *The Lesson*' (1989) is an illuminating example of the latter. This work is useful and has done much to shift the emphasis from describing dramatic language either in impressionistic terms, or not at all, but in order to understand on a deeper level why characters are speaking in a certain way, and why they were stigmatised for doing so, this stylistic work must be supplemented with an understanding of theatrical contexts and of the implications of language, power and ideology.

The cast and the structure

It is inevitable that Harold Pinter and Samuel Beckett loom large in a discussion about language and drama in the post-war period, but I have tried to use them as reference points rather than offer further analysis of their work. My research in this area was originally motivated by a desire to redress both the pessimistic attitude to language and communication expressed by drama critics and reviewers of Beckett and Pinter's work, and to add a depth of dramatic understanding to stylistic accounts of their work.[2] Pinter's work is usually discussed in terms of inadequacy, but also lauded as the most 'life-like', and this schizophrenic critical reception is, in many ways, a model and inspiration for this book. Simultaneously praised and damned for his use of language by contemporary critics, Pinter's style has become the template against which many other dramatic attempts to portray ordinary conversation 'realistically' have been measured. Ideas of linguistic inadequacy and communication failure form an important part of dramatic language minding: as far back as 1962, when Pinter's career as a playwright was still in its infancy, he observed that the 'tired, grimy phrase: "Failure of communication" [...] has been fixed to my work quite consistently', and it has remained fixed ever since (Pinter 1990, xiii). Chapter 1 traces the way in which concerns about language, structure and agency feed into ideas of linguistic 'correctness' and the ideological implications of evaluating language against a 'standard' model. This too can be seen reflected in criticisms of Pinter's work, in particular, observations about 'inarticulate' characters in his early plays (*The Birthday Party, The Room, The Dumb Waiter, The Caretaker* and *The Homecoming*), and the denigration of non-standard language. Chapter 2 examines the way in which these linguistic preoccupations manifest themselves in the theatre, exploring different expressions of this through a series of examples drawn from Beckett, Pinter and Stoppard (among others), and includes a re-reading of Beckett's work which reveals that its underlying structure is as close to 'normal' conversation as Pinter's, rather than a portrait of language in its death throes (a more common perception of Beckett's language in which his *oeuvre* is seen as a chronicle of the inadequacy of language). Chapters 3 to 7 turn to the social, historical and cultural contexts of post-war English theatre from 1945 up until 2000 and relate attitudes to language in these periods with the over-arching concerns of language minders and the plays of the time. Given the chronological and thematic scope under discussion here, the plays, playwrights, directors and critics discussed have been selected on the grounds of their ability to generate linguistic column inches, but I hope that they also offer a representative snapshot of each theatre episteme, albeit with a more specific slant than other surveys of British/English drama. The title refers to English drama to acknowledge the fact that there is no discussion of Scottish or Welsh writers and theatre practices in the book, and they have very different and very specific histories which cannot be encompassed in the space of this volume.

The problematic nature of dramatic speech (i)

i.   What is 'ordinary' language?

Perhaps the most problematic aspect of dramatic speech is finding a satisfactory set of terms in which to describe it. I'm seeking to engage with the forms of dramatic language that are closest to 'ordinary', everyday language, to the kind of language one might hear on the bus, or in the supermarket, rather than rhetoric, or well-made prose. As a result, this work centres on conversation rather than soliloquy, and on dialogue rather than monologue. Linguists have a number of terms for describing this type of conversation: 'naturally occurring', 'spontaneous', 'informal', 'unplanned', but all these terms rely on the understanding that the conversation is not planned and is 'genuine', that is, not scripted for the hearer's benefit. Conversation within a play cannot meet any of these requirements, and so, in order to avoid unwieldy pre- or post-modification of these terms (e.g., 'fictional attempt at naturally occurring conversation'), it seems wiser not to apply them to dramatic dialogue, particularly as Chapters 1 and 2 discuss 'naturally occurring' conversation in some detail. Instead, I will refer to this style of language as 'lifelike-ese', reflecting the fact that such language mimics the structures which underlie 'naturally occurring conversation', such as hesitation, not speaking in full 'sentences' and engaging in conversational repair. Lifelike-ese reflects the fact that, like 'journalese' and (the once popular) 'motherese', it is a contextually specific form of language designed for a specific purpose. 'Lifelike' keeps the connotations of realistic, normal and naturalistic without adding to confusion over the pejorative connotations of 'normalising' and the terminological confusion surrounding Realism and Naturalism (see below).

One does not, as a general rule, overhear many verse conversations, or conversations in invented poetic languages on the bus, or in the supermarket, which puts verse and invented language beyond the scope of the present work. However, comparisons between such language and the conversational style on which I focus are discussed in the next chapter as part of the exploration of how the myth of the 'lacking word' is reproduced in drama criticism of the 1970s.

ii. Naturalism and Realism

The naturalist/realist minefield is not easily negotiated: 'Naturalistic', 'realistic', 'slice of life' and 'fourth-wall' are all terms used to describe attempts in the theatre to reflect life. Both Naturalism and Realism have their origins in a revolt against the declamatory acting style and well-made play structure of the 19th century, and, as the two terms are often used interchangeably, the difference between them is hard to discern. For this reason I follow the particular author's pattern of usage, and observe their distinction between the two or lack thereof; thus where critics used the terms interchangeably I have not attempted to distinguish different meanings. In so far as it is possible to make (if not maintain) a distinction, Naturalism attempts to reflect the psychological processes and societal pressures of an individual in a particular situation, while Realism endeavours to reflect reality in setting, acting style, speech and situation. Styan (1981) suggests that Naturalistic playwrights were 'committed to presenting a specifically angled view of real life', while a Realist playwright 'tried to put on the stage only what he could verify by observing ordinary life', and thus displayed emotion took precedence over feelings (Styan 1981, 5, 6). In respect of the language examined here

Realism and Naturalism are no more useful, taken in isolation, than the linguistic terms discussed above in section (i) above; Beckett is neither a Naturalist nor a Realist, but, as I discuss in Chapters 1 and 4, the language of his characters is recognisably 'lifelike-ese'. What is useful for this discussion is the way in which both terms (Naturalism and Realism) are contingent on the reaction of the audience. As Styan notes:

> It is axiomatic that each generation feels that its theatre is in some way more 'real' than the last – Euripides over Sophocles, Moliere over the *commedia dell'arte*. Goldsmith over Steele, Ibsen over Schiller, Brecht over Ibsen. The claims seem to echo one and other. It is, of course, the conception of dramatic reality which changes, and realism must finally be evaluated, not by the style of a play, or a performance, but by the image of truth its audience perceives.
>
> (Styan 1981, 1)

What is true of Realism is also true of Naturalism and lifelike-ese: what was once regarded as the closest approximation soon appears dated and contrived. In the time span of this study, Coward moves from being contemporary to a subject of parody, as do Rattigan and Osborne, yet each, in their time, was hailed for their 'realistic' ear. This perpetual state of evolution also draws attention to another key facet of Realism and Naturalism: a desire to engage with contemporary issues. Gareth Lloyd Evans (1977) and Stephen Lacey (1995) testify to the importance of this in both naturalism and realism respectively. Evans describes the post-1956 generation as purveyors of the 'new naturalism', echoing Styan's point that each generation reinterprets conventions in the light of their own experiences:

> Those who had found their naturalism heretofore in iambic pentameter, in the custom built obsolescences of 'well-made' language, in the new orotundities of measured prose, were now faced with a 'new' species of dramatic actuality – drawn, as the so frequent phrase had it, 'from life itself'.
>
> (Evans 1977, 85)

Evans's observation here raises a key point about attitudes to language change in general, and to language change in drama in particular: just as there were language minders who perceived new developments in dramatic language as a process of decay, there were also language minders who perceived developments like the 'new' naturalism as a sign of progress. Evans notes that it claimed to be 'nearer to what: most people experience (though of course, patterned, selected and designed) than most drama that had ever been written in theatrical history' (Evans 1977, 85). Lacey (1995) concurs, but suggests that the new dramatists rejected naturalism in favour of a realist style in which engagement with reality was more important than surface approximation:

> In the post-war context, naturalism was, in one sense, simply a short-hand for the practices of the pre-1956 theatre, the chosen form of the directors, dramatists and critics associated with it. To reject 'naturalism' was to reject the creaky plots, artificially manipulated climaxes, the box-sets and lack of 'theatricality' that scarred the old theatre in the eyes of the new. There are social as well as formal characteristics at play here; the assault on 'Loamshire' was an assault on the social basis of the dominant genres. In this way naturalism was a term that focused the problems of an inherited tradition, and the assault on it was connected to the attempt to alter a theatre culture that was perceived to be institutionally and socially, as well as aesthetically, irrelevant.
>
> (Lacey 1995, 100)

Lacey offers an interesting account of the way in which Naturalism and Realism were interpreted post-war, drawing on the work of Raymond Williams, Stuart Hall, Charles Marowitz and others to articulate the way in which the two terms were perceived and defined. Perhaps most usefully for my purposes, he includes Bond, Pinter and Beckett in this discussion, reinforcing once again the point that a play need not have a naturalistic plot to have realistic language.

Studying the language of drama: A brief history

Prior to the 1980s there was very little research undertaken specifically on language in drama. Instead, traditional 'literary' accounts of dramatic language in the 20th century tended to describe language in impressionistic terms (e.g., Brown 1972, Kennedy 1975). Stylistic accounts of language from the theatre of this period tend to concentrate on drawing attention to the way in which verbal interaction in plays is drawn (consciously or not) from knowledge and experience about how people speak in 'real life'. From the 1980s onwards 'linguistic' accounts addressed this problem, stylistic research revealing how meaning is made by reminding us of the unconscious linguistic competence which allows us to derive significance from what may appear to be, at worst nonsense and at best, gibberish, whether this is the oft-quoted 'what time is it?', 'well the milkman's been', or a series of punning advertisements. What is largely missing from stylistic accounts is the synthesis of how dramatic language replicates the pattern of everyday language to a greater or lesser extent, and the historical and cultural context of the plays from which these examples are drawn. In this study I hope to strike a balance between theatrical contexts and linguistic specificity, and, most importantly, to approach both from an informed critical context which will reveal the ideological assumptions that reinforce and perpetuate ideas about language that circulate in the discourses around post-war drama.

i.   Genre trouble: Drama and literature

Stylistic investigations of drama have located the tendency in earlier criticism to discuss drama in impressionistic terms as symptomatic of the failure to recognise the unique status of drama and dramatic language, which had led to its being lumped in with 'literature' and all the connotations of 'literary' that accompany it. Herman (1995) notes that:

> Studies of dramatic dialogue as discourse – as a speech exchange system – are hardly in evidence, even in the investigations of the language of drama. The thrust of the argument has generally been to safeguard the separation of dramatic dialogue from conversation in order to preserve the latter's 'literary' quality.[3]
>
> (Herman 1995, 3)

Culpeper, Short and Verdonk (1998) concur, suggesting that the relative lack of secondary dramatic material:

> may lie in the fact that spoken conversation has for many centuries been commonly seen as a debased and unstable form of language, and thus plays, with all their affinities with speech, were liable to be undervalued.[4] For some literary critics, Shakespeare and some other Elizabethan playwrights were reprieved by the fact that their plays were written in verse. In fact, within the literary-critical movements of New Criticism in the USA and practical criticism in Britain, which dominated the criticism of the mid-twentieth century, such plays were treated as 'dramatic poems'. By denying these plays their status

as 'spoken conversation to be performed', they were considered stable texts worthy of close analysis.

(Culpeper, Short and Verdonk 1998, 3)

I would suggest that the study of Shakespearean and Elizabethan plays as dramatic poems has also had an impact on the way modern drama is studied, and assessed. The hyper-articulate, poetic speech of characters in Elizabethan and Jacobean drama contrasts markedly with the style of much (though not all) modern dramatic dialogue. The Shavian legacy, for all its assertions of realism, barely deviates from this model, and, as discussed in Chapter 6, a great deal of post-war British drama continues to prefer articulacy over realism as a means of conveying messages to its audiences. Indeed, Shaw was candid about the fact that he prioritised the message and the style over realism, giving the following note to Ralph Richardson who was playing Bluntschli in *Arms and the Man* and going to great trouble to emphasise the physical effect of having been chased through the streets and sought refuge on Irina's balcony:

> When you come in you're very upset, you spend a long time with your gasps and pauses and your lack of breath and your dizziness and your tiredness; it's very well done, it's very well done indeed, but it doesn't suit my play. It's no good for me, it's no good for Bernard Shaw. You've got to go from line to line, quickly and swiftly, never stop the flow of the lines, never stop. It's one joke after another, it's a firecracker. *Always reserve the acting for underneath the spoken word.* It's a musical play, a knockabout musical comedy.
>
> (Miller 1995, 41, my emphasis)

In discussing pre-19th-century drama as if it were poetry many of the functions of the language are inevitably overlooked or misconstrued, and critical discussions then become concerned with unpacking meaning, discussing the different meanings and the connotations of certain words in their contemporary context and explaining how effects are achieved, rather than examining language as interaction. Modern drama is not very usefully studied by applying the same criteria; there is little or no need to explain what the words mean and very little 'poetry' to be discussed, and as a consequence the linguistic aspects of modern drama tend to be overlooked. Language that does not differ from the norm in some way tends to be regarded as transparent, or at least as unworthy of comment, and although stylistics has gone some way to redress this tendency at the language/literature interface, it is still generally the case that transparency is assumed to be the natural state of language. Although this notion of transparency has been challenged in certain areas of language study these challenges have been slow to filter into mainstream consciousness. Consequently unremarkable language goes unremarked upon.

ii.   Drama and literary criticism

One of the consequences of the historic idea of drama and literature as superior means of expressing feelings and emotions is that any drama and literature which does not fulfil this function fluently tends to be regarded either as a failure, or as an attempt to show the failure of communication and/or language. Influential literary critic George Steiner is particularly exercised by this failure (which has its roots, in part, in philosophical studies of language). First, he expounds the notion of a 'retreat from the word', the idea that disciplines that traditionally articulated their propositions and investigations in finely honed prose are turning to science and mathematics. Among the subjects he lists are history ('scarcely literate'), economics ('moving from the linguistic to the mathematical, from rhetoric to equation') and sociology ('illiterate, or more precisely, anti-literate') (Steiner 1969, 38, 39). He locates the beginning of this 'retreat' at the beginning of the 17th century with the formulation of:

> analytic geometry and the theory of algebraic functions, with the development by Newton and Leibniz of calculus, mathematics ceases to be a dependant notation, an instrument of the empirical. It becomes a fantastically rich, complex and dynamic language.
>
> (Steiner 1969, 33)

Where the retreat from the word is most pronounced, however, is in philosophy. He offers a somewhat simplistic account of how symbolic logic and its project of 'tidying-up' language and freeing it from ambiguity have made a lasting and decisive contribution to loss of faith/dependence on language. Interestingly, Steiner names Sartre as one of the few who have noticed the inexorable journey towards silence: 'Few humanists are aware of the scope and nature of this great change (Sartre is a notable exception and has, time and time again, drawn attention to *la crise du langage*)', despite the fact that in many critical accounts (including some of Steiner's own), the twin approaches of Existentialism and Absurdism have been repeatedly mentioned as synonymous with propelling language into its final death throes (1969, 36).[5]

The second of Steiner's concerns about language is that of the 'lacking word', outlined in 'Word Against Object' in *After Babel* (1976). This suggests that there was a time when language perfectly articulated our every thought and feeling, expressing the uniqueness of that feeling to us in its very formulation, and that it no longer does.[6] It has become a short-hand, a cliché, for us to say, 'I just can't describe how awful/wonderful it was', 'I don't know what to say', etc, and, as Steiner points out, it has become an equally potent literary myth:

> Those seas in our personal existence in which we are 'the first that ever burst' are never silent, but loud with commonplaces.

> The concept of the 'lacking word' marks modern literature. The principal division of the history of Western literature occurs between the early 1870s and the turn of the century. It divides a literature essentially housed in language from one for which language has become a prison.
>
> (Steiner 1976, 176)

He discusses a number of ways in which philosophers and writers have sought to compensate for, or override, the 'commonplace' nature of the language at our disposal. He reviews the question of 'private' language'; of attempts at building new languages like Esperanto; the anarchy of Dada and the decision taken to lapse into silence. Eventually he locates dissatisfaction with language as it stands, and the failure of attempts to introduce a more structured language of logic, in the (in his opinion) mistaken belief that language is primarily concerned with communication:

> Scarcely anything in speech is what it means. Thus it is inaccurate and theoretically spurious to schematise language as 'information' or to identify language, be it unspoken or vocalised; with 'communication'. The latter term will only serve if it includes, if it places emphasis on, what is *not* said in the saying, what is said only partially, allusively or with intent to screen. Human speech conceals far more than it confides; it blurs much more than it defines; it distances more than it connects.
>
> (Steiner 1976, 239)

The assumption Steiner seems to be making here is that 'communication' does not take account of 'what is not said in the saying'. His reasons for doing so are unclear: it may be 'spurious' to schematise language as communication, but it is a common assumption, and one which certain branches of linguistics have worked on very successfully in order to take account of 'what is not said in the saying'. Pragmatics is a case in point, as is anthropological linguistics. This is a classic example of language minding, extrapolating ideas from several different fields, meshing it with impressionistic accounts and presenting it as a new theory of the problem of language. As with all other aspects of language minding, however, the fact that Steiner is theorising without all the linguistic knowledge should not distract us from the force and effectiveness of his argument. Surveying non-linguistic research on drama which dwells on language in any depth, it becomes clear how pervasive these ideas are. Looking at the work of Bradbrook (1972), Evans (1977), Kennedy (1975), Kane (1984), Russell Taylor (1963) and Russell Brown (1968) it is easy to get the impression that the representation of 'communication failure' is a central feature of the theatre of the period. The phrase 'communication failure' and its collocates are dotted throughout accounts of post-war British theatre and reviews of the plays which constitute it. From Samuel Beckett through to Michael Frayn's *Copenhagen* (1998), described in Ascherson's article in the *The Observer* as demonstrating 'how the language of nuclear physics can convey the agony of human beings failing to communicate', failure to communicate has become a catch-all phrase to describe anything from representations of naturally occurring informal conversation through to Lucky's speech in *Waiting for Godot* (Ascherson 2003, 6). For the most part, the idea of 'failure to communicate' is so widely and unquestioningly accepted that it has become commonplace to describe certain playwrights or types of plays almost exclusively in these terms particularly, Beckett, Ionesco and Pinter, and the entire genre of 'Absurd' plays. The myth is not only pervasive, it is attractive, and, interestingly, it tended to be applied to writers and plays whose work was closer to lifelike-ese than the playwrights of the well-made school.

iii.   Drama and stylistics

The first major stylistic study of dramatic language was Deirdre Burton's *Dialogue and Discourse: A Sociolinguistic Approach to Modern Drama Dialogue and Naturally Occurring Conversation* (1980), written, as Burton points out, because there was no scholarship in the area at all (Burton

1980, 3–4). Quoting Abercrombie (1959) she suggests that there was a bipartite, rather than tripartite, distinction in operation that glossed over the problematic status of dramatic speech, relegating verse drama to poetry, and non-verse drama to 'spoken prose':

> Most people believe that *spoken prose*, as I would call what we normally hear on the stage or screen, is at least not far removed, when well done, from the conversation of real life. [...]
>
> But the truth is that nobody speaks at all like the characters in any novel, play, or film. Life would be intolerable if they did; and novels, plays or films would be intolerable if the characters spoke as people do in life. Spoken prose is far more different from conversation than is normally realised.
>
> (Abercrombie, quoted in Burton 1980, 3–4)

The texts Burton takes for analysis – Pinter's *Last to Go* and *The Dumb Waiter* and Ionesco's *The Bald Prima Donna* – are key examples of the type of drama that provokes criticism about 'failure to communicate'. By taking 'problematic' texts, Burton is able to demonstrate how stylistic analysis enables us to comment usefully on stretches of dialogue that have little apparent content or function. In the introduction, she states that her intention is to show: 'how recent advances in the sociolinguistic description of spoken discourse, or conversational analysis, can be drawn upon to account for reader and audience intuitions about the dialogue in [...] texts' (Burton 1980, ix). Her work is extremely useful in terms of explaining the underlying structure of seemingly random speech, and demonstrating what we are able to infer from it, but her textual analysis adds little to our understanding of the plays. As she observes on several occasions, most audiences, readers and addressees are fairly accomplished at interpreting nuances in conversation, yet she never really addresses herself to this aspect of the plays she analyses. In her discussion of *Last to Go*, for example, she offers coherent accounts of the conversational maxims, implicature, Labov's observations on shared knowledge and the information about status and territory that can be derived from an examination of phatic exchanges; but these explanations do not give us any more information about the interaction of the participants in the text. Similarly, in her discussion of *The Bald Prima Donna*, she devotes a lot of space to explain that it is parody of 'fourth wall', 'naturalist' drama, almost as if she does not realise an audience's capacity for interpreting implicature. For example:

> It is an important issue for any theatre audience to decide whether this sort of writing is 'badly written plot exposition' or a parody of that sort of writing, and a foregrounding of constraints on writers in certain genres. The extremely blatant nature of the bad writing makes it likely that we are hearing or reading the latter.
>
> (Burton 1980, 31)

Burton fails to take account of the fact that even if the audience, or certain members of the audience, were unable to recognise parody at this stage in the play, we do not watch or read in a vacuum. For members of a theatre audience there will be other areas they can gather clues from: previews, newspaper reviews, programme notes and word-of-mouth reports; for readers of the play text, there are introductions, blurbs on the back of the book and experience of other parodies and conventional 'fourth wall' drama. All these elements interplay in our efforts at interpretation, both in spontaneous conversation and in our reception of texts and performances. Since Burton's work appeared, however, stylistic analysis has become much more adept at successfully meshing textual analysis with explication of linguistic phenomena, as more recent works in the field attest, including Burton's own subsequent research. In a later piece of work, 'Through Glass Darkly, Through Dark Glasses', she asserts:

> There is no space here to rehearse the relevant arguments in the philosophy of science [...] but I take it as axiomatic that *all* observation, let alone description, *must* take place within an already constructed theoretical framework of socially, ideologically and linguistically constructed reality whether the observer/describer is articulately aware of that framework or not.
>
> (Burton in Carter 1982, 196)

Burton's point here is a crucial one, particularly in the context of my own argument; the evaluative, intuitive nature of early language-centred criticism of post-war drama makes it very tempting to present stylistic interpretations of dramatic dialogue as the last word in objective, 'rigorous' analysis. By using our knowledge and experience of how language is used, and how we interpret language, we are able to explain how we come to have these 'intuitions', rather than merely attributing it to some sort of literary 'sensitivity', yet we must remain aware that these are still only an interpretation rather than a definitive account. Carter and Simpson (1989) reiterate this point, bearing out the strength of the traditional 'literary' or 'linguistic' approach, even in a hybrid discipline like stylistics:

> The general aims and techniques of literary stylistics remain closely associated with those of practical or New Criticism. In spite of the aforementioned sociolinguistic trends, most literary-stylistic analysis still sees referential, text-immanent language as a primary constituent of the text and as a locus for author-initiated effects and responses to those effects. The existence of an extra-textual world of social, political, psychological, or historical forces is often discounted as being beyond the analytical remit of stylistics. Such forces are also felt to have little influence on the language of the texts as 'language artefacts' which have survived historical change and whose only relevant context is a linguistic one.
>
> (Carter and Simpson 1989, 7)

In *The Real Inspector Hound* (1968) the effect of Stoppard's extraordinarily loquacious characters is to demonstrate the plot devices of a conventional 'whodunnit' by parodying them. At each strategic moment in the play-within-a-play, a character will flout the maxim of relevance and divulge large chunks of information which would normally be filtered gradually into the audience's consciousness through a series of expositions. In the opening scene, for example, Mrs Drudge functions as what Stoppard calls 'an ambush for the audience', because the amount of information she gives destabilises our expectations by usurping the creation of suspense (Trussler 1981, 62):

> MRS DRUDGE: (*into the phone.*) Hello, the drawing-room of Lady Muldoon's country residence one morning in early spring? [...] Who did you wish to speak to? I'm afraid there's no one of that name, this is all very mysterious and I'm sure it's leading up to something, I hope nothing is amiss for we, that is Lady Muldoon and her houseguests, are here cut off from the world.
>
> (Stoppard 1993, 11)

Her consciousness of impending doom deprives us of our role as the omniscient audience; she is capable of interpreting the conventions as we are.

The existence of 'an extra-textual world' is, as noted by Carter and Simpson (1989), essential for an informed study of drama, and how it makes meaning in the world. My aim in this book is to synthesise the study of language as it constructs meaning in the world, with the study of plays as they construct meaning within their social, cultural and historical context. In doing so, I have drawn on the models of recent research in literary and discourse-centred stylistics (Carter and Simpson 1989; Herman 1995; Culpeper, Short and Verdonk 1998); contextually informed studies of theatre and theatre history (Bull 1984, 1994; Lacey 1995; Rebellato 1999; Shellard 1999; Rabey 2003); as well as on basic concepts in literary and cultural theory in order to produce an informed account of how attitudes to language in general and in the theatre influence and constitute each other in post-war English theatre 1945–2005.

The book ends with a coda rather than a conclusion in order to reflect the circularity of minding language in the theatre, and also to emphasise its ongoing nature. It seems improper to suggest closure in terms of theatre reception. Each time a play is revived its language will be perceived differently, and to imply that the reception of its language is fixed is to ignore its dependence on historical, social and cultural contexts. As I hope this book demonstrates, degrees of 'lifelike-ese' are predominantly in the eye and ear of the beholder, and as such always liable to shift. Coward's attempt is superseded by Rattigan; Rattigan by Osborne; Osborne by Wesker; Wesker by Pinter; and even Pinter himself is eventually superseded by the continuing assaults on what constitutes lifelike-ese. Linguistic, and in particular, stylistic research offers the opportunity to show that even Beckett and Ionesco are talking the same language as the naturalistic/realistic school, or at least using the same structures to communicate. The only certain conclusions to be drawn are that language minding will always be with us and that every new generation will spawn a different set of anxieties.

1
Language, Communication and Ideology

This chapter investigates some of the ideological assumptions that underpin language minding. The works discussed here range from expressing specific concerns about communication failure to concerns about clarity, expressivity and 'hidden meanings'; 'deficit' theories; and how and why standard language is privileged. In accordance with Raymond Williams's model of residual and dominant modes, I suggest that the dominance of one attitude does not mean the other is entirely superseded (Williams 1977, 122–127). Concerns about the expressivity of language *per se*, like those expressed by Steiner in the Introduction to this book, are replaced with specific concerns about expressive *varieties* of language, namely, non-standard varieties. This chapter will unveil the internalisation of these beliefs, and suggest that this internalisation has led to what Cameron terms the 'fetish' of communication (Cameron 1995, 25). The interplay of residual concerns about expressivity, in general, and dominant anxieties about standard and non-standard, in particular, is demonstrated by the sheer volume of language minding discourse which encompasses both these preoccupations. For example, Dwight Bolinger's *Language the Loaded Weapon* (1980), Philip Howard's *The State of the Language* (1990), Eric Partridge's *Usage and Abusage* (popular enough to have been reprinted five times since the original 1942 edition), Christopher Ricks and Leonard Michaelis's *The State of the Language I* and *II* (1980, 1990), Lynne Truss's *Eats, Shoots and Leaves* (2003) and John Humphrys's *Lost for Words* (2004) all concern themselves with both the decline of language and the decline of *standards* in language. In order to unveil these processes it is necessary to look at how people view language and their own language use, and how they arrive at these positions in the first place. For my purposes, the key texts for this discussion are Roy Harris's *The Language Myth* (1981) which introduces the idea of language as 'telementation' and Deborah Cameron's *Verbal Hygiene* (1995) in which she elaborates on the ideological force of the telementary model and examines the practices and discourses which go to make up value judgements about language and language usage.

The 'fixed code' fallacy

The theory of language as 'telementation' incorporates a number of assumptions about the structure of language and language use. The first of these is that the structure of language is an invariant system, a grid on which word a = object a, word b = object b and so on, hence the term 'fixed code'. According to this model, each individual in a language community has a copy of this grid in their head which allows them to decipher utterances 'correctly'. Following on from this is the assumption that the grid contains all the words necessary to formulate any utterance regardless of context. The telementary model can only work on the understanding that language is a fixed code, so that the message encoded by the speaker is identical to the message decoded by the hearer. The pervasiveness of the telementary approach is implicit in the metaphors popularly used to describe language and communication, such as the conduit metaphor and its variants, which Harris describes as:

> assum[ing] that 'language functions like a conduit'; through this 'conduit' thoughts are transferred from one person to another. Associated with this assumption are three others. One is that in speaking and writing people somehow 'insert' or encapsulate their thoughts and feelings in the words they use. Another is that the words used have the property of 'containing' the thoughts or feelings, and can thus 'convey' them to others. Thirdly, in listening or reading, people 'extract' the thoughts or feelings from the words in which they are 'conveyed'.
>
> (Harris 1981, 10–11)

Harris's account highlights the extent to which people consider themselves to have a personal connection with the language they use; the idea that they can 'put' *their* thoughts and feelings into these vessels and have their own unique feelings perfectly communicated to another person. The telementary model rejects the idea that 'language "speaks us" ', seeing it instead as something which reflects reality and society, rather than as part of the practices that formulate them (Burke, Crowley and

Girvin 2000, 13). This notion of personal control also highlights another aspect of the fixed code model: the idea that individuals are able to control language. This idea of personal agency over language is something Cameron cites as integral to certain practices of language prescription, proscription and discourses that she terms 'verbal hygiene'. One example of such a practice, and one in which Cameron detects a particularly high degree of personal attachment, is the strength of feeling aroused by politically correct language. In *Verbal Hygiene* Cameron explores the reasons behind hostility to attempts to regulate 'un-p.c' language, concluding that people view their language usage and the impressions conveyed by their usage as synonymous because they regard language as a means of conveying their own thoughts precisely. Therefore if no offence is intended by employing a particular usage then none should be taken; the intention of the utterance should have been preserved in the communication along with the message itself.[1] The fixed code only allows one meaning, so if everyone is abiding by the same code, the meaning should be evident. The telementary model fosters the idea of utterances as something which the speaker can wholly control, not only in their encoding but also in their decoding and so any attempt at interference is seen as an infringement of personal liberty. In addition to this, analysis of the *content* of utterances, as opposed to the *form*, which is what language minders usually comment on, questions the commonsense belief that language is a transparent or neutral medium (language minders refer, in this instance, to people who complain about 'incorrect' or 'poor' usage in newspaper columns, usage manuals, documents for educational reform and so on).[2] As Cameron notes:

> It might with justice be objected that the 'neutrality' of terms like *chairman* was always an illusion. But it was not always apprehended as illusory; and it had a number of important functions. It helped, for example, to sustain the even more fundamental illusion that speakers have total control over the meaning of their own discourse – that when we speak, we engage in individual acts of will whose outcome, ideally, is to communicate our own unique intentions (thus if I don't intend to convey a political attitude by my choice of words, anyone who discerns one is making an illegitimate inference). Reformers have called into question this imaginary omnipotence. At the same time they have questioned another cherished illusion: that although my utterances express my own unique intention, the linguistic code through which those intentions 'were put into words' is unproblematically shared by other speakers of my language. Once again, this

implies that someone who fails to recognise what I 'really mean', or who imputes to me intentions I do not have, is not only in error but in breach of universally accepted rules.

(Cameron 1995, 118)

These 'universally accepted rules' are, of course, another 'cherished illusion' of the telementary/fixed code fallacy. Similarly, the idea of language as a transparent conductor of intention and meaning is not only 'cherished' but pervades most discourses on, about or involving language. Cameron sees the transparency metaphor as an extension and refinement of the conduit metaphor in discourses on language and communication, and as a means of providing justification for many verbal hygiene practices (Cameron 1995, 24). For example, language 'guardians' commonly complain that 'incorrect' usage often leads to ambiguity, making it harder for meaning to be deciphered, easier for misunderstandings to occur and generally hindering communication. The idea that such usages are incorrect implies there is a single correct form from which all others deviate, and also suggests that ambiguity is undesirable (rather than acknowledging that the ambiguity inherent in language makes a nonsense of the idea of one word and one corresponding meaning).

The ideological implications of the 'fixed code'

By adhering to the idea of a fixed code system, verbal hygienists are able to perpetuate the illusion of an ideal and efficient – but fragile – communication system over which speakers have complete control. The fragility of this system resides in the fact that communication easily breaks down if users do not play by the rules, but if they do adhere to them their every unique thought and feeling can be communicated in its entirety to the rest of the community (a community which, in this perfect world, lives entirely in accord). By setting up this paradigm, language guardians are able to hint darkly at the alternative: discord, moral decline and social fragmentation. As Cameron points out

> The social analogue of a 'breakdown in communication' is a breakdown in cultural and political consensus, the eruption into public discourse of irreconcilable differences and incommensurable values. Thus the anxiety gets expressed as 'if we don't obey the rules we won't be able to communicate' might equally be defined as an anxiety

about moral relativism or social fragmentation. Just as 'we speak the same language' is a metaphor for sharing interests and values, so the idea that meaning is contested and relative is metaphorically a recognition of the inevitability of difference and conflict.

(Cameron 1995, 25)

Cameron's observations offer an interesting inversion of the usual perception of language and communication – a perception, it should be added, that is perpetuated largely by verbal hygienists themselves – that there was once a halcyon age when communication was unproblematic, everyone spoke and wrote immaculate prose and everyone was able to express their every thought perfectly in a way that did justice to their sense of uniqueness. Cameron's re-reading suggests that verbal hygienists have always known that language is an arbitrary medium, but contrary to 'professional' linguists who see this indeterminacy as part of its strength and versatility, verbal hygienists see it as a threat to the status quo (Cameron 1995, 24). There are some interesting ramifications for this attitude in the way in which, for example, standard languages are conceived and maintained, and the way standard English has been debated and taught in schools and they will be discussed in later sections of this chapter. For the present I wish to look in more detail at Cameron's discussion of the rhetoric of the 'transparency' of language, and the valorisation of 'plain' language which best exemplifies such transparency.

Cameron cites in-house style guides such as those used by newspapers and publishing houses as excellent exemplars of this rhetoric: 'Here we have a striking illustration of two particularly widespread and powerful beliefs about good writing in English: the belief that it should be *uniform* and the belief that it should be *transparent* (as Orwell put it, "like a window pane")' (Cameron 1995, 38). Significantly, the two professional branches of writing which have the widest public circulation are those which champion what Althusser, in his formulation of ideology, defines as the primary ideological effect:

Like all obviousnesses, including those that make a word 'name a thing' or 'have a meaning' (therefore including the obviousness of the 'transparency' of language), the 'obviousness' that you and I are subjects – and that does not cause any problems – is an ideological effect. The elementary ideological effect.[3]

(Althusser in Rivkin and Ryan 1999, 300)

Not only is the transparency of language the elementary ideological effect, the education system and the media are among the most influential ideological state apparatus, that is, those in the best and most dominant position to naturalise moral, social and political agendas.[4] This makes George Orwell's championing of the values of transparency and uniformity as the only way of defeating the invidious procedures of totalitarian regimes in 'Politics and the English Language' somewhat surprising; yet Orwell's endorsement is also a powerful testimony to the strength of this 'elementary ideological effect'.[5]

As discussed above, transparency is assumed, and/or advocated by many verbal hygienists as the only way to avoid communication breakdown and its concomitant societal implications; for Orwell, transparency is the only way in which we can be sure no unseen agent is tampering with our language, and, by implication, with our minds. Seeing no immediate danger of such shadowy figures manipulating English in this way, Orwell addressed himself to rectifying the slide towards obscurity, caused, in his opinion, by laziness and confused thinking and quickly disseminated by the new forms of mass communication (Cameron 1995, 68–69). Of course Orwell was not the first to advocate plain language, and the reasons for the advocacy of such verbal hygiene practices change over time, but the Orwellian formulation offered a reassuringly patriotic and liberal (as opposed to totalitarian) incentive for proscribing language use.

However, unlike the majority of verbal hygienists, Orwell rejects the idea that enforcing standard language will solve these 'misuses' of language, suggesting that language which will honestly reflect feelings:

> has nothing to do with archaism, with the salvaging of obsolete words and turns of speech, or with the setting up of a 'standard English' which must never be departed from. On the contrary, it is especially concerned with the scrapping of every word or idiom which has outworn its usefulness. It has nothing to do with correct grammar and syntax, which are of no importance so long as one makes one's meaning clear, or with the avoidance of Americanisms, or with having what is called a 'good prose style.' [...] What is above all needed is to let the meaning choose the word, and not the other way around.
>
> (Orwell 1961, 349–350)

Here we see how deeply entrenched the idea of language as a fixed code is and how the concomitant implications of language as nomenclature

and as a reflection of reality have become enshrined. Orwell also articulates here the often expressed language anxiety about originality of
utterance. Cliché is the enemy of clear thinking, allowing the mind
to fall into familiar ruts rather than struggling to give thoughts verbal
shape. He sees such 'lazy' usages as part of a dialectical process of degeneration: sloppy thinking encourages sloppy morals, and sloppy morals
allow sloppy thinking: 'As soon as certain topics are raised, the con-
crete melts into the abstract and no one seems able to think of turns
of speech that are not hackneyed' (Orwell 1961, 339). The correlation
between usage and morals is a favourite of verbal hygienists, yet Orwell
is also making a valid point about the ideological effect of hackneyed
phrases: that they often allow the user, and the hearer/reader to gloss
over the implications of what is being described to them.[6]

   Orwell lists a number of 'dead' metaphors and abstractions (i.e.,
euphemisms) used by politicians and by newspapers to describe political events which 'fudge the facts' to give a particular ideological slant.
The problematic aspect of this is Orwell's failure to acknowledge that all
language portray events from an ideological slant, the 'cherished illusion' of neutral or transparent usage is as much of an ideological slant
as the 'jargon peculiar to Marxist writing (*hyena, hangman, cannibal,
petty bourgeois, these gentry, lackey, flunkey, mad dog, White Guard*, etc.)'
(Orwell 1961, 342). Work in Critical Discourse Analysis by Fairclough
(1989, 1991, 1995 and 2000), Fowler (1991), Fowler et al (1979), Kress
and Hodge (1979) and Wodak (1990) researches this in greater depth,
as well as acknowledging that neither the analyst's methods nor their
language can be neutral. Questioning the neutrality of the analyst is
also key in Bourdieu's work, as John B. Thompson explains in his introduction to *Language and Symbolic Power* (1991). Bourdieu's critique of
Saussurean and semiotic theories is not only based on their failure to
take into account social, cultural and historical factors; 'moreover, such
forms of analysis commonly take for granted the position of the analyst,
without reflecting on this position, or on the relation between the analyst and the object of analysis in a rigorous and reflexive way' (Bourdieu
1991, 4). The notion of transparency then is the 'elementary ideological
effect' for language users, hygienists and analysts alike.

Standard language, ideology and hegemony

Perpetuating the idea(l) of the transparency of language is crucial to
the project of maintaining and promoting standard usage. As Cameron
and others have noted, the most powerful arguments advocating the

teaching of standard English are those that invoke the cherished goal of unproblematic communication.[7] We all understand each other and we all know where we stand; the minute this happy status quo is threatened, hygienists predict the collapse of society. We have seen Orwell's equation of sloppy language use with sloppy morals and Cameron's observation that this equation has become a popular one in discourses on language, its misuse and the decline of standards. In this section I examine what Milroy and Milroy call the 'ideology of standardisation' and how the promotion of standard English has reinforced ideals of articulacy, how certain language guardians have moved from the Marxian formulation of ideology as 'false consciousness' to a more developed position which takes for granted the acceptance of ideology as being in existence, and how this cynical position blurs into a Gramscian notion of hegemony. In *Capital* Marx explains the working of 'false consciousness' as 'Sie wissen das nicht, aber sie tun es' – 'they do not know it, but they are doing it' (quoted by Žižek in *The Sublime Object of Ideology*); Žižek suggests that a more sophisticated formula for these 'enlightened' times is ' "they know very well what they are doing, but still they are doing it" ' (1989, 319). Gramsci defines hegemony as the point where the oppressed classes become complicit in their own oppression, through consenting to received notions of prestige (the consent is 'manufactured' by the ruling classes through their own conferring of prestige on a particular way of life); he describes it thus:

> The 'spontaneous' consent given by the great masses of the population to the general direction imposed on social life by the dominant social group; this consent is 'historically' caused by the prestige (and consequent confidence) which the dominant group enjoys because of its position and function in the world of production.
>
> (Gramsci in Rivkin and Ryan 1998, 277)

Crucially, Gramsci identifies 'the intellectuals' as being part of this 'dominant group', which only serves to strengthen the position for describing standard languages as hegemonic (i.e., because it is usually 'intellectuals, broadcasters and so on who speak and write the standard most fluently').[8] 'Standard' language is the variety of language normally used in academic writing, formal broadcasting and codified in dictionaries thus reinforcing its position as the prestige form.

In *Authority in Language* (1991, 2nd Edition) Milroy and Milroy describe the way in which the hegemonic nature of standard language is maintained as the 'ideology of standardisation'.[9] They use the term to describe the way in which the standard variety of language is privileged over other varieties, ostensibly on the grounds that it is maximally efficient, but more often in practice because it is associated with higher class and levels of education. Milroy and Milroy argue that the prestige and dominance of standard languages (in this case, English) are maintained via education and by 'language guardians' who comment and advise on usage in newspapers and other media, and that this maintenance further contributes to the de-valuing of other language varieties and, as a consequence, the people that use them.

The 'great grammar crusade'

Standard English became a topic of debate in the mid-1980s because of proposals to return to the traditional teaching of grammar by rote, and to correct non-standard usage in *speech* as well as writing. The 'great grammar crusade', as Cameron terms this advocacy of traditional grammar teaching, was the forerunner and eventual executor of the educational reforms that led to the development and implementation of the National Curriculum. In the proposals themselves, and the strategic way in which the government went about implementing them, we can see how attitudes to language can be mutually constituted by opposing sides. The 'grammar crusade' became a battle of right versus left, 'new' orthodoxy versus 'orthodox' orthodoxy; pamphlets and articles by think tanks and academics on either side fuelled the debate and raised additional issues. The spokespersons on the right focused on intensifying the link between declining standards of literacy and declining moral standards, and the danger inherent in liberal left wing academic refusal to proscribe certain varieties of grammar.[10] Among the right's defenders were John Honey, John Marenbon and John Rae, all of whom wrote in response to the 'new orthodoxy's' insistence that linguistics is descriptive not prescriptive (e.g., Deborah Cameron and Jill Bourne (1989), Ronald Carter and Walter Nash (1990), James and Lesley Milroy (1991), Tony Crowley (1991, 2003), Carter (1997) and Tony Bex and Richard Watts (1999)). All these writers subsequently went on to write their own accounts of the debate, challenging the right's correlation of deviation from the standard with moral and social deviance, but the link was successfully made in the mind of the public and the recommendations for English language teaching became policy. The pertinence of this self-perpetuating stream of discourse is that in spite of the left's attempts to demonstrate Althusser's 'primary obviousness' that language, far from being transparent, is actually the primary site of control, the majority preferred to stick with the belief described earlier by Cameron, namely, that their own language is transparent and anything else is 'reading things into words' (Cameron 1995, 119). Yet, at the same time, the successful hegemonic stranglehold of standard language constructs those that hold this view in a cynical position.

The support John Honey (a self-described 'language-expert') expresses for the maintenance and *enforcement* of the standard reflects this position of cynicism. Honey's *Language Is Power* (1998) is a defence of 'the great grammar crusade' on the grounds that the liberal 'new orthodoxy' deprives children of access to power through language. The stance taken by Honey is that standard English has gained prestige and dominance over other varieties because it is the most expressive variety and the one which is used by the greatest English-using thinkers and writers. This is particularly true of dramatists (and pre-1960s dramatists in particular) who, on the whole, want their characters to be able to express emotions and viewpoints in an intelligible way. Thus, Honey's argument follows, if we are to give everyone a chance of social and intellectual advancement, they must be given access to, and an understanding of, the power of standard English. In this respect, Honey situates himself in the cynical position described by Žižek:

> Cynical reason is no longer naïve, but is a paradox of an enlightened false consciousness: one knows the falsehood very well, one is well aware of a particular interest hidden behind an ideological universality, but still one does not renounce it.
>
> (Žižek 1998, 319)

Honey is aware of the ideological apparatus that keeps the standard as the prestige form, and far from ignoring it, he makes their power the reason for retaining them. He argues vehemently that people speaking a particular language variety will only ever be able to understand each other, and since all intellectual discourse takes place in the standard, they will have neither the language nor the exposure to the concepts to take part in this discourse. Language varieties other than the standard, he tells us, are less expressive, less capable of articulating abstract thought, or describing technical processes which is why the standard has been privileged. In his favour, unlike many other language minders, Honey is careful to distinguish between *dialect* and *accent* when he advocates the use of standard language. He characterises accent purely as a matter of pronunciation, whereas dialects may have different grammatical constructions e.g., double negatives in London English (*I haven't seen nothing*), vocabulary, pronunciation and idiom. In spite of the standard caricature of language minders, he is not advocating that everyone should start speaking like a BBC newsreader if they want equal access to power and prestige. The reverse is true of many language minders, to the extent that when the BBC began to allow presenters and newsreaders with regional accents, they were inundated with complaints.[11] Honey is correct in making the point that standard English can be spoken with any accent, but in verbal hygiene debates, accent and dialect are frequently conflated or confused. Stockwell (2002) explains:

> Though, in principle, any dialect can appear in any accent, in practice, some accents tend to accompany certain dialects. RP almost never appears in anything but UK Standard English, though UKSE is usually pronounced in most accents [...] So closely are accent and dialect related in common perception, that the word for the accent (Cockney) and the dialect (Cockney) are often the same.
>
> (Stockwell 2002, 5)

As Cameron noted in the 'grammar crusade' debate, 'expert' opinion has little or no sway against 'common sense'; therefore, to say that correcting non-standard English will not include correcting non-standard pronunciation does not necessarily mean that this is the case.[12] Honey recognises that the standard is privileged over other varieties of speech, he acknowledges that a standard is needed to ensure efficient communication (the language of official documents and negotiations etc.), but his reasons for accepting the privileging of the standard have nothing to do with the economic and social factors in which the development of a standard language is grounded. Instead, they are an acceptance of the process of naturalisation as a justification in itself: since this is the standard, since this is privileged, since non-standard forms are dis-valued (sometimes even by their own speakers, thus proving Gramsci's point about the manufacturing of consent) and since it is the means of access to power, education and wealth, then we should accept its elevated status as natural. Linguists do not deny there is a need for a standard language, what the 'liberal orthodoxy' objects to is that the idea that this standard is any way 'superior' to other language varieties on any intrinsically linguistic grounds, for example, complexity.

Collapsing definitions: Standards, written and spoken forms and articulacy

> in so far as spoken communication has resources which do not appear in written representations of it, it will seem impoverished compared with purely visual communication, expressed in writing. Quite unconsciously, a community which is defined by its mastery of the written medium disvalues the resources of oral and gestural language, and hence the culture of its users.
>
> (Kress and Hodge 1979, 10)

> the most fully described and codified forms of language are those appropriate to public, formal, and, especially, written usage. One effect of this has been a neglect of the structure and social dynamics of spoken forms and hence a tendency (in the absence of adequate descriptions of speech) *to evaluate spoken usage on the model of written usage.*
>
> (Milroy and Milroy 1991, 55, emphasis added)

Milroy and Milroy's *Authority in Language* gives over several chapters to the topic of written and spoken discourses, in particular, the way in which standardisation practices originally intended for written language have been (mis)applied to spoken language, resulting in the problematic treatment of non-standard spoken forms. The supplementary effect of this is that the most highly valorised spoken form is that which apes the characteristics of written language. As a result, articulacy and fluency become the norm from which other forms deviate. The difficulty with this tendency, as the quotation above suggests, is that the 'structure and social dynamics' of spoken forms are at the core of their difference from written ones, and so any account which fails to recognise this becomes an account of why the forms are not the same, rather than how and why they differ. Milroy and Milroy point to the strength of historical precedent for evaluating the spoken and written by the same criteria, hence the tendency in English to characterise one in terms of the other (e.g., describing words as having 'silent' letters). During the standardisation of English attention was focused on the written medium because it was more permanent and easier to standardise and codify. Speech conventions were gradually subsumed by the rules which governed written language and so the most prestigious register of speech became that which was most like written language: fluent, well-organised and explicit. Work done in the field of conversation analysis since the 1970s has documented how misleading this subsumption was. Unplanned, informal speech is governed by different rules and assumptions to written language or planned, formal speech (e.g., public addresses or lectures). Lack of fluency in unplanned speech is accommodated and compensated for by the rules and strategies discussed in the Introduction.

Crowley's *Standard English and the Politics of Language* (2003) gives a history of the standard which, again, can be seen as tracing the movement of standard English to its present hegemonic status. Crowley reviews the project of linguistics from the 18th century onwards to unravel the meanings of 'standard' conflated in the idea of a standard language. As he points out, 'standard' has military connotations as a flag representing a state or city, the function of which is to act as an 'authoritative focal point, a marker and constructor of authority'; or it can be used in the sense of an 'exemplar of weight or measure', it is also seen to be the language of literature (Crowley 2003, 77, 78, 83). In the idea of standard language the two senses merge, it is both a badge of authority and a mark against which other varieties are judged. The famous adage used by linguists to explain the relationship between language and politics, and especially, languages and dialects – 'a language is a dialect with an army and a navy' – can be amended here to 'a *standard* language is a dialect with an army, a navy and a flourishing culture of language minding'. Crowley traces the transition of standard English from being exclusively concerned with the written form (necessary for the keeping of records, state communication, etc.), to the encompassing of speech as well as writing in the 18th century which is evidenced by the increase in the number of elocution manuals. The promotion of standard pronunciation came about (as the standardisation of spelling did) by suppressing variability and privileging one form and devaluing others through the twin processes of prescription and proscription. By the mid-19th century the goals of the standardisers had become far more ambitious than a mutually recognisable and understandable written form. The standard language was to be both uniform and unifying, as Fairclough notes (harking back to the adage quoted above):

> Modern armies and navies are a feature of the 'nation state', and so too is the linguistic unification or 'standardisation' of large politically defined territories which makes talk of 'English' or 'German' meaningful. When people talk about 'English' in Britain, for instance,

they generally have in mind British *standard* English, i.e., the standardised variety of British English. The spread of this variety into all the important public domains and its high status among most of the population are achievements of *standardisation* as a part of the economic, political and cultural unification of modern Britain.

(Fairclough 1989, 21)

Gradually, attempts to standardise spoken as well as written language resulted in the formation of Received Pronunciation. The standard moved from being a supposedly neutral form derived for ease of communication which effectively erased geographical and social origins to a benchmark of excellence and social standing to be emulated. Crowley describes the twin emphases of the 18th and 19th century on standardisation and on dialects heightening the preoccupation with speech (and pronunciation in particular):

Later in the [19th] century the 'distinct specific character' of both standard English speech and dialectal speech was to be evaluated according to pronunciation rather than to any lexical characteristics and this is a clear line of continuity with 18th century concerns.

(Crowley 2003, 114)

Received Pronunciation (RP) was codified by 19th-century phonetician A.J. Ellis who explicitly linked the idea of a standard written language with a standard form of pronunciation through his proposal of 'the theoretical existence of two phenomena: first, the nationally recognisable written form of English (the standard literary English), and second, a "received pronunciation" of that form (standard spoken English)' (Crowley 2003, 114). We can see here how the distinct meanings of 'standard' outlined above have all been absorbed into the ideal of a standard language. It also becomes evident (as Crowley hints) how the term 'received' aptly describes the process through which most people became familiar with RP – passively hearing it spoken by their 'betters': teachers, doctors and politicians, later on 'received' via the medium of radio, stage and then television. The spread and valorisation of RP operates as a 'top-down' system in the same way as hegemony does (and performed by largely the same group of people). It also connotes interestingly with the idea of 'received wisdom': both achieve their status based on historical precedent and unquestioning acceptance.

Crowley explains how Ellis hoped RP would efface geographical and social origins:

> [Ellis] asserted that 'in the present day we may, however, recognise a received pronunciation all over the country, not widely differing in any particular locality, and admitting a certain degree of variety' (ibid, 23). Within this term there are again important distinctions to be made since RP is not 'received' all over the country if by this it is meant all linguistic subjects hear it constantly [...the sense of received that's at work here] is rather that sense of the term that signifies 'generally adopted, accepted, approved as true or good, chiefly of opinions, customs, etc'. Rather than the 'common' form of the spoken language, 'RP' is that particular form that is counted as 'generally adopted, accepted, approved as true or good'. It is not made clear who has made such evaluations or even the basis for describing them as 'general', yet there is a clear argument here for a form of the spoken language that is counted (at least among certain quarters) as a superior form.
>
> (Crowley 2003, 114)

It is at this point that the link between standards, articulacy and criteria becomes manifest. RP, the variety of speech closest to standard written English, the variety spoken by the 'best people', becomes a marker of intelligence because it most closely resembles the written form characteristic of intellectual, academic and literary discourse. Thus the development and maintenance of the variety is dialectically formulated, the more the standard is valorised, the more powerful it becomes, thus the more disadvantaged the speakers who are farthest away from the speaker become. Though it may be difficult to sway people's opinions about what talking 'properly' means, it is doubly important that language testers are able to describe without prejudice the difference between someone using a non-standard variety and someone who is unable to string a sentence together in an intelligible way (e.g., in terms of word order, c.f. *John likes coffee* and **John coffee likes*) (Milroy and Milroy 1991, 82). This is one of the reasons so much work has been done on standard language, and is often cited as a factor in the work of Labov, Bernstein, Trudgill and Milroy and Milroy, all of whom are concerned to remove the stigma of speaking 'normally' (i.e., in ways consistent with informal, spontaneous speech, rather than aping the characteristics of spoken, planned writing).

Following Ochs (1979) who distinguished between planned and unplanned discourse, Milroy and Milroy suggest two forms of speech event: planned and unplanned ones. The salient characteristics are described below:

- In relatively unplanned discourse more than in planned discourse speakers rely on the immediate context to express propositions (Ochs 1979, 62).
- In relatively unplanned discourse more than in planned discourse, speakers rely on morpho-syntactic structures acquired in the early stages of language development. Relatively planned discourse makes greater use of morpho-syntactic structures that are relatively late to emerge in language (Ochs 1979, 68).

(Milroy and Milroy 1991, 146–147)

As they point out, the two modes are also very similar to Bernstein's elaborated and restricted code (discussed at length in the next section) in the assertion that unplanned discourse tends to be simpler, more abbreviated, makes use of deletion, ellipsis and other context-dependent features. The link between planned discourse and literacy is also made explicit in this chapter ('Planned' and 'unplanned' speech events'), bringing us back to the position stated by Kress and Hodge at the beginning of this section: a culture based on literacy tends not to value the features associated with orality. A culture that bases its idea of speech on the norms of an artificially created and maintained written form is likely to see literacy as the key to speaking 'properly' (particularly, as Crowley notes, when the standard written form is based so closely on literary language). Milroy and Milroy note that as well as the work of Stubbs (1980) and L. Milroy (1973):

> Brown has noted the similarities of her message-orientated speech to Bernstein's elaborated code, and argued 'that this highly structured language is parasitic upon written language and that it is extremely hard to develop it in the absence of control of written language skills' (Brown 1982, 82).

(Milroy and Milroy 1991, 147–148)

Non-standard speakers, or speakers using unplanned speech events, are likely to be labelled as inarticulate precisely because we base our notions of articulacy on the fluent, elaborated and reasoned mode of (at worst) the written form, or (at best) planned speech in which all the thinking time needed to construct a well-reasoned position or well-turned phrase has taken place before the speech event rather than during it. The Radio 4 game-show *Just a Minute* demonstrates just how difficult it is to speak even for a minute without 'hesitation, repetition or deviation' on a pre-scribed topic, let alone for longer than this on a variety of topics, yet this is the criteria against which most people unconsciously judge/d verbal performance. In *Language as Ideology* (1979), Kress and Hodge note that not only is the speaker disadvantaged when being heard, but also when their speech is transcribed:

> Transcribers of oral discourse have the choice between transmitting the oral forms as closely as they can, thereby exposing the discourse to the judgement 'oral therefore inferior', or normalising it in the direction of the written form. The person transcribing Freda's language could have emphasised its oral nature more, by attempting to approximate the sound of the utterance, writing *must of, yuh know, woz*, etc. The effect of this convention is to imply that the speaker is illiterate, and in doing so it introduces, covertly, a host of negative judgements about the speaker.
>
> (Kress and Hodge 1979, 66)

It is precisely this response to attempts to represent speech more 'faith-fully' in post-war drama that has led to many dramatic characters being labelled as inarticulate, monosyllabic or embodying the breakdown of communication.

Speaking 'properly'

Having examined above more recent work on the re-evaluation of spo-ken language, I would like to look at two of the pioneering studies undertaken in conversation analysis during the late 1960s and 1970s by Bernstein and Labov. Their work was vital in demonstrating that context is the key factor in evaluating and describing the speech of supposedly 'under-performing' speakers. Bernstein's work has frequently been accused of reinforcing the 'deficit' model of language, that is, that one form of speech is intrinsically 'better' than another; Labov's work is generally more sympathetically received, although as I discuss later, not without its problems. I hope that an analysis of their work will provide a framework/terminology for describing modes of 'dysfluent', 'inarticu-late' and other 'problematic' forms of speech in drama of the post-war period.

Bernstein's theories, collected in four volumes of *Class, Codes and Control*, draw heavily on linguistic relativism as explored by Sapir and Whorf, as well as on the pioneering work in ethnography done by Dell Hymes, in order to trace the 'transmission' of culture through language (Bernstein 1971, 119). He began to develop the notion of restricted and elaborated codes in the late 1950s when teaching basic Maths and English to apprentices and attempting to 'connect' with his students (Bernstein 1971, 5). From this he set out to discover why students from 'working-class' backgrounds scored poorly in tests for verbal dexterity. He concluded that there are two basic speech variants (one restricted, the other elaborated) which can be distinguished by the predictability of certain syntactical and lexical features. 'Code' (originally employed as the name of the variant) came to have a separate meaning as the means by which one determines whether the restricted variant is being employed as a context-dependent register, or is the usual form of speech, and thus determines the distribution of these variants across class:

> I found it necessary to disconnect the notions of elaborated and restricted speech variants from the concept of code; that is, when is a restricted or elaborated speech variant no more than a switch in register, and when are such speech variants an indication of code?
>
> (Bernstein 1971, 12)

He then went on to relate the distribution of these two variants to access (or perhaps exposure) to higher social classes. The restricted variant is characterised by context dependency, is implicit and particularistic; the elaborated is capable of abstraction, is explicit and independent of context. More significantly in terms of its application to post-war drama, the restricted variant is not predicated on intelligence, but to a large degree on familiarity, hence the wider context of the utterance will be implicit between the speakers – a characteristic more in keeping with the idealised 'community' by which the working-classes were characterised in decades after the war. Both Paul Atkinson and Ralph Fasold have commented on this aspect of Bernstein's work in their attempts to rehabilitate his critical standing. Atkinson, writing in 1985, draws attention to the cultural and temporal proximity of Bernstein and Richard Hoggart's work (discussed in detail in the next two chapters):

> the sociological sources which seem to have informed his [Bernstein's] thinking in the late 1950s portrayed an unwarrantably romantic version of 'the community'. It is noteworthy that Bernstein

cites Hoggart (1957) who, while distancing himself from cosy associations of 'the word community' itself, did much to promote a fashionably *gemeinschaftlich*[13] view of the working classes. There is more than a hint of *nostalgie de la boue*. Hoggart's working-class members have a strong sense of group which they express proverbially: 'Y've got to share and share alike; y've got to 'elp one another out'.

(Atkinson 1985, 48)

Fasold is more business-like in his evaluation, pointing out that Lesley Milroy's *Language and Social Networks* (1980) articulates less problematically Bernstein's conclusion that working-class interaction tends to be particularistic and context dependent. Milroy's theory, based on fieldwork in Belfast, is that:

Dense and multiplex networks, where an individual's friends and relatives are likely to be friends and relatives of each other, are common in working class societies. Conversational participants do not have to actually say a lot of what will be understood with people they know well and with whom they share a lot of the same background. Much of what would have to be explained to an outsider can simply be assumed within a tightly knit group. If this is true, then dense, multiplex networks like these would be a natural environment for a 'restricted code' and not a very good one for 'elaborated code'.

(Fasold 1990, 271)

A dramatic analogy might be the mocking description of the typical characteristics of an Ibsen play in David Hare's *The Great Exhibition*, first performed in 1972:

the characters would come on stage and tell each other what they perfectly well knew already. 'It is ten years ago today, Mrs Rummell, since the terrible snowdrifts during which Eywolf fell off the table while Gregers and I were copulating thereby damaging the nerves in his leg, which account for the limp, with which he now walks'. And in would come Eywolf, limping like mad.

(Hare 1992, 153)

The significance of these findings for Bernstein – significance which has been overlooked by his critics – is that variant usage is not conditioned by intelligence but by background:

because a restricted code is universalistic with reference to its models, all people have access to its special syntax and to various systems of local condensed meanings; but because an elaborated code is very likely to be particularistic with respect to its models, only some people will have access to its syntax and to the universalistic character of its meanings. Following this argument, the use of an elaborated code or an orientation to its use will depend *not* on the psychological properties of a speaker but upon access to specialised social positions, by virtue of which a particular type of speech model is available. Normally, but not inevitably, such positions will coincide with a stratum seeking or already possessing access to the major decision making areas of society.

(Bernstein 1971, 130)

Bernstein's work is usually interpreted as a simplistic and problematic correlation between articulacy and class (as Bernstein himself has acknowledged in the Introduction to the first volume of *Class, Codes and Control*) and has been criticised on ideological and methodological grounds (1971, 18). I do not intend to rehearse all these criticisms here but confine myself to those concerned with ideological reservations/ protestations. The most commonly levelled of these objections is that Bernstein's thesis supports the 'deficit' model of describing non-standard language, that is, that non-standard speech is the result of a 'lack' (of parental interaction, exposure to 'well-spoken' language, 'good' literature) in the environment of the non-standard speaker. Inevitably, this 'lack' is judged against the 'norms' of white middle-class society, and again, inevitably, the notion of 'lack' soon collapses into a judgement on the inferiority of one set of conditions over another. Labov criticises this model, and Bernstein in particular, in 'The Logic of Non-standard English' (1969):

Bernstein's views are filtered through a strong bias against all forms of working class behaviour, so that middle-class language is seen as superior in every respect – as 'more abstract, and necessarily somewhat more flexible, detailed and subtle'.

(Labov 1972, 183)

This is a somewhat unfair, if familiar, criticism of Bernstein's work. Bernstein is at pains to stress that, as a relativist, he does not subscribe to the idea that one language variety is superior/inferior to another one. In 'Social Class, Language and Socialisation' he asserts: 'the code the linguist invents to explain the formal properties of the grammar is capable of generating any number of speech codes, and there is no reason for believing that any one language code is better than another in this respect' (Bernstein 1971, 172). What he does acknowledge is that middle-class language is likely to be judged as the superior form because of the prestige that accrues to middle-class mores in other aspects of society. As quoted above, the position given to the elaborated code in the pecking order 'will [normally] coincide with a stratum seeking or already possessing access to the major decision making areas of society'. The unravelling of the conflation of spoken and written norms in the 1980s and 1990s also helped to rehabilitate Bernstein's reputation. As Milroy and Milroy note:

> speech events which require prior organisation are, like Bernstein's elaborated code, associated primarily with speakers who are of relatively high status and have control over society's major resources. Since planned discourse and written language are closely associated with one another, it is likely, as Stubbs (1980) and L. Milroy (1973) have pointed out, that acquisition of the elaborated code is tied up with acquisition of literacy.
>
> (Milroy and Milroy 1991, 148)

In 'The Logic of Non-standard English' Labov explores how the deficit model has further disadvantaged 'ghetto' children at school. By continually judging them as lacking the verbal skills of their (white) middle-class counterparts, Labov argues, language testers are overlooking the verbal skills the lower-class black children do possess. Labov's findings are no longer ground-breaking research for us in these enlightened, politically correct times; far from being 'illogical' as language testers in the 1960s and 1970s had thought, Nonstandard Negro English (NNE, now renamed BE – Black English, or BVE – Black Vernacular English) is just as logical and consistent as Standard (American) English. What is more striking about his paper now is the way in which he reinforces the logical/illogical binary by reversing it, rather than challenging the grounds for constituting the relationship in this way in the first place. In the famous comparison of interviews with Larry, a 15-year-old gang member and 'paradigmatic speaker of non-standard Negro English' (Giglioli 1972, 194), and Charles M., 'an upper-middle-class, college educated Negro man' (Giglioli 1972, 197), Labov judges Larry to be the more effective speaker, because he is more emphatic, less reflective and uses fewer fillers and hedges, grounds just as spurious for privileging speech varieties as those offered by those who champion the deficit model. The comparison is intended to illustrate that the supposedly 'restricted code' of NNE is just as capable of discussing abstract concepts as the 'elaborated code' of Standard English, and as an exercise in positive discrimination it must have been highly effective at challenging preconceptions. However, in the course of this illustration Labov sets up a problematic distinction between 'verbality' and 'verbosity', which further reinforces the binary distinction between superior/inferior. 'Verbality' is described as 'the child's total verbal capacity'; 'verbosity' is pejoratively constructed, as evidenced in Labov's description of Charles M.'s speech:

> His language is more moderate and tempered than Larry's; he makes every effort to qualify his opinions, and seems anxious to avoid any misstatements or over-statements. From these emerge the primary characteristic of this passage – its *verbosity*. Words multiply, some modifying and qualifying, others repeating or padding the main argument.
>
> (Giglioli 1972, 198)

The characteristics Labov identifies here are those which Milroy and Milroy have since identified as being typical of most unplanned speech irrespective of class. It is easy to point this out with the benefit of hindsight (and 20 years of linguistic research); what is more germane is Labov's failure to mention the difference in context of the two interviews. He goes into great detail about the changes that were made to reduce the formality of interview situation in order to encourage the verbality of the NNE speakers (interviewer sitting on the floor, inviting friends to accompany the interviewee or offering crisps). Under what conditions was Charles M.'s interview conducted; how have the different ages of the interviewees been factored in? As a 'college educated man' is Charles M. not more likely to have had the impulsion behind the project explained to him; is he not going to do his best to give carefully thought out answers to the 'great question' of life after death which will have more cultural and intellectual resonance for him than for a 15-year-old boy? The differing conditions are hinted at when Labov explains:

> The reader will notice the speed and precision of Larry's mental operations. He does not wander, or insert meaningless verbiage. [...] It is often said that the non-standard vernacular is not suited for

dealing with abstract or hypothetical questions, but in fact speakers from the NNE community take great delight in exercising their wit and logic on the most improbable and problematic matters.

(Giglioli 1972, 196)

What seems to have been presented to Larry as an opportunity to demonstrate knowledge and wit ('What happens to you after you die? Do you know?', 193) is presented to Charles M. as anthropological research into the occult ('Do you know of anything that someone can do, to have someone who has passed on visit him in a dream?' 197). And if one were going to comment on verbosity and clarity, the question put to Charles M. is not exactly the best example of unequivocal plain speech. It seems that Labov is more guilty of making evaluative judgements of speech than Bernstein; Bernstein's work may be more open to misinterpretation (e.g., giving rises to stances like Honey's: that children need to be given access to the privileged code, rather than questioning the innate superiority of this code), but Labov's is far more effective at maintaining the evaluative binaries. Bernstein's formulation of elaborated and restricted codes is referred to throughout the rest of the book as a framework for understanding why non-fluent dramatic speech has been so variably received and interpreted. His theories also go some way to explaining why the dense multiplex networks which characterise much New Wave drama allow for a greater degree of accommodation of the restricted code, than the universalistic world of Coward's social whirl.

Conclusion: The fetishisation of communication

> Taken literally, this [communicative breakdown] is an unfounded fear. Humans have always managed to communicate to their mutual satisfaction for various purposes in the absence of a shared language, and the differences which provoke most anxiety on this score are in any case too trivial to pose any serious threat to meaningful interaction. But the underlying fear is not the literal fear of being unable to make yourself understood. It is the fear that the meanings which anchor your own view of the world are not, after all, shared by everyone; which in turn expressed a more general fear of difference, otherness and relativity.
>
> (Cameron 1995, 219)

We have seen in this chapter how communication is invoked, revered and anxiously protected in discourses on language and by language minders. In particular I have been concerned with uncovering what lies beneath this obsession with communication and communication breakdown, its origins and the means by which it is perpetuated. In *Verbal Hygiene* Cameron terms these processes the 'fetish of communication' and notes that:[14]

> The speciousness of the arguments put forward to justify particular verbal hygiene practices might lead us to suspect that the fetish of communication is really just a cover for some other obsession. We are back once again to the way verbal hygiene is not just about ordering language itself, but also exploits the powerful symbolism in which language stands for other kinds of order – moral, social and political.
>
> (Cameron 1995, 25)

The verbal hygiene practices she examines centre on written language rather than the spoken form (with the exception of the 'great grammar crusade' in which it was mooted that children's pronunciation and 'spoken grammar' was corrected as well as their writing), and it is interesting to note that it is possible to discern a faint pattern in discourses about language complaints where the focus alternates between the written and the spoken form. As discussed in the brief history of standard English above, in the 19th and early 20th century the focus was initially on the drive to standardise the written form for political and economic reasons; then to standardise spoken forms through the introduction of RP, primarily for social reasons, though it was dressed up as concern for the moral and educational welfare of the poorer classes; then a return to the written form in the drive to increase literacy. In the late 20th century the focus turned again to speech (as seen in the work of Labov, Bernstein and Milroy and Milroy), this time in arguing for the equality of all forms rather than imposing a standard; and now in the 21st century, speech has become a professional resource. In *Good to Talk?* (2002), in which Cameron sets out to explore new attitudes to the spoken form, she states that the object of her enquiry is:

> basically 'ordinary' talk: spontaneous as opposed to planned, interactive rather than monologic. And what interests me is precisely the novelty of approaching this sort of talk in the way we have

traditionally approached writing, and more recently other 'literacies'. The norms of written language have been codified and taught for centuries; literacy has always been an acquired skill – albeit in modern times one that is expected of almost everyone. In the case of spoken language, by contrast, only the most formal and ritualised instances have been extensively codified and their rules explicitly taught. Judgements of skill have undoubtedly been made, but the criteria have been variable and largely implicit. Now it seems that things are changing.

Changing attitudes to and practices of talk are the subject of this book, and I will ask two main questions about them. One is, *how* are people being exhorted or required to talk in contemporary society? What linguistic and social norms define 'good' and 'bad' communication? By whom, and for whom, are the norms constructed, and how are they enforced? The other question is *why*. Why is there a perceived need to regulate, codify and make judgements on even the most banal forms of spoken communication? What motivates the contemporary belief that communication is both the cause of all problems and the cure for all ills?

(Cameron 2002, 2–3)

Cameron is documenting here the re-emergence of the fetish of communication as a mammoth marketing drive, masquerading as an initiative that is for the good of the individual consumer, and for the good of society, in this case understood as the consumer. The moral, social and political concerns which usually lie behind practices of verbal hygiene are now augmented by economic ones. The new texts for Cameron to study are manuals from British Telecom (BT), self-help guides etc., not the expected ideological state apparatus of education and media. The next chapter discusses the way in which this shift in the fetishisation of communication is reflected in the reception of language in drama. As capitalism becomes a global language, the tenor of dramatic discourse has shifted, so that from the late 1980s onwards, self-help guides and the spread of 'therapy culture' mean that the majority, including characters in soap operas, tv drama and on stage, are capable of expressing their worries and problems in a suitably therapeutic discourse. In the theatre, this tendency is exemplified in Mark Ravenhill's *Shopping and Fucking* (1996),[15] when Mark is forced to drop his therapeutic register in order to make his position clear:

Gary: You God Squad?
[...]
Mark: No. I'm not God Squad.
Gary: Just got a thing about druggies?
Mark: I have a history of substance abuse.
Gary: You're a druggie
Mark: I'm a recovering substance abuser.
Gary: You're not a druggie?
Mark: I used to be a druggie.
Gary: Got you.

(Ravenhill 1996, 22)

2
Fetishising Communication on Stage

> people attach considerable importance to 'communication'.
> Good communication is said to be the key to a better and
> happier life; improving communication 'would improve every-
> thing else'.
>
> (Cameron 2002, 1)

Cameron is quoting here from British Telecom's first National Communication Survey, 'Listening to the Nation' in 1996. The quotation
demonstrates perfectly the 'fetishisation of communication' Cameron
has described elsewhere, that is, the processes by which the primarily
social and casual activity of talking has been reconstituted as a commodifiable skill: communication (Cameron 1995, 2000). In using the
term 'fetish of communication' here I am broadening this definition,
suggesting that communication, or more precisely, the success or failure of communication, has become the dominant concern of most
metalinguistic discourses and that drama is no exception. Theatre is
particularly well situated for an examination of such discourses because
it historically occupies a position of cultural supremacy among forms
of drama (as opposed to television drama, for example). Despite the
fact that most people's experience of drama now comes from watching it on television (as does their experience of reading writing about
drama), theatre has a consistent body of documented discourse around
it.[1] Not only are there reviews in newspapers and other media, and academics and institutional heads all contributing to this discourse, theatre
practitioners – actors, directors, dramaturges, playwrights, set designers,
costume designers and dressers – frequently comment on their field in

books, interviews, lectures and newspaper articles. Such a wealth of discourse provides a rich field for an investigation into the different ways in which communication is fetishised.

This chapter examines the specific ways in which the 'fetishisation' of communication, or 'language minding', manifests itself in the theatre, through the foregrounding of non-standard language and through metalinguistic discourses about the 'problem' of language. The 'flagging up' of these fetishised forms is designed to provide a framework for the following chapters in which plays, playwrights and critics are historically, socially and culturally contextualised to provide a snapshot of the way in which the attitudes of language minders in general, and theatre language minders in particular, interacted during the period 1945–2015.

Foregrounding the non-standard in the reception of drama

To suggest that the entirety of post-war British drama is concerned with, or perceived in terms of, communication is, of course, a huge exaggeration. What is striking, however, is that those instances in which communication is mentioned, it is nearly always characterised as faulty, in need of repair, failed, or in some way 'othered'. Praising a dramatist for the 'realistic' nature of their dialogue is to constitute that dialogue in opposition to the norm of unrealistic dialogue, else why comment on it? The ability of Standard English (and later, RP) to mask any trace of social or geographical origin is reflected in the theatre in the way in which, up to the 1960s, lead characters spoke RP (or a close approximation of it), and servants and 'local colour' adopted variations on what theatre critic Kenneth Tynan referred to as 'Stage Rustic', 'Stage Dublin' and presumably Stage Cockney, Welsh and Glaswegian depending on the actor and the part (Tynan 1961, 29). Before the 'watershed' of 1956, this division of accents was part of the status quo, and most theatre (knowingly or not) perpetuated it (indeed, even the 'New Wave' post-1956 barely deviated from the RP norm). John Elsom notes that during theatre impresario Binkie Beaumont's dominance of London theatre before and immediately after the Second World War, actors were encouraged to adopt an RP accent. 'Leading parts were written with such an accent in mind', and not simply because it could be clearly heard and understood in the back stalls and upper circles, but also to ensure that:

> the Aristotelian principle was observed that the public identified with those who are better than average. With the right accent in

Britain, you signalled to others that you came from a good family, had received a classical education, and could thus speak with authority. The best-known upper-class accents on the English stage came, however, from those who had no such social advantages. Ivor Novello was brought up in Cardiff, Noel Coward in Teddington, Edith Evans in Pimlico.

(Elsom 1992, 25)

Elsom's comment not only serves to reinforce the complex and mutually constitutive relationship between accent, class and power, it also foregrounds the *performative* nature of this relationship. The monopoly of RP on the English stage is additionally indicated by the reception of non-RP, non-Cockney lead characters who emerge in the 1950s and 1960s. Frequently cited examples are Shelagh Delaney's *A Taste of Honey* (1958) and *The Lion in Love* (1960) and Arnold Wesker's *Roots* (1959), portraying Mancunian (specifically Salford) and Norfolk dialects respectively. It is striking that the reception of non-standard accents in these plays blurs accent into content, and that the reception of this content is characterised by an attitude of 'could do better', as if the playwrights were letting down the working-class by portraying them as too stupid or lazy to speak 'properly'. In *Anger and After* (1963), Russell Taylor remarks of *The Lion in Love*:

One would not question Shelagh Delaney's ear, which seems, as far as a non-Salfordian can judge, impeccable, nor her skill in noting down precisely what she hears, but in this play her critical sense and her ability to select seem to have at times deserted her. A lot of the writing here not only seems like the small change of unintelligent everyday conversation, but actually is just that, virtually untouched by the dramatist's art.

(Taylor 1963, 118)

The connotations carried by the accent and 'restricted code' style of speech seem to automatically nullify the content. Walter Allen's reception of *Roots* in the *New Statesman* is even less complimentary:

The characters, all but one, are dumb oxen in Wyndham Lewis' sense of the word; moreover their vocabulary is so sparse as to make them almost inarticulate; and it must be admitted, the Norfolk dialect is the slowest means of expression outside Texas.

(Allen 1959 in Elsom 1981, 95)

Here we see an explicit link being made between articulacy and intelligence. In Taylor's commentary on Delaney's characters 'non-Salfordian' is in close proximity to 'unintelligent everyday conversation'. In Allen's review, the link is represented even more forcefully: 'dumb oxen', 'sparse vocabulary', 'inarticulate' and 'slowest' forming a collocational range worthy of the verbal hygienists who commented on the 'Great Grammar Debate'.

The performative dimension of accent, register and other styles of speech is essential to perceptions of language and power, and is aptly demonstrated by the conflicting reception of non-standard accents on the stage. Performativity, in the sense used here, refers to the theory developed by Judith Butler to challenge the dominant models of gender and sexual identity as fixed and stable categories, suggesting instead that this fixed appearance is the result of a 'regulatory fiction' (Butler 1990, 136). Any behaviour occurring outside these norms troubles this fiction: 'that regulatory ideal is then exposed as a norm and a fiction that disguises itself as a developmental law regulating the sexual field it purports to describe' (Butler 1990, 136). Gender is thus an act, a performance constituted in, by and through its repetition. Butler describes it thus:

> As in other ritual social dramas, the action of gender requires a performance that is *repeated*. This repetition is at once a re-enactment and re-experiencing of a set of meanings already socially established; and it is the mundane and ritualised form of their legitimation. [...]
>
> Gender ought not be construed as a stable identity or locus of agency from which various acts follow; rather gender is an identity constituted in time, instituted in an exterior space through a *stylised repetition of acts*.
>
> (Butler 1990, 136)

Thus, once the ideology of standardisation became a fixed category, the associations that went along with it: articulacy, wealth, power, educatedness and clarity become part of the 'regulatory fiction'; hence any deviation from the standard repetition is marked as other, or deviant, as is the case with non-standard accents on the stage, in broadcasting and education.

Cameron's appropriation of Butler makes the link between these regulatory fictions and the fictional representation of language in drama explicit. Cameron employs the notion of performativity to demonstrate how understanding of language and class can be understood outside the traditional quantitative paradigm of sociolinguistics:

> Whereas sociolinguistics would say that the way I use language reflects or marks my identity as a particular kind of social subject – I talk like a middle class white woman because I am (already) a middle class white woman – the critical account suggests language is one of the things that *constitutes* my identity as a particular kind of subject. Sociolinguistics says that how you act depends on who you are; critical theory says that who you are (and are taken to be) depends on how you act.
>
> (Cameron 1995, 15)

This has obvious implications for a study into language, theatre and ideology. In the history of post-war British theatre, the way in which a character speaks is an essential to their identity. Having a dustman speak like Noel Coward (or a character from one of his plays) is an obvious challenge to our comfortable prejudices, but also suggests that there is some 'story' as to why the person who speaks like this is a dustman, or why the dustman has chosen to speak like this. The shifting registers used by Vladimir and Estragon in Beckett's *Waiting for Godot* (1955) illustrate this conflicting set of expectations perfectly. The play opens with Estragon struggling to take his boots off and giving up with the words 'Nothing to be done'. Vladimir responds to this pragmatic utterance with a speech pondering on the meaning of life:

> **Vladimir**: I'm beginning to come round to that opinion. All my life I've tried to put it from me saying, Vladimir, be reasonable, you haven't yet tried everything. And I resumed the struggle. [*He broods, musing on the struggle. Turning to* **Estragon**.] So there you are again.
>
> (Beckett 1990a, 11)

Vladimir's ability to conceive of abstract relations (himself out of his present situation in time and space), and his ordering of 'yet tried' rather than the more prosaic 'tried yet' suggest him as a speaker of 'elaborated code', and thus, if we follow Bernstein, an educated speaker, one who has had 'access to specialised social positions, by virtue of which a particular type of speech model is available' (Bernstein 1971, 130). The dislocation between this register and the conversation that follows forms the basis for countless interpretations of the play by audiences, directors, journalists and academics (including Muriel Bradbrook's suggestion that the play is based on Beckett's experiences in the French Resistance, and so Vladimir and Estragon must be Resistance members too (Bradbrook 1972, 19–21)). Immediately after Vladimir greets Estragon with 'So there you are again' the conversation turns to the fact that Estragon spent the night in a ditch and was beaten by the 'same lot as usual'; this exchange strengthens the common assumption that the two men are tramps (in typically enigmatic fashion, Beckett offers no stage directions as to costume or circumstance, leaving the director to come to their own decision about these matters, apart from references to those items necessary for stage business such as boots, trousers, and bowler hats (Beckett 1990a, 11). It is the origin of these items that fixed them as tramps in the popular imagination).[2] What is the story behind the lives of these two tramps? Were they really artists, poets? Did they really try to throw themselves off the top of the Eiffel Tower, or are these merely the delusional fantasies of two lonely old men? This shift between formal and demotic modes of speech, between mundane and 'intellectual' topics has led to general critical assumptions that the two characters must be part of some allegorical treatise about the existence of God and/or the meaning of life. These assumptions appear to result from a lack of context for Vladimir and Estragon and the play as a whole – for it is scarcely ever suggested that characters firmly situated within a particular social milieu are operating on an allegorical or metaphorical level. Yet, if we examine similar exchanges of register and topic-switching patter in Harold Pinter and Joe Orton (both of whom owe an obvious debt to Beckett), these scenes are almost inevitably interpreted as social satire or music-hall style 'turns' introduced for comic relief rather than serious meditations on the meaning of life.

The first example is from Pinter's *No Man's Land* (1975) and occurs early on in Hirst and Spooner's encounter. Despite the fact they have only just met, the garrulous Spooner, *'dressed in a very old and shabby suit'*, has accepted the *'precisely dressed'* Hirst's invitation to come back for a drink and is holding forth about his brilliance on a variety of subjects to his host.

> **Spooner:** [...] I'll ask you another question. Have you any idea from what I derive my strength?
> **Hirst:** Strength? No.
> **Spooner:** I have never been loved. From this I derive my strength. Have you? Ever? Been loved?
> **Hirst:** Oh, I don't suppose so.

Spooner: I looked up into my mother's face. What I saw there was nothing less than pure malevolence. I was fortunate to escape with my life. You will want to know what I had done to provoke such hatred in my own mother.

Hirst: You'd pissed yourself.

Spooner: Quite right. How old do you think I was at the time?

Hirst: Twenty eight.

Spooner: Quite right. However, I left home soon after.

(Pinter 1994a, 90–91)

The conversational register moves from Spooner's romanticised version of his own life, and the revelation of an emotionally debilitating childhood experience, full of Latinate vocabulary and couched in poetic terms, to the uncompromisingly Germanic and scatological. To further debunk Spooner's self-important tone, tragedy turns into comedy with the revelation that he was a grown man, rather than a baby when this occurred. The switch from an elevated tone to a more vulgar one is reminiscent of many passages in *Waiting for Godot*, yet *No Man's Land* is not considered to be a parable on the essence of humanity, the writer's craft or the future of language as we know it (although some of Pinter's early work is considered to do just that). Similarly, Orton's *Entertaining Mr Sloane* (1964) is described as black comedy rather than 'absurdism' or any other portentous intellectual endeavour. As with the passages discussed above, Orton's style is arresting because of the discrepancy between the register of language used and the situation of the user. So often his characters are debunked by their own words, especially when they slip from their refined register to an earthier one, as in the discussion between Ed and Kath about his business meetings:

Ed. […] I live in a world of top decisions. We've no time for ladies.

Kath. Ladies are nice at a gathering.

Ed. We don't want a lot of half-witted tarts.

Kath. They add colour and gaiety.

Ed. Frightening everyone with their clothes.

(Orton 1995a, 90)

Ed moves easily from the mannered register of a 1960s cigar advertisement to bald declarations of misogyny, and in doing so emphasises the difference between the positive face he likes to present to the world and the reality. Similarly, Kath, intent on keeping up her appearance of refinement in the hope of being invited to Ed's penthouse, speaks in a style straight from the fashion pages of *Woman's Own*, but still fails to convince (as she fails to convince anyone that she is still a 'girl', or that she surprised anyone with the suddenness of her engagement and subsequent pregnancy). These examples make it clear that much of our expectations of drama, and of language within drama are predicated precisely on the performative aspect of language. In aping the conventions of the positions they aspire to Kath and Ed seek to perform themselves into being as members of the urbane and sophisticated ranks. Similarly, Spooner, Estragon and Vladimir seek to construct themselves as writers and thinkers rather than itinerants through their appropriation of, or usage of, linguistic registers 'appropriate' to such discourses.

Performativity, performatives and cliché

The concept of performativity also offers a useful way of re-reading the 'problem of cliché' so often foregrounded in discussions of 'loss of faith in language', from Orwell's horror of 'hackneyed' phrases via Steiner's 'sunless sea [...] loud with commonplaces' and beyond. Both Derrida's and Butler's refinement of the performative speech act, as developed by Austin and Searle (see below) into performativity, allow us to re-work constant anxiety about lack of 'originality' lessening the impact of our speech, into strengthening the impact of our speech by drawing on the power of its collective background. Thus, because cliché is just a repeated stylisation, when we say 'I can't express how I feel', we are already doing something with words, with the apparently useless language that does not allow us to express ourselves, we are expressing the magnitude of what we feel. In Derrida's interpretation outlined in *Limited Inc* (1988), Austin's theory suggests that a performative utterance constitutes itself; 'It does not describe something that exists outside of language and prior to it. It produces or transforms a situation' and as such, is set apart from other communicative acts (Derrida 1988, 13). Derrida suggests instead that performative acts only work (as does the rest of speech) through a process of iteration. That is, that one must have a framework, a context, before one can understand that the utterance is performative:

> Could a performative utterance succeed if its formulation did not repeat a 'coded' or iterable utterance, or in other words, if the formula I pronounce in order to open a meeting, launch a ship or a marriage were not identifiable in some way as a 'citation'? Not that 'citationality' in this case is of the same sort as in a theatrical

play, a philosophical reference, or the recitation of a poem. That is why there is a relative specificity, as Austin says, a 'relative purity' of performatives. But this relative purity does not emerge *in opposition to* citationality or iterability, but in opposition to other kinds of iteration within a general iterability which constitutes a violation of the allegedly rigorous purity of every event of discourse or every *speech act*.

(Derrida 1988, 17–18)

In other words, we identify a performative utterance by distinguishing it from other types of utterance, not by recognising it as an original act in itself. Austin imposes a 'relative purity' onto the category of performatives through the imposition of felicity conditions, some of which are referred to by Derrida above, that is, a performative utterance in a play, or in the recitation of a poem, would be disqualified on the grounds that the speaker does not mean what they say, the utterance is not genuine:

A performative utterance will, for example, be in a *peculiar way* hollow or void if said by an actor on the stage [...] Language in such circumstances is in special ways – intelligibly – used not seriously, but in ways *parasitic* upon its normal use.

(Austin 1962, 22)

Derrida's point is that *all* speech, *all* communication is parasitic upon itself, and that meaning is forged from acknowledgement of, and referral to, this parasitic nature through the examination of context. To extrapolate this then, it is only through their knowledge of context and past usages, past citations, that a theatre audience can recognise (a) that a performative act is being performed on the stage, and (b) that such an act is not binding because it takes place on the stage in the context of a fictional story. An actor 'named' 'Romeo' on stage in a production of *Romeo and Juliet* does not become 'Romeo' offstage, anymore than he becomes married to 'Juliet', because 'Friar Lawrence' has pronounced them married in the context of the play.

Derrida names this parasitic process 'iteration'; that for a 'mark' (word, expression, etc.) to have any valency as a referent, that is, to have any significance in an act of communication it must be recognisable or authenticated as having been used before. He gives the analogy of signing a cheque to validate a purchase: in order for the cheque to succeed, the signature must be authenticated by a similar signature on the corresponding cheque guarantee card. In order for the signature to have any significance in the transaction, one's signature must have been previously authenticated, on the card, on the slip you sign in the bank. Similarly, the anguished 'I can't describe the horror' only retains its performative force if the audience recognise that the strongest possible description of something is to label it as 'indescribable'. In this way then, Derrida effectively negates the validity of the debate about the 'lacking word' and corresponding anxieties about the originality of expressions referred to in the Introduction. There is no such thing as entirely an original expression, because for the expression to succeed in having its effect it must contain enough 'traces' of former/similar expressions to be recognisable, yet the idea of clichéd or moribund language continues to be a potent and seductive myth in studies of drama, particularly in studies of 'absurd' drama.

In theatre studies, Martin Esslin's *The Theatre of the Absurd* (1962, 1980) remains an influential text, concentrating on the type of drama associated with the names of Samuel Beckett, Eugene Ionesco, Arthur Adamov, Jean Genet and a number of other avant-garde writers (Esslin 1980, 15). Esslin subsequently updated the book in 1980, including a chapter on Pinter and commenting on the impact of the Absurd in 1970s, as well as offering an account of how 'absurd' became such an influential concept and reference point. He asserts that the book was:

> mainly intended as a polemical contribution to the then current debate on what seemed to many an aberrant and debased form of drama. As it continued to be reprinted, read, and used as a text in colleges and universities it gradually changed its nature. For what had been a hotly controversial intervention in the give and take of the argument increasingly turned into a book which was used as the definition of a new approach (often mistakenly thought to be a school, a movement or even a new *genre*), into a history or a reference handbook.
>
> (Esslin 1980, 15)

It is fittingly ironic that Esslin's concern to defend an 'aberrant and debased form' should consist mainly in pointing out that the language used by the characters in these plays is aberrant and debased and that such use of language is 'merely a satirical magnification of the existing state of affairs' (Esslin 1980, 407). Despite dealing with the apparently timeless philosophical concepts of existence, religion and death, *Theatre of the Absurd* is, of course, as historically grounded as every other

cultural artefact, and was as direct a result of the post-war period as the more transparent link between the New Wave and New Left was. The book is largely responsible for foregrounding the preoccupation with 'communication failure' and the 'inadequacy' of language for expressing existential anxiety rather than the more prosaic business of talking to one's neighbour that so exercised Raymond Williams and Richard Hoggart. Instead, Esslin draws on Steiner's 'The Retreat from the Word' (1960) and Wittgenstein (among others) to corroborate his theory of universal disillusionment with language:

> In its devaluation of language, the Theatre of the Absurd is in tune with the trend of our time. As George Steiner pointed out [...] the devaluation of language is characteristic not only of the development of contemporary poetry of philosophical thought but, even more of modern mathematics and the natural sciences. [...] 'The world of the word has shrunk'.
>
> (Esslin 1980, 407–408)

Interestingly, despite his own role in the mass media as Head of Drama for BBC Radio, he seems to regard the 'newer mass art' – to borrow Hoggart's term – as a pernicious influence. His explanation as to why 'communication between human beings is so often shown in a state of breakdown in the Theatre of the Absurd' is reminiscent of the concerns expressed by the New Left about the impact of mass culture on 'community', as is his call for 'authenticity' (discussed in the next chapter):

> Language has run riot in an age of mass communication. It must be reduced to its proper function – the expression of authentic content, rather than its concealment. But this will be possible only if man's reverence toward the spoken or written word as a means of communication is restored, and the ossified clichés that dominate thought [...] are replaced by a living language that serves it. And this in turn, can be achieved only if the limits of logic and discursive language are recognised and respected, and the uses of poetic language acknowledged.
>
> (Esslin 1980, 409–410)

Belief in a 'proper function' of language, and language as fallen from its former glory are part of the 'language myth[s]' outlined by Harris (1980, 1981, 1987), and Esslin's statement further highlights the ideological assumptions behind this myth. The idea of reverence towards language, particularly towards 'poetic language', is a common theme among language minders, and his displeasure at 'the ossified clichés that dominate thought' brings to mind Orwell's 'Politics and the English Language'. Esslin's acceptance of these aspects of the language myth makes it a simple matter for him to interpret the use of language in absurd drama as evidence of loss of faith in language on the part of the playwrights and their characters, and he is by no means alone in doing so. In his chapter on Beckett, for example, Esslin uses a thesis called *The Inadequacy of Language* to reinforce his assertions about Beckett's continual attempts to 'devalue' language.

> Niklaus Gessner has tabulated ten different modes of disintegration of language observable in *Waiting for Godot*. They range from simple misunderstandings and *double-entendres* to monologues (as signs of inability to communicate), clichés, repetitions of synonyms, inability to find the right words, and 'telegraphic style' (loss of grammatical structure, communication by shouted commands) to Lucky's farrago of chaotic nonsense and the dropping of punctuation marks, such as question marks, as an indication that language has lost its function as a means for communication, that questions have turned into statements not really requiring an answer.
>
> (Esslin 1980, 87)

From a pragmatic perspective of course, none of these 'modes' indicate the 'disintegration' of language. Both Gessner and Esslin are conflating the literary effect of these devices with their function in communication. Misunderstandings do not necessarily indicate that language is disintegrating, or that communication is breaking down; there are a number of pragmatic features of language use that prevent this from happening, such as conversational repair and Grice's cooperative principles. Similarly, monologues indicate nothing about the state of language and everything about the dramatic, or narrative use to which they are being put. Repetitions of synonyms can indicate many things, for example, supportive conversational strategy, or in the case of *Waiting for Godot*, the device is primarily used as part of a game of phatic exchanges or for comedic effect. 'Inability to find the right words' is a common feature of informal, spontaneous spoken discourse, as are so-called performance errors like repetition, hesitation and losing one's thread. Esslin's uncritical use of terms like 'disintegration', 'loss of grammatical structure' and the 'dropping of punctuation marks' argues for the strength of the ideological hold of standard language previously discussed, suggesting an acceptance of the prescriptive ideals of language against which non-standard forms can only be judged as failures, and in which spoken language continues to be judged by written norms (understandable in Esslin's case given that no one really knew about the differences between the two outside of linguistics departments in universities). Viewing clichés as a form of debased language is also part of the prescriptive and 'lacking word' ideologies, feeding from the view that all thought should be expressed as originally and individually as possible, and that 'second-hand' or 'hackneyed' phrases are therefore necessarily inferior. To simply conclude that these common linguistic features are evidence that 'language has lost its function as a means of communication' is reductive. Esslin's persistent conflation of theories about language with literary representations of spoken language on stage, of playwrights' pronouncements about their 'art' and their relationship to language, with the modes through which they communicate, is paradigmatic of much drama criticism, more examples of which will be explored below.

In his essay on *Endgame* (first performed in English in 1958) in *Must We Mean What We Say*? (1976) Stanley Cavell proposes a way to read through and around the characteristic Beckettian obfuscations of language, meaning and motivation. According to Cavell, Beckett is trying to 'uncover the literal', thus a less nihilistic reading of the play can be achieved by taking every word literally, breaking open the clichés and curses and taking the meaning of the words at face value (120). Accordingly Cavell reads Clov's '[*exasperated*] What in God's name could there be on the horizon?' (1990b, 107) as showing 'Hamm [*sic*] really asking whether anything on the horizon is appearing in God's name, as his sign or at his bidding' (Beckett 1990b, 120):

> Beckett removes this curse by converting the rhetoric of cursing; not as traditionally, by using the name in prayer (*that* alternative, as is shown explicitly elsewhere in the play, is obviously no longer open to us) but by turning its formulas into declarative utterances, ones of pure denotation – using the sentences 'cognitively', as the logical positivists used to put it. Beckett (along with other philosophers recognisable as existential) shares with positivism its wish to escape connotation, rhetoric, the noncognitive, the irrationality and awkward memories of ordinary language, in favour of the directly verifiable, the isolated and perfected present.
>
> (Cavell 1976, 120)

According to this interpretation then, *Endgame* shows Beckett not despairing of language as, for example, Esslin, Steiner and Gessner would have it – indeed, Cavell dismisses Esslin's interpretation as nothing more than 'impositions from an impression of fashionable philosophy' – but rejoicing in the simplicity of language, 'our inability *not* to mean what we say' (Cavell, 115, 117). Although this position offers a welcome change to the more traditional one outlined by Esslin and others, both Cavell's and Esslin's interpretations seem to ignore an additional branch of 'fashionable philosophy' of the period in which Beckett wrote: J.L Austin's Speech Act Theory.

How to Do Things with Words was the title of Austin's William James Lectures delivered at Harvard in 1955, and in contradistinction to the traditions of logical positivism and existentialism, they were, as their title suggests, concerned with exactly how much words were capable of, rather than their limitations. As with the discussions of Derrida and Butler earlier in this chapter, it is important to acknowledge that the original context of Austin's work and Searle's elaboration of Speech Act Theory are concerned with the workings of language within the domain of philosophy, but their influence on linguistic and, in particular, stylistic research cannot be too strongly stated. In simple terms, the basic principle of Speech Act Theory is that within the category of locutionary acts (i.e., the act of making an utterance) there are two types of speech act: the illocutionary and the perlocutionary.[3] Illocutionary acts are those utterances which by virtue of being spoken perform an act, for example, christening a child; swearing an oath; issuing a warning; making a promise. Perlocutionary acts are the acts performed as a result of what is said, for example, persuading. In order for an illocutionary act to be performed it must fulfil certain felicity conditions: there 'must exist an accepted conventional procedure, having a certain conventional effect', the persons and circumstances must be 'appropriate for the invocation of the particular procedure invoked', the procedure must be correctly and completely executed, the individual in question must be sincere in their invocation of the procedure, and must 'actually so conduct themselves subsequently' (Austin 1962, 14–15). Three domains which very obviously fall outside these felicity conditions are spoken exchanges in plays, poems and novels, and both Austin and, later, Searle were adamant that these domains were among the conditions which deemed an illocutionary act 'unhappy', that is, invalid. It is these three 'unhappy' categories which have captured the attention of many philosophers and theorists, notably, as discussed above, Derrida and Butler.

In addition to the idea of 'unhappy' or infelicitous speech acts, Austin's work is also useful for the study of language and drama thanks to his discussion of misunderstandings, in particular his introducing the notion of 'uptake'. In his elucidation of infelicities, Austin classifies the use of vague or inexplicit utterances as coming under the general heading of 'incorrect procedure', that is, flouting the rules which constitute a speech act. Hence, if I refer to 'my house' when I have two, I am being deliberately misleading:

> This is a different question from that of misunderstanding or slow uptake by the audience; a flaw in the ritual is involved, however the audience took it. One of the things that cause particular difficulty is the question whether when two parties are involved '*consensus as idem*' is necessary. Is it essential for me to secure *correct understanding* as well as everything else?
>
> (Austin 1962, 36)

As mentioned briefly at the beginning of this chapter, slow or incorrect uptake often forms the basis for entire plot structures, stage business and general merriment. What makes Austin's work useful in this respect is that it places misunderstandings in a context in which they can be rectified, repaired, rather than seeing misunderstandings as symptomatic of communication failure – volitional or otherwise. Conversation may go awry if we assume a character has one house, when, in fact, they have two, but in a play, this fact will be revealed in order to propel plot, resolve dramatic tension and so on.

The problematic nature of dramatic speech (ii)

As discussed in the Introduction, many of the ambivalences expressed about dramatic language are the result of the very ambivalence of its position within the study of both language and literature. The study of drama has gone through a number of changes over the course of its academic life, and has only recently come to be studied as both text and performance rather than as deviant poetry or prose. Similarly, early studies of non-verse dialogue concentrated on its lack of eloquence and rhetorical artistry when compared to the verse-drama which preceded it. Subsequently, when non-standard dialogue began to appear, the expected standards of articulacy plummeted still further in the eyes of a nation of critics raised on the verbal intricacies and bombast of Shakespeare, Wilde and Bernard Shaw. Allardyce Nicoll saw the writer's job as making the inarticulate articulate. In 'Dramatic Dialogue' (1968) he argues for a return to dialogue in verse (what he calls 'patterned speech'), because the language of everyday conversation is simply not dramatic enough, or sufficiently emotionally stirring:[4]

> The dramatist should be an artist in words, [...] the drama itself should deal mainly with emotional material, and if its limitations demand that playwrights should have the most perfect of instruments available for their use, then certainly the employment of our common familiar speech, even when carefully selected and manipulated, is not sufficient for dramatic dialogue. It is, of course, the realisation of this that has led to the recent pleas for 'poetry'.
>
> (Nicoll in Calderwood and Tolliver 1968, 344)

He continually uses metaphors of debasement and impoverishment to discuss modern dramatic dialogue, and advances the theory that one cannot produce stirring drama without using stirring language. He attempts to lend weight to his argument for a return to 'patterned language' by illustrating the widespread nature of his support:

> Peculiarly impressive is the fact that these pleas have come not only, or even chiefly, from the poets, who might be though to have a vested interest in the matter, or from academic critics, whose opinions might be deemed influenced by their affection for bygone tradition, but also from within professional theatre itself.
>
> (Nicoll in Calderwood and Tolliver 1968, 340)

It is interesting to note here that Nicoll credits theatre 'professionals' with more critical distance than poets and academics, as if they are somehow immune to 'affection for bygone tradition' (Nicoll 1968, 340). He also suggests that everyday language has become so debased since the halcyon days of poetic drama, that it will be a struggle to restore either to their former glory.[5] The main thrust of his argument is that 'ordinary speech' is both unexciting to listen to, and incapable of communicating emotional depth and intensity, yet, the answer is not just to abandon prose drama, but also to abandon prosaic subject matter:

> There is of course no doubt that a play set in familiar, contemporary surroundings and presenting characters who are made to behave in a lifelike manner must properly make these characters speak in an equally lifelike manner. The one thing which is anathema for plays

of this sort is anything which savours of the 'literary' or 'artificial'. Where this formulation of ordinary speech is concerned with situations which are commonplace and unemotional, it provides a perfectly satisfactory, if often, unexciting medium. The world of drama however, is, or could be, the world of emotions, and every one knows that our common speech has no power to express our passions intimately. In ordinary life passion tends to make us tongue-tied or incoherent; the trite phrases, 'stunned with grief', 'spluttering with anger', and the like, testify to universal recognition of this fact.

(Nicoll in Calderwood and Tolliver 1968, 341)

Nicoll is here appealing to the 'commonsense' view that there are some ways of expressing ourselves which are more 'authentic' than others; and that communicating through language consists only of the words themselves, with no contextual or paralinguistic features to supplement them. Vimla Herman takes issue with such commonsense assertions in her introduction to *Dramatic Discourse: Dialogue as Interaction in Plays* (1995):

> The assumption appears to be that the relation between conversational and dramatic speech must be predicated upon reflections of surfaces and textures of the one in the other. A mirror or a glass is thus inserted between the two domains without respect to the transformations that are wrought when context and function are taken into account. The binary divide separating the two erases the variety which characterises speech forms in daily life which are at least as remarkable as those found in plays.
>
> (Herman 1995, 5)

Nicoll's objection then is not really so much about realistic dialogue, but about realism, *per se*. His expectation that dramatic dialogue should intensify emotion is based on a different genre and period of drama and its forms of dialogue; he seems unable to consider that enacting the effect that emotion has on articulacy might be just as acceptable to an audience as somebody elaborating on the state of their emotions in a seamless, fluent way. He asserts that trying to express extremes of emotion in everyday speech limits the dramatist to reducing his characters to silence, to depicting characters who are deranged (and therefore, according to Nicoll, more loquacious); or to making them speak in fragmentary exclamations: 'The resultant sense of inadequacy becomes amply apparent when we note how the texts of these scenes are commonly bespattered with as many exclamations and underlinings as might disfigure a schoolgirl's letter' (Nicoll in Calderwood and Tolliver 1968, 342). He fails to take into account the difficulty of conveying intonation, and conveniently does not draw a distinction between the written representation of formal, planned discourse where punctuation is used to break the text up into comprehensible units, and the representation of informal, unplanned discourse. As discussed in the previous chapter, in everyday spontaneous conversation people tend not to talk in complete, grammatical sentences, and whereas 'patterned' speech might have a rhythm to guide sense and intonation, 'unpatterned' speech has to rely on explicit stage directions, for example, '*gives an anguished cry*', or '*nastily*', and 'disfiguring' punctuation.[6] In describing informal language as 'lacking' and 'inadequate' Nicoll is reinforcing prescriptive attitudes about 'right' and 'wrong' language use. Such prescriptive attitudes tend to have lasted longer in dramatic criticism than in other areas of literary studies, precisely because drama spans a problematic area between planned and unplanned discourse. In the greater part of modern drama, the dialogue is a written, planned representation of spoken, spontaneous discourse; and as such, until recently, the dialogue has always been analysed as a 'literary' artefact, rather than an oral one. Also, because the 'great' literary dramatist is Shakespeare, ways of studying poetic language have become the dominant mode for studying dramatic language. This affective way of examining language is so pervasive that some dramatists describe their characters' speech in this way. In *Look Back in Anger*, for example, Osborne refers to Jimmy Porter's extended monologues as 'arias', thereby foregrounding the affective nature of the speech, rather than the content of it (Osborne 1993, ix).

The notion that dramatic speech is always a 'tidied up' version of naturally occurring spontaneous conversation is occasionally mentioned during the 1960s and 1970s but does not really get any in-depth consideration until the 1980s and the formulation of stylistic discourse analysis. Up to this point, drama/theatre critics seem wary of the linguistic tools available for the study of dialogue, as Andrew Kennedy's *Six Dramatists in Search of a Language* (1975) demonstrates. The book stands at the intersection between traditional evaluative drama criticism and the acknowledgement of the role linguistic and contextual factors have to play in discussions of language and drama.[7] This intersection is problematic, both for Kennedy and the reader, for while he acknowledges a number of important considerations hitherto ignored in mainstream drama criticism, his basic vocabulary and attitude is still that of prescriptive, practical criticism. In the Preface he explicitly states that he will be 'testing the texture of the dialogue of six dramatists on a linguistically informed but ultimately evaluative basis' (Kennedy 1975, xi); and typically, he does not set out the criteria by which he will be forming these evaluations. All the preceding drama criticism seems to adopt this consensual, unspoken ideal of what is to be evaluated, and how it should be judged, which in itself suggests a dominant ideological position. Yet at the same time, Kennedy does not endorse the idea of the author as sole creator and interpreter of meaning, or see the author as a conduit of human experience as Esslin seems to, although there are certain similarities between the two studies. Kennedy uses many of the same sources as Esslin: Mauthner's *Critique of Language* (which Beckett read aloud to Joyce), Vannier's 'Theatre of Language' and also talks about what he terms, a 'crisis of expressiveness', which he also sees as a reaction to prevailing literary traditions (Kennedy 1975, 1). Yet while Esslin links this 'crisis' to philosophical trends and questions of validity, Kennedy sees it as having been precipitated by naturalistic drama, and as being part of the 'myth' of the creative writer's plight. In his conclusion he asserts:

> In what sense, then, can we speak of 'crisis of language' in drama? (The phrase itself is for shorthand, and should be avoided in glib company.) First, the various versions of the linguistic 'fall' – the experience of a new Babel in our time – seem to have had value more as myths *for* verbal creativity than as generally valid statements about language or literature. It is a particular writer in a precise situation who experiences language as 'exhausted' (Eliot) or 'abstracted to death' (Beckett) or as a cause for nausea and paralysis (Pinter). The experience is authentic and disturbing; it is transformed when it is allowed to enter and shape the act of writing, the texture of dialogue. then the crisis becomes a condition of creativity.
>
> (Kennedy 1975, 231)

Kennedy makes several important points here: the first of which is that although he may see the idea of the 'crisis of language' as 'shorthand', in dramatic criticism up to this point the phrase is neither questioned nor used as shorthand. Instead it has become the main object of study in accounts of dramatic language. His emphasis on its mythical (or we might more accurately say, 'mystifying') status is long overdue, but at least has the effect of giving some historical perspective to the apparently chronic condition of writers' dissatisfaction with language, which

Kennedy traces back to Symbolism. He isolates those areas which seem to trouble modern dramatists in particular:

There seem to be three main areas of critical self-consciousness about language in drama:

1. The dramatist's awareness of naturalism as a tired or exhausted style which yet survives – since the dramatist cannot wholly lose touch with everyday speech without sterility – as a constant pull towards mimetic dialogue.
2. His awareness of a whole 'imaginary museum' of possible languages, usually conjoined with a self-imposed and restless search for a 'new' language, worked out in and for his own drama.
3. His awareness of the shrinking uses and powers of language itself, as the mediator of thought and feeling, and as the meaningful counterpart of action.

(Kennedy 1975, 1)

His explicit naming of these feelings as 'critical self-consciousness' at last distances the authors in question from 'truth'; these are merely their own personal issues, rather than linguistic facts. Kennedy is also one of the first of the critics represented here to discuss the ambiguous position that dramatic dialogue occupies between spoken and written language:

There is another aspect of dramatic language that needs to be studied: the interaction between 'everyday' and 'literary', the spoken and the written language. The whole question of 'shaping' in dialogue is involved here: how do fragments of utterance fit into a dramatist's grammar? Roland Barthes remarked, at a recent symposium on literary style: 'the opposition of speech and writing has never been completely clarified'.[8] He sees the opposition inherent in both philosophy (different ontologies of speech and writing) and in linguistics (it has a lot to say about sentences, but little about 'subsentence' language).

(Kennedy 1975, 242)

In spite of his sharing certain sources with Esslin, Kennedy also appears to have been reading further afield; the following comment representing an excellent definition of iteration in action:[9]

A new dramatic language so to speak leans against both an 'old style' and the 'common language'. Even at an extreme point – Lucky's

pathological speech, with its deviant syntax and diction – dramatic
language connects with all language (the 'public' language we have
at various levels, learned and shared, from babble to rhetoric, from
symbolist poem to advertisement).

(Kennedy 1975, 232)

Despite Kennedy's enlightened stance, we see how entrenched the
prescriptive vocabulary is; despite his repudiation of the idea of 'inadequate' or 'failing' language, Kennedy still refers to 'deviant syntax and
diction'. Kennedy's study is an important step in changing perceptions
of language in drama criticism, his assertion that 'the Retreat from
the Word' is a myth is an important one, in that language is finally
being recognised and analysed as interactional rather than merely rep-
resentational. The timing of the study is also significant inasmuch as
it coincided with the advent of tape recorders being used to facilitate
close analysis of 'everyday' speech; for the first time it became possible
to listen to how people really spoke; all the pauses, fillers, and so-called
performance errors.[10]

Communication breakdown on stage: Can't, or won't, communicate?

Thus far I have outlined the compelling myths about the state of language and communication failure that preoccupy language minders.
This section considers a factor much overlooked in previous accounts of
communication breakdown, namely, that many instances pinpointed as
'breakdown' are wilful instances of refusal to communicate, or deliberate miscommunications, rather than demonstrations of an inability to
do so. If we exclude the existential angst which renders the majority of
Absurd protagonists apparently unable to communicate (or, in the case
of Victor – the protagonist of Beckett's first play *Eleutheria* (not published
until 1995) – unwilling to even try), it becomes apparent that unwilling-
ness to communicate is often associated with class and/or intelligence
by theatre critics. As we saw above in section 'Foregrounding the non-
standard', and as shall we see in future chapters, collocations often occur
(albeit perhaps unwittingly) linking non-communication to stupidity.
In *Anger and After*, for example, Taylor once again links intelligence and
articulacy in his discussion of Pinter:

in ordinary conversation Pinter's characters twist and turn, profoundly distrustful of any direct communication, and even when

they attempt it are generally constitutionally incapable of achieving it: hardly ever in his work does one encounter two people at the same level of intelligence in conversation – there is nearly always one leaping ahead in the exchange while another stumbles confusedly along behind – except at the lowest end of the scale, where both are so stupid that communication is virtually impossible anyway. And out of these confusions and conversational impasses Pinter creates his characteristic forms of comedy.

(Taylor 1963, 294)

Taylor's commentary raises several interesting points. Firstly, given the circumstances in which Pinter's characters find themselves, their being 'profoundly distrustful' and evasive is entirely understandable. In a 'real' conversation most people would behave in a similar way. Secondly, Taylor is conflating reluctance to tell the truth with reluctance to say anything, as if most people only ever spoke to express a 'true' sentiment, or as if we used an entirely different sort of language to tell lies. Thirdly, it is hard to imagine what 'constitutionally incapable' of communication can mean in this context. Even people physiologically incapable of speaking or suffering from speech disorders like aphasia or dysphasia have other forms of communication available to them. Finally, Pinter is not the first or the last dramatist to have mined language-based misunderstandings for a comic purpose; it has formed an essential part of comedy for centuries. What is 'new' is that the characters in Pinter's early plays misunderstand in a more 'realistic' way, as people do in everyday conversation, rather than in an excessively 'staged' way. As Coupland, Giles and Wiemann note, this reductive attitude towards less fluent communication is not merely stigmatised in the evaluative discourses so characteristic of early theatre studies, more recent, 'objective' and 'empirical' linguistic research falls into exactly the same category:

Communication research typically has been couched in prosocial terms with little regard for the fact that most communicators are sometimes of necessity sceptical, crafty and less than veracious (Giles and Wiemann, 1987) and that sharing a disclosure is an inherently constrained exercise of semantic transfer and strategic selection. Intentionally hostile or dissociative strategies of talk have even been seen as the product of unskilled individuals and, in the extreme, as symptoms of psychopathology (c.f. Watzlawick, Beavin and Jackson, 1967).

(Coupland, Giles and Wiemann 1991, 2)

In theatre as in life, the purpose of language is not simply to communicate 'truths', hence Austin's 'quarantining' of language spoken during the course of a play. In fact, in many of cases it is precisely the disjunction between what is said, and what is happening, that makes theatre dramatic. David Hare's example of the 'most basic dramatic situation' picks up on this:

> A man steps forward and informs the audience of his intention to lifelong fidelity to his wife, while his hand, even as he speaks, drifts at random to the body of another woman. The most basic dramatic situation you can imagine; the gap between what he says and what we see him do opens up; and in that gap we see something that makes theatre unique: that it exposes the difference between what a man says and what he does.
>
> (Hare 1992a, 2–3)

The gaps between what people do and say onstage is, of course, often the main source of dramatic tension within a play, but it is also one that language minders often overlook. The tendency for this to go unnoticed results in quantities of papers agonising over, for example, Mick's intentions towards Davies in *The Caretaker*; the precise nature of the relationship between the protagonists of *Old Times*, and the nature of Isabella's decision in *Measure for Measure* (will she marry the Duke?).

Metatheatrical, metalinguistic discourses

> **Player King**: [The dumb-show is] a device, really – it makes the action that follows more or less comprehensible; you understand, we are tied down to a language which makes up in obscurity what it lacks in style.
>
> (Stoppard 1968, 56)

Thus the Player King in Stoppard's *Rosencrantz and Guildenstern Are Dead* (1968) epitomises the last of the ways in which communication is fetishised in drama – through metalinguistic – and in this case – metatheatrical, commentary. Both are, and always have been, standard theatrical fare. The reason for analysing them here is to draw a parallel between the way in which the metatheatrical and the metalinguistic interact, and how standard metalinguistic expressions about being lost for words are taken literally, rather than performatively, in some contexts, but not in others. I will be taking the reception of Beckett and Stoppard as an example of this. Beckett's professions of linguistic decay are usually taken literally, as in Cavell's article discussed above, while Stoppard's are interpreted performatively, and praised for adding to the theatrical experience.

In *Endgame* (1958) Hamm, the great raconteur spends the play warming up for his 'last soliloquy'; his parents, Nagg and Nell, are continually engaged in retelling stories, two of their favourites being 'how we lost our legs' and Hamm as a boy (Beckett 1990b, 130). In common with *Waiting for Godot*, many of the characters' interactions take the form of reviews of the other's performance, or foiling the other's attempt to dominate the conversational (as well as the physical) stage. For example, in the following scene, Hamm and Clov are in the middle of another of their stalemate discussions about their future. As in *Waiting for Godot*, these discussions never have any effect on the actual state of affairs, and have an air of ritual about them:

Clov: What is there to keep me here?
Hamm: The dialogue. [*Pause*] I've got on well with my story.
[*Pause*] I've got on with it well.
[*Pause. Irritably*] Ask me where I've got to.
Clov: Oh, by the way, your story?
Hamm: [*Surprised*] What story?
Clov: The one you've been telling yourself all your ... days
Hamm: Ah, you mean my chronicle?
Clov: That's the one.
[*Pause.*]
Hamm: [*Angrily.*] Keep going, can't you, keep going!
Clov: You've got on with it, I hope.
Hamm: [*Modestly*] Oh not very far, not very far. [*He sighs.*]
There are days like that, one isn't inspired. [*Pause.*]
Nothing you can do about it, just wait for it to come. [*Pause.*]
No forcing, no forcing, it's fatal. [*Pause.*]
I've got on with it a little all the same. [*Pause.*]
Technique, you know. [*Pause. Irritably.*] I say I've got on with it a little all the same.
Hamm: [*Admiringly.*] Well I never! In spite of everything you were able to get on with it!

(Beckett 1990b, 121)

Hamm's prompting during this exchange exposes the cues which are normally acted on in conversational interaction to keep the process moving. Clov's reluctance to engage in this process is sharply counter-pointed by Hamm, the great soliloquiser, literally 'hamming' it up. Yet this standard music-hall style patter, in which one partner sabotages the other's act, was derided for being 'unoriginal' when first produced. Writing in the *Manchester Guardian*, Philip Hope-Wallace implied that the jokes actually made the play more depressing:

> This wry comment on the hopelessness of our human situation with our failing faculties and futile fidgets, accumulates almost impercepti-bly a leaden weight of despair which the occasional little jokes, some perhaps rather too puerile, only increase.
>
> (Hope-Wallace *Manchester Guardian*, 28 October 1958)

The quandary articulated by the Player-King about language, expres-sivity and theatre is a common theme in Stoppard's earliest plays – *Rosencrantz and Guildenstern Are Dead, The Real Inspector Hound* (1993a), *Jumpers* (1972) and *Travesties* (1974) – and the main means of deriving comedy. There is an obvious debt to *Waiting for Godot* in the games of linguistic 'tennis' in *Rosencrantz and Guildenstern*, in the 'playing' at being Guildenstern and Hamlet, as Vladimir and Estragon 'play at [being] Pozzo and Lucky', but Stoppard's meta playfulness is usually interpreted as virtuoso grandstanding (Stoppard 1968, 31–33, 35–36; Beckett 1990, 68), rather than Absurdist anxiety. Reviews of these plays emphasise the *theatrical* nature of Stoppard's achievements in a way that completely eluded contemporary reviews of Beckett's work. Mil-ton Shulman's review of *Rosencrantz and Guildenstern Are Dead* praises the play for avoiding the gloom of its philosophical and theatrical antecedents: 'Easy as it is to find echoes of Sartre, Beckett and Kafka in the introspective exchanges of R. and G., it is an exceedingly funny play' (Elsom 1981, 89–90), while Michael Billington's 1974 review of *Travesties* acclaims it as:

> a dazzling pyrotechnical feat that combines Wildean pastiche, politi-cal history, artistic debate, spoof-reminiscence, and song-and-dance in marvellously judicial proportions. The text is a dense web of Joycean allusions, yet it also radiates sheer intellectual joie de vivre, as if Stoppard were delightedly communicating the fruits of his own researches.
>
> (Billington 1992, 51)

And this is in spite of the dangerous heresy of Dadaism that the play investigates, which one would have thought was every bit as degenerate as existentialism. Perhaps the difference in these critical responses can be attributed to the different contexts in which these metalinguistic debates occur. As discussed above in the case of *Waiting for Godot*, it seems to be the removal of any identifiable surroundings that contributes most to the 'nihilism' of Beckett's plays, whereas Stoppard's usually take place in a recognisable context, for example, *Hamlet* for *Rosencrantz and Guildenstern* and *The Importance of Being Earnest* for *Travesties*. His characters are always from the educated classes, so it is natural for them to be articulate, and to reinforce the expectation of Wildean and Cowardian levels of wit in everyday conversation. In addition, as Billington identifies, Stoppard delights in letting his audience know what Stoppard the playwright has learned about for his latest play, thus the audience feels that they are learning from the play, rather than being asked questions by the play, or being forced to confront their own *ennui* – something Beckett's plays tend to foreground quite strongly.

Conclusion

The forms of fetishisation discussed in this chapter form an over-arching structure for the rest of this book. The proceeding chapters elaborate and expand upon the forms of fetishisation shown here tying them into wider concerns of language minding specific to the periods covered in detail in the book (1945–1955, 1956–1962 and 1963–1975, 1976–1989 and 1990–2000). For example, in the next chapter, which deals with the immediately post-war era, I investigate the place of slang, and the dissociation of sensibility, as well as elements of the fetishisation of communication outlined here. In the chapter following that, I examine the way in which language minding is co-opted into the New Left project, giving rise to a concern for vital language; and in the fourth chapter, I look at the way in which language minding becomes less important as political engagement in the arts and on through the century until theatrical language minding, to all intents and purposes, comes to an halt.

3
1945–1955: The 'Dissociation of Sensibility' and 'the Jewelled Epigram'

This chapter focuses on language and theatre in the immediate post-war period up until the 1956 'revolution'. As the first chronological chapter it also attempts to give a sense of activity in the theatre and language minding up to this point by referring to texts and ideas from pre-1945. To do so is to risk reinforcing the stereotypical notion that drama during this period formed a continuum with the pre-war period, which, like all stereotypes, has elements of truth in it, although the whole picture is never, of course, as clear as the constraints of periodisation suggest. What I hope does emerge from the discussion of the pre-war period is the degree to which both language minding and concerns about new forms of theatre are as dominant then as they were to be post-1956 and indeed, post-1976.

The historical context

The end of the Second World War in Europe in 1945 is, of course, the dominant historical event in this period. The election of a Labour government, the establishment of the National Health Service and the Butler Education Act, which made education up to the age of 15 compulsory, are other decisive events in the socio-cultural fabric of the time. The Newbolt Report on *The Teaching of English in England* (published in 1926) provides us with some background on attitudes to language in the period before the Second World War. In terms of language minding, some of the dominant assumptions about linguistic 'correctness', propriety and felicity that manifest themselves in the theatre between 1945 and 1955 have their roots in this earlier period. For example, the education of theatre practitioners, audiences and critics in the 1940s and 1950s, as well the wider cultural dissemination of these idea(l)s via the media, seems to stem from the 1920s, where concern with language is focused principally on misuse rather than inadequacy. The Butler Education Act of 1944, although within the chronological remit of this chapter, is dealt with in subsequent chapters, simply because its effects do not really become apparent until the late 1950s onwards. Indeed, some of the writers discussed here are too old to have been influenced at school by the Newbolt Report, let alone the Butler Act.

i. Equal opportunities for 'speaking proper': The Newbolt Report

The Teaching of English in England (referred to as the Newbolt Report after the Chairman of the committee) was commissioned by the Government in 1919 to:

> inquire into the position occupied by English (Language and Literature) in the educational system of England, and to advise how its study might best be promoted in schools of all types [...] including Universities and other Institutions of Higher Education, regard being to –
>
> 1. the requirements of a liberal education
> 2. the needs of business, the professions, and public services; and
> 3. the relation of English to other studies.
>
> (HMSO 1926, 1)

This list represents the scope and ambition of the Report – it runs to 378 pages and covers everything from the history of the English Language through to teacher training via the current situation in all educational establishments from Elementary Schools to Universities. The pertinence of the Report to language minding 1945–1955 is the extent to which language is recognised as a means of social engineering, and recommended to be used for such a purpose. Other prominent members of the committee besides Newbolt – described by Terry Eagleton as a 'minor jingoist poet' – were Arthur Quiller Couch, novelist and professor of English at Cambridge, and Franz Boas, early linguistic relativist and tutor to Edward Sapir (Eagleton 1983, 28). The Report reflects this diversity of interests: reflecting not only Newbolt's 'jingoism', but also the insistence on the teaching of English language as well as literature, and the idea of teaching children to appreciate literature. Tony Crowley includes an extract from the Report in his study of language, ideology and nationhood, *Proper English* (1991), and both he and Eagleton point out that the Report's explicit political agenda was to make the teaching of English language and literature a lesson in nationhood, morals and cultural identity, in order to reaffirm national values and standards in the aftermath of the war. Crowley comments that the Report's:

> whole thrust is to view education as a possible means of intervening in history in order to restore harmony and peace. The aftermath of the First World War, the bitter class antagonism of the period, the rebellion in Ireland and the ongoing struggle of the suffragettes, created a tense and fragile social order.
>
> (Crowley 1991, 193)

The Report aimed to unify classes and English speakers by teaching them all to speak their language 'properly' – that is, to speak Standard English (although it was at pains to stress that children could be 'bilingual'; rather than 'suppressing' dialect, the intention was to remove it from the schoolroom) (HMSO 1926, 348). The Report sympathises with the difficulty of Elementary School teachers in some areas, acknowledging that 'they have to fight against the powerful influence of evil habits of speech contracted in home and in the street' (HMSO 1926, 59). In order to counteract this evil influence, it is suggested that English take pride of place among the subjects in Elementary School, reasoning that there is no point trying to impart knowledge to a child who is not yet fully human, or at least, not a civilised one:

> Plainly, then, the first and chief duty of the Elementary School is to give its pupils speech – to make them articulate and civilised human beings, able to communicate themselves in speech and writing, and able to receive the communication of others. It must be remembered that children, until they can readily receive such communication, are entirely cut off from the life and thought and experience of the race embodied in human words.
>
> (HMSO 1926, 60)

As is so often the case, the reasons given for using (and imposing) the standard were its efficiency, clarity and general desirability as a mode of communication. This attitude towards language – a simple conduit which safeguards civilisation and articulacy by teaching everyone how to make themselves clearly understood – is the doctrine which would have been drummed into George Devine (b.1910), Terence Rattigan (b.1911), Joan Littlewood (b.1914), Lindsay Anderson (b.1923), John Dexter and Peter Brook (both b.1925), Kenneth Tynan (b.1927), Tony

Richardson (b.1928) and John Osborne (b.1929) at school. However, the Report is not an entirely conservative document; it urges that an equal standard of education should be available to everyone, regardless of class, and that an enjoyment of literature can cross class divides. The following extract, which argues for education as a means of arriving at 'fullness of life', anticipates Leavis's conviction (as outlined in *The Great Tradition* (1962 [1974])) about the role of literature in the accomplishment of a 'full and rich life':

Both the idea that the man who works with his hands ought not to have a humane education, and the idea that when he has got one he cannot continue to work with his hands, grew out of the idea that education is exclusively an affair of vocation. [...] The first thought of education must be fullness of life, not professional success. That is the only universal educational ideal.

(HMSO 1926, 62–63)

This idea is stressed throughout the Report: perhaps naively, the Committee seemed to think that education in general, and in the enjoyment of literature in particular, all 'men' should be equal. The Report's progressiveness can also be seen in their enlightened attitude towards 'the Drama' as a means of teaching appreciation of great works, proper speech, and by osmosis, proper thoughts. Many of the practitioners and critics cited above would have been encouraged to compose plays, act at school, and even permitted visits 'to professional performances of suitable plays' (HMSO 1926, 315). Taking pupils to see suitable plays was also supposed to inculcate a love of suitable plays over unsuitable ones, thereby safeguarding their morals for all time, 'the sooner a child becomes familiar with the best forms of theatrical amusement the less likely he is to be permanently attracted by the worst' (HMSO 1926, 315). The overall aim of the report could be described as an exercise in releasing English children from the yoke of 'dissociation of sensibility', to enable them to articulate their feelings in a way that would do justice to their emotions:

What a man cannot clearly state he does not perfectly know, and, conversely, the inability to put his thought into words sets a boundary to his thought. Impressions may anticipate words, but unless expression seizes and recreates them they soon fade away, or remain but vague and indefinite to the mind which received them, and incommunicable to others.

(HMSO 1926, 20)

The Report also pre-empts George Orwell's anxieties expressed in 'Politics and the English Language' (1946) about the pernicious implications of vagueness (discussed below), as well as the New Left emphasis on communication.

ii.   The dissociation of sensibility

T.S. Eliot's notion of 'dissociation of sensibility' suggests that expressing oneself eloquently is only desirable if one has the feeling to match the words. Newbolt's *The Teaching of English in England* tried to remedy this by encouraging the development of the sensibility and vocabulary of all students and teachers, irrespective of class and prospects, through a liberal education. Eliot's hostility to universal education, however, makes it unlikely that he would have welcomed such a move. Indeed, it could be argued that augmenting linguistic ability could lead to an even greater 'dissociation of sensibility', moving people farther away from meaning what they say. Eliot coined the phrase in his 1921 essay on 'The Metaphysical Poets', suggesting that the Metaphysical Poets represented the apotheosis of sensibility matched to language, and that after their passing a disjunction between thought and feeling, emotion and expression came in to existence:

> The poets of the 17th century, the successors of the dramatists of the 16th, possessed a mechanism of sensibility which could devour any kind of experience. [...] In the 17th century a dissociation of sensibility set in, from which we have never recovered [...] while the language became more refined, the feeling became more crude.
>
> (Eliot 1932, 287–288)

It is interesting to note that this gap between thought and feeling exists in one direction only, confirming my earlier assertion that what troubled language minders during this period was propriety rather than inadequacy. Eliot is not suggesting, for example, that feeling has become more refined and that language has been unable to keep pace with it. Set against the background of the expansion of education and the egalitarian ideals espoused by the Newbolt Report, it is hard to read the dissociation of sensibility as anything other than an attempt to move the goalposts once again to elude any aspiring lower-class students.

As education opens up and refined language (supposedly) becomes within the remit of the chambermaid as well as the member of the Diplomatic Service, this is matched by a decline in sensibility. In this respect, dissociation of sensibility can be compared here to John Carey's (1992) argument in *The Intellectuals and the Masses: Pride and Prejudice among the Literary Intelligentsia, 1880–1939*. Carey suggests that every step forward in mass literacy and mass education was regarded by the intelligentsia as an encroachment on the citadel of civilisation, and was thus countered by the production of literature which made increasingly stringent demands on the reader, for example, Modernism. Carey offers the delightful symbolism of Leonard Bast's death in *Howard's End* as a 'reader beware'. Bast, a cockney clerk who strikes up a friendship with the intellectual Schlegel sisters and subsequently gets one of them pregnant, is attacked when the pregnancy is announced and 'symbolically grabs at a bookcase for support, and it falls over on top of him, so that he dies of a heart attack. Such are the dangers of higher education, we gather, when it is pursued by the wrong people' (Carey 1992, 19). It is fitting then, that the New Left should appropriate the sentiment behind 'dissociation of sensibility' as a means of promoting vitality of feeling and language among all classes, thereby rejecting Eliot's top-down model of education and literary arbitration.

'Dissociation of sensibility' can also be traced in part of the New Wave rationale for disliking the well-made comedy of Coward, and, to a lesser degree, of Rattigan's oeuvre too. Flippancy was the height of fashion in the 1920s and 1930s, but post-war, sincerity became more highly valued, and overly sophisticated or figurative language was under attack from a variety of sources. J.B. Priestley should have been popular with the writers of the New Wave: he was left-wing, blunt speaking with a bluff Yorkshire persona and a deep suspicion of mass culture, but his plays declined in popularity from the 1950s onwards alongside those of his contemporaries: Maugham, Coward and Rattigan. In spite of their experiments with shifting time frames, and plain-speaking, Priestley's plays remained set in drawing rooms, dining rooms and hotels. His most famous plays combine naturalistic dialogue with a subject matter which frequently makes reference to a fourth dimension, or 'other world' beyond the rational. In *An Inspector Calls* (1946) this is hinted at through Inspector Goole's pre-knowledge of the death of Eva and the Birlings' involvement in it. The play takes place in 1912 in 'Brumley, an industrial city in the North Midlands' and begins with the Birlings celebrating the engagement of their daughter Shelia to Gerald Croft. Their celebrations are interrupted by the arrival of a mysterious police inspector (Birling) who announces the death of a young woman called Eva Smith and then proceeds to demonstrate that every person present at the table has been instrumental in her downfall and subsequent suicide. Having reduced their complacency to rubble, and having exposed the son as a thief, the son-in-law as an adulterer and the rest of the family as selfish and vindictive, the Inspector leaves. As they sit contemplating the evening's revelations, the Birlings receive a phone call telling them 'a girl has just died – on her way to the Infirmary – after swallowing some disinfectant. And a police inspector is on his way here – to ask us some – questions' (Priestley 1947, 73). This is the moment that propels the play beyond the norms of naturalistic and moralistic drama into the familiar Priestleyean realm of other dimensions: perhaps the action of the play is beginning again, or Birling is an otherworldly avenger, or it has all been a dream. What is striking is the way in which Priestley uses the conventions of naturalism to criticise the complacency and selfishness of the 'respectable' Society. In a letter to Michael MacOwan published at the beginning of the 1947 edition, Priestley rather acerbically criticises the press and public for their inability to see through the naturalistic setting to the message beneath:

> Basil Dean's production [...] had more realistic detail and more solidity in it than Tairov's;[1] and there was a strong suggestion of pre-1914 Manchester Repertory drama about the Birling family in the first half-hour, a suggestion that I for one rather enjoyed; but I can see that, set as it is against this weighty naturalism, the play's symbolism tends to be under-emphasised; so that perhaps there is an excuse for those London daily grumblers who really thought the play is merely concerned with a bit of excitement in one night in 1912 and is not an attempt to dramatise the history of the last thirty years or so making everything cast a long shadow.
>
> (Priestley 1947, vii)

Priestley's disappointment is not altogether surprising. The bell announcing the Inspector's arrival rings as soon as Birling has finished denouncing the New Left's ideal of cooperation and community:

> **Birling**: [...] the way some of these cranks talk and write now, you'd think everybody had to look after everybody else, as if we were all mixed up together like bees in a hive – community and all that nonsense. But take my word for it you youngsters – and I've learnt in the

good hard school of experience – that a man has to mind his own business and look after himself and his own – and –

We hear the sharp ring of a front door bell. **Birling** *stops to listen.*

(Priestley 1947, 10)

For all the subtlety of this gesture, Goole might as well have appeared in a puff of smoke, but there are other, less crude clues to the rottenness at the Birlings' moral core. The stage directions describe the Birlings as '*a heavy-looking, rather portentous man in his middle fifties with fairly easy manners but rather provincial in his speech. His wife is about fifty, a rather cold woman and her husband's social superior*' (Priestley 1947, 1) and throughout the opening scene both give the impression of being fixated on financial and social success at the expense of everything else. Mrs Birling in particular is concerned on keeping up appearances and constantly upbraids the rest of the family for slips of etiquette.

When he does appear, Inspector Goole's speech and manner is anything but symbolic: he continually cuts through the family's attempt to finesse their way out of their responsibility for Eva Smith's death by rephrasing their blustering into 'plain fact'. An example of this unvarnished style is the way in which he breaks the news of Eva's death to Sheila Birling:

Inspector (*impressively*). I'm a police inspector, Miss Birling. This afternoon a young woman drank some disinfectant and died, after several hours of agony, tonight in the infirmary.
Sheila. Oh – how horrible! Was it an accident?
Inspector. No. She wanted to end her life. She felt she couldn't go on any longer.

(Priestley 1947, 17)

The most common adjectives used to describe Goole's speech style in the stage directions are 'massively', 'steadily', 'impressively' and 'with authority' or 'authoritatively'; the Birlings and Gerald, after Goole arrives, tend to speak 'miserably', 'abruptly' 'uneasily', 'sharply', 'angrily' and 'sulkily'. Thus we gather that blunt speech belongs to the righteous, a point that Orwell affirms in 'Politics and the English Language' published in the same year.

The Linden Tree, first performed in 1947, also centres on a family gathering in which unpalatable truths come to the surface and are finally acknowledged. Professor Linden teaches History at a university in the 'provincial city of Burmanley' (Priestley 1948, iii). The university (and society) are changing and his style of teaching and the values he upholds are no longer welcome. His wife and older colleagues are hoping for an honourable withdrawal so that he can return to 'civilisation' (i.e., Oxbridge or London). His older children – Jean, a doctor at a London hospital; Marion, married to a French aristocrat; and Rex, who does something mysterious with money – arrive to help persuade him to leave. They fail, and Mrs Linden leaves with them, hoping that the Professor and their youngest daughter Dinah will follow eventually. In the time it takes for this to happen, nearly everyone has had some kind of emotional outburst. However, despite the rather conventional plot, the play is remarkable for two things: the way in which Priestley represents characters from differing social classes and regions, and its use of overlapping dialogue.

One of the first characters to appear is Mrs Cotton, described by Priestley as *'the Linden's woman-of-all work and looks it. She is middle-aged and has a curious confused manner, which must be played seriously and not for laughs'* (Priestley 1948, 1). She is also a stereotypically garrulous Cockney: when she shows Lockhart (the University Secretary) into Professor Linden's study, she answers his protest: 'Oh – I say – is this right?' with a torrent of information:

> **Mrs Cotton**: Right? It's as right as we can make it. Nothing's right now, nor ever will be, if you ask me. Half the sitting-room ceiling come down yesterday – no warning – just come down in the night – and when I see it, I stood there – ice-cold, turned to stone, I was an' couldn't speak for ten minutes
> **Lockhart**: I'm afraid I don't understand – I meant –
> **Mrs Cotton**: It took me right back – see? Lived in Croydon – an' went out one Saturday morning for a bit o' fish – and one o' them buzz-bombs came – and when I gets back – it's all over – finished for ever – all three of'em – and the home of course.
>
> (Priestley 1948, 1–2)

Mrs Cotton's eccentricities, we gather, are the result of her traumatic experience during the Blitz, hence, presumably, Priestley's instruction that she should not be a figure of fun. Her non-standard usages, 'come' instead of 'came', 'gets' instead of 'got', elided 'd' in 'and' and 'f' in 'of' all remind us that she is one of the chirpy cockneys who cannot be kept down, even by bombing. Her spirit manifests itself at several points in the play, but most amusingly when she is trying to instruct Dinah in the mysteries of rationing:

> **Mrs Cotton:** 'Alf the time it isn't difficult – it's just bloody impossible. Minute I think o' them shops, up the language comes. I come out with it at Frost's, greengrocer's Tuesday mornin', an' e' says 'You're no lady to talk like that'. An' I says 'I know I'm not- but you're no greengrocer neither, though you've got it up outside you are', I says.
>
> (Priestley 1948, 74)

Alongside Mrs Cotton's cockney outbursts and the genteel tones of Professor and Mrs Linden is the 'provincial' speech of the Professor's scholarship student Edith Westmore. Interestingly, for all his own provincial roots, Priestley's stage direction once again indicates that having a provincial accent, while a disadvantage, does not necessarily make someone a bad person.[2] Whether this is emblematic of Priestley's unresolved feelings about his own accent, or of a pessimistic attitude towards actors and directors who might interpret a provincial character wrongly unless instructed otherwise, is impossible to tell, but it does attest to the fact that a marked accent needed an explanation. Edith is described thus:

> *She wears spectacles, has untidy hair, rather shabby wrong clothes, but is not altogether unattractive and must not be grotesque or comic. She has a provincial accent, which must not be overdone, and has a strained manner, a mixture of shyness and defiance.*
>
> (Priestley 1948, 12)

Actually, in terms of the text, she speaks in exactly the same way as the Lindens, only without their confidence. Unlike the Birlings, most of the Lindens feel that they must speak their mind all the time. Rex is the exception, at first he seems to have sauntered in from a Noel Coward play: he makes flippant jokes, is incredibly rich and apparently unserious about money and thinks nothing of offering Edith advice about her make up and clothes, or of kissing her. Yet it soon transpires that this raffish demeanour is nothing but a façade he has erected after his experiences during the war. We learn all about this during his own heart-to-heart with his father in which he explains the change that has come over him:

> First, losing Jock – and some of the other chaps. Then that spell at the War House – and war-time London. But even then I was still ready to

put my shoulder to one of the back wheels of the big chariot – and be as dusty as hell – if somebody big enough had shouted 'Come on, chaps. Throw in everything you've got. Either we'll work miracles or go down fighting.' Something like that. The words don't matter. But the mood does, and the inspiration – just to have one good crack at it before the bombs came again – or perhaps they would never come if we showed the world a great example – gave'em all hope again. Look I'm talking too much – and most of it bullsh [*sic*], I suppose.

(Priestley 1948, 33)

Rex's disillusionment with post-war Britain was shared by many, and was to be explored in great detail by the writers of the 1950s and 1960s. In this speech however, he sounds much more like one of the thoughtful servicemen that turn up in the plays of Rattigan – fearful of losing their stiff upper lip and bewildered by the world in which they find themselves after the war. This bewilderment and shift of moral perception also affected the way in which people viewed language in the post-war period as explored in the following section.

The linguistic context

As discussed in the preceding chapters, there are various theories that illuminate the notion of 'communication failure'. There are also many theories as to when 'lack of faith' in language became manifest. For Steiner, it is knowledge of the death camps and man's inhumanity to man that has contaminated language, but also made language inadequate. For other language minders, such as Orwell, the problem is not so much inadequacy but misuse. The gap between Orwell and Steiner also marks the gap between language minding which focuses on the impropriety paradigm, and minding which focuses on an inadequacy paradigm. The impropriety paradigm focuses on misuse of language; the inadequacy paradigm on the fact that language has not kept place with sensibility, and that slang, jargon and other non-standard usage imperil the purity and clarity of speech.

This idea of 'contamination' in particular the way in which slang and other non-standard forms of language occupied language minders in the immediate post-war period.

i.   Orwell and linguistic impropriety

Orwell's concerns about language expressed in 'Politics and the English Language' (1946) are a reflection not only of the link between language and nationhood, but also of the link between language and morals. The link has exercised language minders for centuries, and continues to do so today, manifesting itself in complaints about debased values and people who are incapable of making themselves clear without resorting to slang. For Orwell, linguistic perversion arises out of laziness but it is a short step between using contaminated language and embracing the contaminated ideals that lurk behind it, hence Orwell's dictum: 'Never use a foreign phrase, a scientific word, or a jargon word if you can think of an everyday English equivalent' (Orwell 1961, 351). Vagueness in language enacts a form of dissociation of sensibility, particularly with regard to politics. The horrors of the war still fresh in his mind, Orwell laments the way in which 'political speech and writing are largely the defence of the indefensible'. To defend them would be to engage in too brutal a discourse (Orwell 1961, 347):

> Thus political language has to consist largely of euphemism, question-begging and sheer cloudy vagueness. Defenceless villages are bombarded from the air, the inhabitants driven out into the country, the cattle machine-gunned, the huts set on fire with incendiary bullets: this is called *pacification*.
>
> (Orwell 1961, 347)

Orwell's polemic updates dissociation of sensibility for the atomic age, anticipating the writings of Steiner and others on the way in which the atrocities of the Second World War shaped literary attitudes towards language. It is interesting that Orwell's objection to jargon is the way it obscures meaning, whereas Ross (below) is concerned with describing how jargon and slang can be used to differentiate class.

ii. Ross and linguistic impropriety

Adam Ross's 'Linguistic Class-Indicators in Present-Day English' (1954) first appeared in *Neuphilologische Mitteilungen*, then as 'U and Non-U. An Essay in Sociological Linguistics' in Nancy Mitford's collection of essays *Noblesse Oblige* (1956), alongside Mitford's explanation of the English Aristocracy, 'Strix's' article on 'Posh Lingo' and Betejeman's 'How to Get On in Society'. Ross's descriptions of slang tie in very well with the way in which slang and U-phrases are deployed in Coward and Rattigan, and his interest in both the Navy and the Diplomatic Service makes him a peculiarly apt choice, given the playwrights' predeliction for these professions in their plays. According to Ross, although improvements in social welfare and education, along with class mobility during the war, mean that 'a member of the upper classes is, for instance, not necessarily better educated, cleaner or richer than someone not of this class'. He also asserts that most professions are now open to all classes, with two notable exceptions:

> It may, however be doubted how far the Navy and the Diplomatic Service will in practice (in contradistinction to this theory) be 'democratised', even if there should be a succession of Labour Governments; foreigners seem to expect English diplomats to be of the upper class.
>
> (Ross 1956, 11)

Ross also comments that U speakers tend not to use as much slang as they did previously, with the exception of those in the Services during the war. However, he notes that: 'Since the War, there has been an unfortunate tendency for non-Service personnel to use Service slang and it is clear that Service personnel regard such use in very poor taste' (Ross 1956, 33).

Rattigan's *French Without Tears* (1936) deals with both the Navy and Diplomatic Services, as well as public school slang, and as such, is an irresistible dramatic collocate of Ross's theories, in spite of its pre-war status. Lieutenant Commander Rogers comes to a French crammer's to learn the language alongside a group of young men hoping to join the Diplomatic Service. He is constantly ridiculed by the other students because of his use of Service Slang, and his actions are frequently characterised in terms of them, yet, as Rogers points out during a drunken bonding session, their own use of language is equally marked and exclusive:

> **Rogers.** [...] From the moment I arrived, you all treated me like some interesting old relic of a bygone age. I've never known such an unfriendly lot of blighters as you all were.
>
> **Alan.** We thought you were a bumptious bore.
>
> **Rogers.** Oh, I may have seemed a bortious bump, but that was only because I was in a blue funk of you all. Here was I who'd never been away from my ship for more than a few days at a time, suddenly plumped down in a house full of strange people, all talking either French, which I couldn't understand, or your own brand of English, which was almost as hard, and all convinced I was a half-wit. Of course I was in a blue funk.
>
> (Rattigan 1981b, 56–57)

'Your own brand of English' is public school slang. The younger men deplore 'hearties' (sportsman) because they are 'high-souled' (Rattigan 1981b, 15). When one of the men is discovered to have gone for an early morning swim with his girlfriend, another teases him:

> **Kit.** [...] I had hoped you wouldn't be here, Alan, to witness my shame.
>
> **Alan.** You of all people an early morning dipper.
>
> **Kit** (*shuddering*): Don't put it like that. You make it sound worse than it is. Say a nine o'clock bather. Oh, hell, this coffee's cold. Marianne!
>
> **Alan.** Mere toying with words can't hide the truth. Do you know I think that girl could make you go for a bicycle tour in the Pyrenees if she set her mind to it.
>
> [...]
>
> *Slight pause.*
>
> **Rogers.** I once went for a bicycle tour in the Pyrenees.
>
> (Rattigan 1981b, 16)

These passages very clearly illustrate the extent to which registers are used to form and maintain social bonds, and in an environment as small as the French crammer's house, in order for bonds to be maintained they must be tightly and explicitly controlled. Not only is Rogers older than the other students in the house, he is clearly from the 'hearty' tradition, has already had a career in active service whereas the others are cramming to pass a language test in order to get into the Diplomatic Service, and so they deliberately try to distance him. As Rogers points out in the first passage, his age makes it difficult for the others to know how to treat him; he is not a contemporary, and cannot be jocularly insulted as they insult each other, so deference is mixed with mockery. He is also suspected of being 'po-faced' because of his formality; an early attempt at camaraderie fails when Rogers flouts the maxim of quantity. Alan and Brian are trying to warn Rogers of Diana's man-eating skills:

> **Rogers.** (*Politely.*) I don't quite follow you, I'm afraid.
>
> **Alan.** I'm sorry sir. I was forgetting you're of an age to take care of yourself.
>
> **Rogers.** (*Testily*) There's no need to call me 'sir', you know.
>
> **Alan** *raises his eyebrows.*
>
> **Rogers.** What you're implying is that this girl is – er – rather fast.

Alan. I'm not implying it. I'm saying it. That girl is the fastest worker you're ever likely to see.

(Rattigan 1981b, 12)

Alan's apology suggests that Rogers is being deliberately obtuse, either because he feels he can take care of himself, or because of the lack of chivalry shown in impugning the character of a 'lady'. In the light of Rogers's comments on the impenetrability of their language later on in the play (quoted above), it seems entirely plausible that he is not entirely sure what is being suggested, or, more likely still, that he thinks they are joking. However, Alan's switch to a formal tone, as indicated by 'sir', is interpreted by Rogers as a sign of his stuffiness. He rises to this by employing a colloquialism, 'rather fast', possibly to try and fit in with the other men. Alan seems to view the colloquialism as a euphemistic attempt to avoid a distasteful subject, and strengthen his own formulation accordingly. This kind of repair and correction seems extremely rude, as if he is shoving the fact down Rogers's throat, implying that he is both po-faced and naïve.

'Strix's' 'Posh Lingo' offers some useful insights into the way in which Coward's characters often seem to be speaking slightly tongue-in-cheek. Concurring with Ross's assertion that slang among U-speakers has been in decline since 1914, he suggests that U speakers have developed another mode of speech 'the frequent use, by those who in fact know better, of non-U words as a joke;' adding that 'I am sure that a sense of parody is a formative influence in the case of U-slang' ('Strix' 1956, 85). This sense of parody, and the use of non-U words by characters who 'know better', also ties in with the 'dissociation of sensibility'; that as language has become more refined, feeling has become less so. As Nigel so acerbically comments to his mother in *Relative Values* (1951): 'I suppose all this laboured flippancy is just to cover up what you really feel?' (Coward 1983c, 53). In the opinion of the critics, Coward seemingly personified this essence of style over substance, wit over 'genuine' feeling. In Hoare's 1995 biography *Noel Coward*, a friend of Coward remarks: 'Ginette Spanier, recalled that *The Vortex* "started a whole new form of conversation – until November 1924 nobody called anyone 'Darling' except as a declaration of love"' (1995, 140). By calling everyone 'darling' then, Coward managed to simultaneously trivialise the endearment, declarations of love, and imply a repugnant degree of promiscuity both in his affections and in his attitudes. In addition to this, he was feted among his own circle and in the press for his innovative use of fashionable slang, both on and off the stage. Coward was the epitome of everything Eliot, Leavis, Orwell and the advocates of 'genuine expression' most despised and feared. His characters are articulate and witty, but defiantly unconventional, and not above satirising the aspirations of others in the way 'Strix' has suggested. The flamboyancy of Coward's language, both in his plays and in his speech, is frequently commented on, and suggests an enjoyment of exploiting the 'playful' possibilities of language. As Gray (1987) notes: 'With Maugham or Wilde characters are witty, epigrammatic and lively, but it is a fact they themselves take for granted. Coward's characters visibly enjoy their own cleverness; they make language into a game, irresistible even at moments of emotional crisis' (Gray 1987, 197). This 'playfulness' in Coward's use of language is discussed in greater detail in a later section of this chapter, but first, a general introduction to theatre 1945–1955.

The theatrical context

> The theatre, in the first half of the century, was effectively dominated by figures like Galsworthy (Oxford), J.M. Barrie (Edinburgh), J.B. Priestley (Cambridge), Somerset Maugham (Heidelberg, though he was supposed to go Oxford), Auden and Isherwood (Oxford & Cambridge respectively), T.S. Eliot (Harvard, Sorbonne, Oxford), Greene (Oxford), and Rattigan (Oxford) – a tradition in stark contrast to that offered by the Irish playwrights like Shaw, Synge, Yeats and O'Casey. It is no wonder, then, that the emergence of young, working class writers should present the appearance of a social and artistic revolution. Indeed there was a clear messianic tone in Bernard Kops' enumeration, in 1962, of Arden, Wesker, Owen, Bolt, Willis Hall and himself as writers who had ensured that the theatre would never again be the 'precious inner sanctum for the precious few', and for his belief that by tackling issues of immediate social concern they could change the face of things, 'we hope for all time'.
>
> (Bigsby 1981, 12)

This is the stereotypical image of English theatre up until the seismic shift of 1956: an 'inner sanctum' of sleek, evening-jacketed men writing chic, slick comedies for a sumptuously dressed, perfectly enunciating cast in a variety of wooden poses over the course of a weekend house-party: at breakfast; playing croquet; at lunch; at cocktails; at dinner; standing near pianos and wafting through French doors exchanging well-bred commonplaces or acid witticisms. The plays are as perfectly arranged as a formal dance, or an elaborate masonic ritual with partners coming together, moving apart and coming together again as secrets are concealed, revealed and discussed (rather like the dance scene at the beginning of Act II of *The Vortex*).[3] The characters always seem above mundane concerns like money, jobs or any of the concerns of 'man in the street', they are solely concerned with the 'precious few' referred to above. As Harold Hobson notes, however, even this 'precious few' had slipped a few rungs down the social ladder by the 1930s and 1940s:

> Throughout the twentieth century the English drama has, in general, been about the ruling class. When the aristocracy dominated government, people of title besprinkled the cast list of West End entertainments, entertainments that then proceeded to tour the whole country without rousing any resentment. But when the aristocracy gave way to the middle class, then drama itself became middle class. In 1930 Somerset Maugham declared that it was no longer possible to introduce aristocratic characters into a play unless there was some special and compelling reason for doing so.
>
> (Hobson 1984, 18)

As Hobson observes, the fact that plays featured predominantly upper, or upper middle class characters had been an uncontentious issue, and despite Maugham's protestations, the 1930s hardly saw a decisive break from this formula. If Maugham and his contemporaries seem to have had difficulty in manufacturing circumstances compelling enough to slide in a few aristocrats, they certainly managed to portray a new class with the same stageworthy eccentricities and flamboyances, what Lahr refers to as the 'talentocracy' (Lahr 1982, 42). The conduct and values of this 'talentocracy' was just as scandalous to contemporary audiences as the unsavoury behaviour of the New Wave figureheads (e.g., Jimmy Porter, Jo in *A Taste of Honey*), just as their standards and attitudes seem as mundane or reactionary to us now in the era of *Blasted* (1995) and *Shopping and Fucking* (1997). An even bigger social shift was to come, and the idea of an upper and middle class monopoly was violently assaulted by the arrival of the New Wave, and its ironing boards, bedsits and squalor. The very different ways in which the two generations of playwrights articulated their very different ideas of dramaturgy, and the artificial distinction that has been imposed upon them, have merely served to reinforce the idea that the New Wave was a decisive break in the historical continuum.

Style over substance – (mis)representations of pre-war drama

Well into the 1950s theatre was dominated by a series of well-known figures, comprising what Shellard refers to as the 'theatrical triumvirate' of actors, dramatists and producers/entrepreneurs (e.g., Basil Dean, C.B. Cochran, Binkie Beaumont, Coward, Rattigan, Maugham, Olivier, Gielgud and the Lunts) (Shellard 1999, 16). The right combination in a triumvirate could be a potent box-office draw and ensure a long-running success. There was no subsidy and this inevitably curtailed the practical encouragement of experimental drama. The well-made play, and the variations on it created by Coward, Rattigan, Priestley and Maugham, was good for the box office, and, indeed, continued to be so throughout the New Wave (which was, after all – barring transfers to the West End – generally confined to the Royal Court, the Theatre Royal at Stratford East and a handful of theatre clubs). The general consensus (among critics and New Wavers) was that pre-New Wave drama looked good, but lacked substance, or engagement with any 'relevant' issues. Tynan's 'Summing Up' of 1959 illustrates the typical attitude to the dominant mode of drama at this time:

> As recently as five years ago, popular theatre in the West End of London was virtually dominated by a ruthless three power coalition consisting of drawing-room comedy and its two junior henchmen, murder melodrama and barrack-room farce. Although competitive among themselves, the members of the combine were united in their determination to prevent the forces of contemporary reality from muscling in on their territory. [...]
>
> Nobody except the gardener was ever called Sidney or Bert, and names like Enid and Myrtle were reserved for housemaids, paid companions, and pets. To pour the drinks, there was usually somebody's tweedy, middle aged stick of husband, who grinned tolerantly at his wife's caprices, offered brandy to her lovers, and never raised his voice

above street level; a symbol of sanity in a collapsing world, he was described by other characters as 'damn decent' or 'rather dim'.

(Tynan 1961, 229–232)

The virulence with which the New Wave attacked the values and style of its predecessors has led to a very skewed notion of theatre history. Tynan's summary is accurate to a degree, but the evening dressed 'inner sanctum' was under attack as early as 1945 – as Priestley's *An Inspector Calls* demonstrates. By 1954 (the 5 years before Tynan's 'Summing Up' of 1959), Rattigan's characters had slipped down the social ladder since the war, and Coward's talentocracy had all but fled the realistic play and moved into musical comedy. The tweedy husbands and prosaically named staff might still have been appearing in the West End, but the plays themselves were written in the 1920s, 1930s and 1940s. To overlook this fact is to shift responsibility entirely onto the playwrights without taking into consideration the audiences, producers and general economic conditions. Until the revisionist trend began, the fact that these plays had once been considered as provocative as *Look Back in Anger, Saved* or *Blasted* seems to have been overlooked. Similarly, the idea that the New Wave injected 'realism' into mainstream drama by introducing regional and 'working class' accents, and less articulate characters is also open to debate in the light of subsequent innovations in stylistic discourse analysis (as discussed in the Introduction). The rest of this chapter will focus on two of the biggest 'victims' of New Wave and post-New Wave scorn, Coward and Rattigan, both of whom have been vilified and ridiculed for their 'irrelevant' plays and artificial dialogue. As discussed in the previous chapter, many of the assumptions about what constitutes 'life-like-ese' are defined against the mannered, upper-class exchanges that are perceived to characterise theatre pre-1956, and in particular, against the dominant model presented by Coward and Rattigan. While this chapter focuses on the work of these two playwrights, it also seeks to acknowledge the historical disjuncture often glossed over when their work is discussed. First, Coward and Rattigan are not exact contemporaries, Coward's first play was produced in 1916, Rattigan's in 1934. Second, during 1945–1955, Coward's output was predominantly in revue or 'Musical Play': *Sigh No More* in 1945 (revue), *Pacific 1860* ('Musical Romance') in 1945, *Ace of Clubs* ('Musical Play') in 1950, and *After the Ball* ('Musical Play') in 1954. *Peace in Our Time* (1947), *Relative Values* (1951) and *Quadrille* (1952) are the non-musical offerings. The film *Brief Encounter* was released in 1945 enshrining the cut glass vowels of Trevor Howard and Celia Johnson for all time as the epitome of Cowardian pronunciation (even Coward's own appearance as Captain Kinross in *In Which We Serve* cannot match it). In 1947, *Present Laughter* was revived with Coward once again playing the role of the ageing, sexually irresistible, terminally witty playwright Garry Essendine. Third, Rattigan's plays (with the exception of *French Without Tears*) are more serious than Coward's, his characters engage in less wordplay, and usually do so in dingier surroundings. As Anthony Curtis puts it:

> Instead of cocktail parties there are pub-crawls; instead of elegant hostesses dripping in diamonds, a fat garrulous landlady; instead of White's or Boodle's, drinking clubs that stay open in the afternoon where former officers may fritter away what remains of their gratuity payments.
>
> (Rattigan 1985a, ix)

In sum, apart from Coward's *The Girl Who Came to Supper*, a musical comedy which he based on Rattigan's *The Sleeping Prince* (filmed as *The Prince and the Showgirl*) in 1962, the playwrights had little in common professionally other than the opprobrium they attracted from the New Wave.

Coward's critical fortunes

> Coward knew how to be popular, but he was no longer pertinent. The English New Wave was pertinent but would never quite learn how to be popular.[4]

Coward's work epitomises everything the New Wave set out to challenge. He wrote plays to a certain formula, with lavish sets and costumes, and made no secret of, or apology for, the fact that he intended to earn as much as possible for his efforts. Famously, he wrote most of his works in a matter of days, the bulk of the hard work being done during rehearsals and negotiations for contracts. In line with the spirit of the time, in which star actors could have a decisive effect on box-office takings, he usually wrote excellent parts for himself and his friends (similarly, Ivor Novello wrote and starred in his own plays). Before he became famous, he wrote the parts to showcase his talents and get himself noticed. As his fame increased, who better to write parts for him to shine in than himself? In his biography of Coward, Philip Hoare recounts the brazenness with which Coward pursued this policy in an account of one of his early plays:

> Depending on a slim plot (Uncle Daniel's promise to leave his money to whichever of his nieces or nephews makes good in the world) *I'll Leave It to You* is self-consciously clever. Full of effects and 'brilliant' ripostes, the play resembles Bobbie, bright, witty and effusive, but ultimately without definition or intent. Noel remarked that he 'at least had the sense to write a part in the play for myself, in which I should undoubtedly, when the moment came, score an overwhelming personal triumph'.
>
> (Hoare 1995, 82)

Similarly, when the Second World War interfered with the production of two of his new plays *Sweet Sorrow* and *This Happy Breed* Coward determined to defer their opening until he could make himself available: 'Both were written by me for me, and must wait until after the war. No matter how long the war lasts it won't affect my suitability for either role, since I could play both wearing a long white beard' (Hoare 1995, 307). As luck would have it, Coward did not have to wait until after the war, but this determination to do so if necessary speaks volumes about Coward's plays (and ego).

Coward's critical trajectory (along with Rattigan's) is symptomatic of the re-evaluation of the intellectual wasteland that was allegedly British theatre before 1956. He has recently undergone something of a renaissance after being vilified for representing an artificial class, lifestyle and register of speech, and for being so unashamed about his desire for commercial success. It is now more widely acknowledged that his plays challenged many conventional mores with their portrayal of cocaine abuse, adultery and homosexuality. Innes notes that *The Vortex* 'is a significant play, which in 1924 challenged social conventions. It extended the theatrical range in the same way as Osborne's *Look Back in Anger* would do just over a quarter of a century later, creating an equivalent effect of shock and instant recognition' (Innes 1992, 240). Lacey locates the vital difference between pre-1956 and post as the fact that up until that point there was little or no idea of a 'contemporary' drama on the stage.[5] Re-examinations of Coward, and a glance at the press commentary of the time, shows that this is simply not the case. Hoare's account of the reception of *The Young Idea* (1921) confirms this:

To have captured his peer group was an essential step in Coward's rise to fame. Sholto and Gerda, those archetypal bright young things, were irresistible models for a generation ready to accept their values: nearly amoral, certainly modern, always smart. The flapper craze – born of female liberation and the German *backfisch*, 'a compromise between pederasty and normal sex', and the post-war boy – cynical, smart talking and effeminate – were the extremes of type to which Coward's pop culture aspired. It was a time of emancipation: birth control and sexual liberation; drink drugs and dance-crazy clubs; divorce and adultery. Here his fans thought, was the playwright for their time: no fusty Edwardian dramatist, but a man to inherit the mantle of Oscar Wilde. His languid urbanity, his elegant witticisms and his innate understanding and experience of the turbulent era in which he had grown up made Noel a perfect anti-hero of his time.

(Hoare 1995, 114–115)

Certainly, later in his career Coward's work lost its claim to contemporaneity, but this was not the only complaint levelled against his later work. A review of *Nude with Violin* (written 1954, first performed 1956) in *Tatler and Bystander* commented that: 'The author who could [once] whip off a rollicking funny line [...] has dwindled into a mere playmaker who can still hold the stage, but whose dialogue all too rarely achieves those little shocks of surprise which make all the difference' (Russell 1987, 76–77). By the 1950s Coward had obviously ceased to appeal to youth but in his own youth, he was as contemporary as any of the New Wave. As Lahr points out, the New Wave reaction against Coward was based as much on objections to form as to subject matter, whereas Coward's reaction against his own predecessors had been based on a rejection of subject manner. One generation upped the scandal quotient, but kept the settings, the next lowered the social tone of both:

Coward's charm had long ago begun to wear thin with the Young Turks of English theatre.[6] Coward's boulevard theatre embodies the triumph of technique over content against which the New Wave was rebelling. Coward's was a theatre of enchantment; and the New Wave wanted disenchantment.

(Lahr 1982, 137)

The issue of 'technique over content' is at the heart of the clash between the Young Turks and the Old School. The availability of subsidy gave the next generation a greater degree of freedom to experiment with form and content without the possibility of commercial failure looming over them. This in turn is influenced by the high art/popular culture distinction in which what is popular could not possibly have any literary merit (a position advanced by Eliot and Leavis, as well as the New Left contemporaries of the New Wave). Thus, once George Devine announced the 'right to fail', the idea of failure as an indicator of intrinsic quality was reinforced: the Court's policy gave credence to the idea of the underappreciated genius, unwilling to prostitute artistic integrity. In such a climate, Coward's and Rattigan's colossal commercial success (in 1931 Coward 'was declared the world's highest-paid writer, with an estimated annual income, since 1929, of £50,000') became shorthand for their artistic shortcomings.[7]

Regardless of whether Coward had any real aspiration to produce so-called literary drama or not, his ability to write a popular and successful play is undeniable. He understood that in order to get a play performed and make it successful, it had to conform to certain expectations. This is not to say that he did not try to experiment, or subtly alter the formulae (*Cavalcade*), or that he did not have his share of critical opprobrium – not to mention run-ins with the Lord Chamberlain's office nearly as frequent as the Royal Court's. His concern for producing plays that could be performed well, that were 'actable' is well-documented; he prided himself on having learnt how to do it from his years on the stage.[8] The oft-quoted advice offered by playwright, actor, producer and dressing-gown wearer extraordinaire Garry Essendine to his protégé Roland Maule in *Present Laughter* (written 1939, first performed 1943) is often seen as Coward's clearest statement of his creed:

> If you wish to be a playwright you just leave the theatre of tomorrow to take care of itself. Go and get yourself a job as a butler in a repertory company if they'll have you. Learn from the ground up how plays are constructed and what is actable and what isn't.
>
> (Coward 1979c, 173)

The reconsideration of Coward and Rattigan is linked to the realisation that, as Bull pointed out, the 1956 'revolution' at the Royal Court was one of content, or even delivery, rather than of form:

> With the exception of Arden, the new writers of the 1956–60 generation, and in particular Wesker and Osborne, offered no real threat to the traditional format of the well-made play. Their political protest

was contained within existing theatrical models. Their characters may have proclaimed a refreshingly abrasive form of radicalism at the audience – although Osborne's increasingly less so – but they did so in plays which were remarkably unthreatening in format.

(Bull 1984, 3)

Having acknowledged that the form had yet to change radically, and that the content was not significantly different once allowances for class have been made, all that remains are the accusations levelled at the dialogue.[9]

'The jewelled epigram'

> The day of the jewelled epigram is past and whether one likes it or not one has moved into the stern puritanical era of the four-letter word. There is a slight danger that the language of gentility may be imposed upon dramatists who are sincerely trying to evoke the manners and modes of different classes in society.
>
> (Annan, cited in Browne 1975, 66)

Thus spoke Lord Annan in 1966, the man who proposed to the House of Lords that a joint committee of enquiry should be set up to investigate the practice of stage censorship and the law. Although the abolition of censorship was still someway off in the crisply enunciated days pre-1956, the 'jewelled epigram' sums up popular preconceptions about the standard and style of dialogue in these pre-'revolutionary' times. Kenneth Tynan was one critic who did much to keep these preconceptions alive; his keen ear for language, and even keener ear for an opportunity for pastiche did much to draw public attention to the gulf between stage speech and 'real' speech. The two extracts below are a representative sample, the first comes from 'The Lost Art of Bad Drama' (1955), the second from a review of Rattigan's collected plays (1954):

> at no point may the plot make more than superficial contact with reality. Characters earning less than £1000 a year should be restricted to small parts or exaggerated into types so patently farcical that no member of the audience could possibly identify himself with such absurd esurience. Rhythm in dialogue is achieved by means either of vocatives ('That, my dear Hilary, is a moot point') or qualifying

clauses ('What, if you'll pardon the interruption, is going on here?') and irony is confined to having an irate male character shout: 'I am perfectly calm!'.

[on Rattigan's *Adventure Story*] After reading the play one is forced to conclude that Alexander's real crime, in Rattigan's eyes, was to have been guilty of conduct which would get him expelled from any decent club. His pagan legionaries move like gods and talk like prefects: 'Been cheeking Alexander again, I expect,' says a general of his son; the language will not rise to the occasion.

(Tynan 1961, 91, 74)

The main misconceptions about the relationship between class and language use in English drama arise from the conflation of accent with articulacy and articulacy with expressiveness. Accent *per se* has no bearing on articulacy or expressiveness, but can be indicative of class. For example, it is perfectly possible to have an extremely 'posh' accent, but still be inarticulate, or to have a very 'common' accent (the usual connotation of common being 'marked'), but be extremely articulate. As previously discussed, conflation of accent with elaborated code is common, but based on a misunderstanding perpetuated in drama because it is a written medium masquerading as a spoken one. Combined with the conflation of drama and literature our expectation of dramatic speech is somewhat skewed. As Esslin points out: 'Traditionally stage dialogue always tended to err on the side of assuming that people have the right expression always ready to suit the occasion' (Esslin 1987a, 145). The plays of Wilde, Shaw, Coward – and much later, Stoppard – are classic examples in which the characters are never lost for an intelligent, articulate phrase. As Coward wrote in his defence of the South London life-like-ese he attempted in *This Happy Breed* (1942), expectation has much to answer for:

They [the critics] implied that in setting the play in a milieu so far removed from the cocktail and caviare stratum to which I so obviously belonged, I was over-reaching myself and writing about people far removed from my superficial comprehension. Having been born in Teddington, having lived respectively at Sutton, Battersea Park and Clapham Common during all my formative years, I can confidently assert that I know a great deal about the hearts and minds of South Londoners than they gave me credit for.

(Coward 1979e, 6)

Having discoursed at length about his equally 'sound working knowledge of the Navy, the Army and the Air Force', Coward goes on to give his own criticism of the play (Coward 1979c, 6). 'The character "Frank Gibbons" is a fraction more than life-size' in the ease with which he expresses his views, 'his articulateness throughout the play concedes too much to theatrical effectiveness' (Coward 1979c, 7). Articulacy and theatrical effectiveness are all very well it seems, but not from the mouth of a South London travel agent's clerk. Stoppard admits that his plays are constructed along similar principles: 'I don't think I've ever written anything where the main characters are inarticulate because my reason for writing about a subject is to say certain things and somebody has to be there to say them' (Gussow 1995, 57). The strength of this tradition has led to more realistic representations of speech – as in Pinter's plays – being perceived as inarticulate and described as demonstrating communication 'failure', when in fact they are merely a more realistic rendering of normal speech. Hedging, topic-switching and pausing are all indications that we are thinking on our feet.

Yet as dated as dialogue like Coward's seems to us now, and as mannered and contrived as Coward sometimes prided himself on it being, as Gray points out, for some, this style was ultra-naturalistic. Although Coward is hardly a by-word for naturalism now, in the 1920s it seemed to Somerset Maugham that:

> It was inevitable that some dramatist should eventually write dialogue that exactly copied the average talk, with its hesitation, mumblings and repetitions, and broken sentences of average people. I do not suppose that anyone can ever do this with more brilliance than Mr Coward.
>
> (Gray 1987, 23)

Maugham's judgement is testimony to the effect of time on judgement. Just as the content of some of Coward's plays was challenging and shocking to their original audiences, compared to the fare they were used to, so too was his language. Such a claim is reminiscent of the reception of Pinter's work in the 1960s and 1970s when those who did not label him an Absurdist, feted him for his 'realistic' dialogue. In *Anger and After*, John Russell Taylor pronounces: 'the language which the characters use is an almost uncannily accurate reproduction of everyday speech' (1963, 287), and many other critics comment on the 'authenticity' of the pauses, hesitations and stumblings which characterise Pinter's early dialogue (see, for example, Esslin 1977; Dukore 1982 for more examples). In a nicely ironic twist, Coward – praised by Maugham for his depiction of mumbling – nicknamed the 'naturalistic' style employed by the New Wave as the 'Scratch and Mumble School', obviously having forgotten the praise he had garnered for doing the same thing.[10] The point of these comparisons is not so much that neither Coward or Pinter (or indeed anyone else similarly praised) produced convincingly 'natural' dialogue, but that they were perceived to have done so by certain critics, while for others their dialogue was the epitome of artificiality (over-polished in Coward's case, and full of non-sequiturs in Pinter's).

Coward at play with language

> All you do with talent is to wear dressing gowns and make witty remarks.[11]

This section seeks to provide a stylistic analysis of Coward's hyper-articulate style, and to suggest that the self-reflexivity of this style may have some subversive potential. With a few exceptions (the plays Coward wrote to stir patriotic fervour during the Second World War, *Cavalcade* (1931), *This Happy Breed* (1942), and films such as *In Which We Serve* (1942)), the unapologetic flippancy with which Coward's characters greet every kind of scandal, sexual proclivity and non-conformist behaviour offers a serious challenge to social mores. Particularly when this *sang-froid* is matched with an extremely high degree of articulacy. To refer back to the link between slang and low morals discussed earlier in this chapter, it seems that, in the case of Coward's characters, their cavalier use of language is a reflection of their cavalier morals. Linguistic laxity is an extension and reflection of moral laxity, and an inability to take anything seriously, unless it is something trivial. Certainly, Coward managed to inject even the most prosaic remark with a degree of flippancy – the famous balcony scene in *Private Lives* (written 1929, first performed 1930) comes to mind. On being told that her ex-husband met his wife at a house-party in Norfolk, Amanda ignores the maxim of relevance to observe: 'Very flat, Norfolk' (Coward 1979, 30). While at first glance we might take this as a polite attempt to avoid a contentious topic, it is clear from the rest of the exchange that both speakers are fully aware that Amanda was equating Norfolk's flatness with other possible collocational sets: dull, boring, without life or fizz, and by implication, suggesting Elyot's new wife shares these qualities:

Elyot. How old is dear Victor? [. . .]

Amanda. I wish you wouldn't go on calling him 'Dear Victor'. It's extremely irritating.

Elyot. That's how I see him. Dumpy, and fair, and very considerate, with glasses. Dear Victor.

Amanda. As I said before I would rather not discuss him. At least I have good taste enough to refrain from making cheap gibes at Sibyl.

Elyot. You said Norfolk was flat.

Amanda. That was no reflection on her, unless she made it flatter.

(Coward 1979, 30–31)

There are similar exchanges throughout Coward's work. Flippancy acts as social bonding; the many bickering couples in the plays (Amanda and Elyot, Gilda and Otto, Gilda and Leo, Leo and Otto, the Blisses, the Essendines) know exactly how to interpret the comments, yet outsiders are either baffled or offended. In *Present Laughter* (1942), for example, Garry Essendine, the famous playwright and actor, tries to put Roland Maule (an aspiring dramatist) at ease with some phatic communion, but ruins it through flippancy:

Garry. You've come all the way from Uckfield?

Roland. It isn't very far.

Garry. Well, it sort of sounds far, doesn't it?

Roland. (*defensively*): It's quite near Lewes.

Garry. Then there's nothing to worry about, is there?

(Coward 1979c, 171)

Garry's attempt to play 'host' and indulge in some meaningless chitchat to allow his guest to appreciate the effort he has made in coming all this way to see him backfires because he assumes Maule will be complicit in his metro-centric attitudes, if not because he really holds them, then in order to ingratiate himself with his star host. Instead Garry merely sounds rude and (literally) ignorant, and Maule sounds parochial, and even Garry's majestic rejoinder is not convincing enough to make us believe the conversation has turned out the way he had hoped it might. At least one contemporary critic was alert to the fact that Essendine is not always flippant just for the sake of it: 'Mr Coward plays the character as a man who is aware of his own temperamental sentimentality and masks it whenever possible with a defensive frivolity' (quoted in Russell

1987, 62). The fact that Coward so often played the leading role in his plays suggests another level of playfulness in his work; by writing characters so like his own public persona he further blurred the distinction between authorial pronouncement outside the text (of which there are many) and characters' opinions inside the text, and encouraged critics and audiences to do so too.

Coward's awareness of the reception of his work brings a highly metatextual, metalinguistic element to many of his plays (particularly those which feature actors and writers). In a climactic argument scene from the (at the time) highly controversial *Design for Living* (1932, not performed in London until 1939), Coward simultaneously satirises drama critics, dramatic conventions of the time, and his own highly developed 'bracketed' style. Leading up to this exchange, Otto has just found out that Gilda (his lover) once had an affair with Leo (his best friend).

> **Otto.** Don't speak to me – old, old Loyal Friend that you are! Don't speak to me, even if you have the courage, and keep out of my sight from now onwards –
> **Leo.** Bravo, Deathless Drama!
> **Otto.** Wrong again. Lifeless Comedy. You've set me free from a stale affection that must have died years ago without my realising it. Go ahead, my boy, and do great things! You've already achieved a Hotel de Luxe, a few smart suits, and the woman I loved.
>
> (Coward 1979d, 32)

Leo, it should be noted here, is a dramatist, Otto, an artist. This is typical in content, if not context of the play as a whole. The three main characters (the other, 'the woman I love', being Gilda, an interior decorator) use the vocabulary and register of criticism and evaluation reminiscent of the reviews their own work receives; indeed, the stock phrases employed by Leo and Otto are an eerie pre-echo of Tynan's 'Summing Up' of 1959 discussed above. This self-reflexive commentary on drama is pursued in the opening of the next act when Leo and Gilda read aloud from the reviews of Leo's latest play. It hardly requires much imagination to detect the similarities between Leo's reviews and Coward's own:

> **Leo**: (*reading the 'Daily Mirror'*): '*Change and Decay* is gripping throughout. The characterisation falters here and there, but the

dialogue is polished and sustains a high level from first to last and
is frequently witty, nay, even brilliant –'
Gilda: I love 'Nay'.

(Coward 1979, 32–33)

On the page the capital letters on the nouns 'Loyal Friend', 'Deathless
Drama' and 'Lifeless Comedy' suggest these are stock phrases, clichés.
In performance intonation would presumably convey this suggestion.
Certainly, 'You've set me free from a stale affection' sounds like the kind
of cliché we might find in 'Deathless Drama' or 'Lifeless Comedy'. The
knowing references to frame in this exchange serve both a comedic and
a bathetic effect. In real-life situations we may often unwittingly employ
phrases and gestures that seem the most suitable for conveying the
effect that we want, but these things are instilled through culture and
may well have originated in fiction/drama/media. However, that does
not necessarily mean they are less genuine because of this. Therefore,
the suggestion that our feelings are insincere because the expression
is not original tends to be doubly insulting – not only are we sham-
ming, but we cannot even do it in an original and convincing way, so
to draw attention to someone's choice of phrasing tends to be either a
very aggressive strategy or a humorous one (because of the implications
involved for face). A humorous intervention might well look like Leo's
'Bravo, Deathless Drama!' an attempt to break tension by introducing
a joke (especially as, in this case, the joke is against himself (no doubt
he has been described as a purveyor of 'Deathless Drama'), but given
the context of their argument it seems a highly inappropriate intervention. Otto's correction of the genre suggests a further Face Threatening
Act. He uses Leo's joke against him to insult him further by suggesting
there is a degree of veracity in the damning descriptions of dramatic
(sub)genres.[12] The bathos of the exchange is intensified by the order in
which Otto lists Leo's achievements. Although at face-value this seems
a perfectly normal order in that it is chronological (Leo having only
just stolen the woman he loves), it would seem that this being the most
heinous of Leo's offences, it might rank a little further up the pecking
order than it does here.

A review of the first New York production of *Design for Living* (1932)
reminds us, however, how contingent Coward's playfulness is on [in this
case British] cultural knowledge. Brook Atkinson, writing in *New York
Times*, has seemingly missed the parodic overtones of the characters'
dialogue: 'unfortunately for the uses of artificial comedy, establishing

this triangular situation involves considerable sobriety. All through the first act, Mr Coward writes as earnestly as a psychologist' (quoted in Russell 1987, 52). As discussed above, there seems to be nothing 'earnest' about the writing of the first act at all. If anything, Leo, Otto and Gilda seem to revel in aping and taking advantage of the serious manner of their friend, the aptly named Ernest, the man Gilda eventually marries, only to elope again with Leo and Otto.

Rattigan's stiff upper lip

> There was not a single sentence in it that would surpass the emotional level of a railway time-table.[13]

Thus Harold Hobson praises Rattigan's *The Browning Version* (first performed 1948), for the subtlety with which the audience is reduced to tears without being made to endure any histrionics. Hobson is writing in 1984, at the end of his career, having witnessed more unfettered hysterics, temper tantrums and naked emotion during the last 30 years of his career than he could possibly have hoped for. And he did hope for them, and was not alone in this hope, if the rest of his account of *The Browning Version* is to be believed:

> For some time we had been listening wearily to the banal, clipped, naturalistic dialogue of modern drama with impatience, and we thought our hearts cried out for writing of courage and colour, for the evocative word, and the bannered phrase. It was one of the elements in the popularity of Novello that he gave us something approximating to, or at least thematically and scenically, suggesting these. But *The Browning Version* made us momentarily doubt (for *Look Back* was not far in the future) the necessity for this cry.
>
> (Hobson 1984, 148)

Rattigan's position, then, is between the polished riposte of Coward and the screamed insults of *Look Back in Anger*. His plays are famed for depicting emotional restraint and inner turmoil, and it was this very English style which so alienated the New Wave with its insistence on vitality and expression. Like Coward, he was seen as snobbish because he wrote almost exclusively about middleclass and upper middleclass characters (staff excluded), but his most heinous crime was to posit a typical play-goer 'Aunt Edna', a nice middleclass woman whom he described as 'a hopeless lowbrow' (Rattigan 1953 vol. 2, xi–xii). The suggestion that an audience might go to the theatre purely for entertainment, rather than to educate and improve themselves, is something Coward and Rattigan frequently repeated, particularly when discussing the New Wave and its incorporation of political and social issues.[14] It was also anathema to the would-be educators of the New Left, who were intent on erad- icating all things 'low-brow'; the last thing they needed was a public declaration that there was someone out there happy to feed the masses' vast appetite for un-political, un-ideological 'entertainment'. However, Rattigan never suggests pandering to Aunt Edna; in fact, he categorically advises against it, proposing instead what Rebellato describes as 'the playwright [...] engaged in a kind of *pas de deux* with Edna, with whom he or she must maintain a certain distance, working with and push- ing against the limits of her tolerance and understanding' (Rebellato 1999, 108).

Rattigan's work certainly seems very dated, perhaps even more dated than Coward's, simply because his plays tend to be quite serious thus negating the possibility that there is a degree of self-parody at work. It seems plausible that self-parody and self-conscious wit is what makes Coward and Wilde revivals popular and feasible – the enjoyment derived from listening to people 'playing' with words. The delight the characters manifest in their own verbal dexterity is shared by the audience – as Gray describes in Coward:

> A new phrase to most of Coward's eccentric charmers, is like a bright pebble to a baby, something to be played with and examined and put in the mouth even if the circumstances are not very favourable; Elyot and Amanda stop in the middle of a fight to debate whether adders could be said to snap or sting.
>
> (Gray 1987, 135)

With the exception of *French Without Tears* and the *Harlequinade* (which follows the fortunes of a theatrical family and is awash with 'darlings' and 'perfectly sweet of yous') this playful element is lacking in Rattigan's work. What his characters do share with Coward's is a high degree of awareness about the way they use language and language is used by others.

The understatedness of language in the majority of Rattigan's plays is now usually interpreted as a virtuoso demonstration of the use of sub-text. Shellard comments that *The Winslow Boy* (1946) 'demon- strated Rattigan's brilliance at creating characters masking emotional vulnerability with public stoicism (as in *Separate Tables* (1954))' (Shellard 1999, 15).[15] Rebellato's thesis about the reality of the 'stiltedness' of pre-1956 'Loamshire' speech is refracted through the lens of gay studies:

> This is why these writers [Rattigan, Ustinov, Huxley] have been censured by gay critics. The emotional repression in these plays 'reflects the internalised homophobia of the playwright' (Clum 1994, xviii) and thus they 'dramatise and maintain the closet' (85). [...]
>   Except that the reverse is true. In each of these cases, what we actually have presented before us *is* emotion, emotion which is perhaps immediately hidden, but in the moments when tears are dabbed away, when characters are tongue-tied with grief, or left alone on stage with their feelings, we *are* given clear signs of emotion.
>
> (Rebellato 1999, 166)

The 1956 watershed merely meant that as youth was getting in touch with, talking about and examining their feelings, it was not good theatre to have people keeping it all in. It was time for people to bare their souls verbally, not through a muscle going in the cheek, or a manly silence. Yet, Tynan, who criticised both Coward and Rattigan for their artificial, out-of-touch dialogue, was also the first to note that Coward's mannered dialogue was a significant influence on Pinter, the playwright acclaimed as the master of naturalistic dialogue.[16] Perhaps the similarity was why Coward singled out Pinter for praise in his address to the 'old-fashioned revolutionaries', that and the fact that like Osborne, Pinter had followed Essendine's advice to Roland Maule to 'learn from the ground up how plays are constructed and what is actable and what isn't' (Coward 1979c, 173):

> Mr Pinter is neither pretentious, pseudo-intellectual, nor self-consciously propagandist. True, the play [*The Caretaker*] has no apparent plot, much of it is repetitious and obscure; but it is written with an unmistakable sense of theatre and is impeccably acted and directed.
>
> (Coward 1961, quoted in Russell 1987, 91)

Pinter, here, is being praised at the expense of the 'Scratch and Mumble' school of the New Wave, whose vitality did not, in Coward's eyes, make up for their lack of a sense of theatre. The New Wave was equally unimpressed by Coward and Rattigan and their impeccable sense of theatre, rejecting the artifice inherent in this for being against their agenda of voicing the concerns of the new contemporary generation. Where the Old Guard elevated flippancy on the one hand and restraint on the other to an art form, the New Wave was to elevate earnestness on the one hand and anger on the other. The way in which the New Wave constructed itself against the template of drama made by the Old Guard is the subject of the next chapter.

4
1956–1964: Moribund and Vital; Demotic and Epic

For some 1956 is the point at which theatre threw off (and threw out) the social niceties of the drawing room in favour of a style variously described as 'kitchen-sink' or 'new wave'.[1] For others, 'kitchen-sink' was simply another string to the theatrical bow (along with other standard West End fare), taking its place alongside the new 'absurdist' work of Beckett and Ionesco, and the epic theatre practised by Brecht. All three styles attracted critical commentary for their use of language: kitchen-sink plays because they appeared to show people as they 'really' spoke; absurd ones for their dramatisation of the breakdown of communication; and epic theatre because of its combination of gestus and non-naturalistic conventions. This chapter will examine these theories of linguistic engagement in the broader cultural contexts of the period, and, in particular, the extent to which plays reflected how people 'really' spoke. It will also discuss the emergence of working class and regional speech varieties on stage and the reception of these unfamiliar forms.

Historical context

The disillusionment with Britain's post-war state expressed by Priestley and others in the 1940s and early 1950s found a distinct identity post-1955 in the persona of the angry young men and women who were demoralised by events in Suez, disgusted by Kruschev's confirmation of the Stalinist purges and determined that the future would be different. The New Left was one of the products of this disillusionment, and the intellectuals who made up the group – E.P. Thompson, Raymond Williams, Stuart Hall and Tom Milne – became central to the study of popular culture and everyday life. Richard Hoggart's work in this area meant that he was often co-opted in New Left rhetoric and project and his work, and the work of Raymond Williams is crucial to this study.

Williams's work can be broadly characterised as examining the interface between community, culture and communication. His dramatic criticism is concerned with communication and with challenging antipathy towards naturalistic drama and its apparent inability to communicate anything very much. He attributes the rise of naturalism to the shift in perception of humankind's relation to the universe, a shift that he characterises in terms of the work of Leavis, and more specifically Eliot. As discussed in the previous chapter, Eliot's theory of the 'dissociation of sensibility' and its implications for the relationship of language, thought and feeling was to resonate throughout the 1940s and 1950s. Williams makes just such a link, citing 'a response to certain changes in *language* and in *feeling*' as the most pertinent reason for the move towards naturalism (Williams 1954, 23).

In the introduction to *Drama from Ibsen to Eliot*, he addresses the dilemma facing naturalistic dramatists regarding the communication of feeling, and in doing so makes some interesting assumptions about the role of the writer and their responsibility for communicating *feeling*. In his antecedent discussion he has already engaged with the notion of naturalistic dialogue as 'tidied up speech', describing the suspension of belief necessary on the part of the audience to accept that they are 'overhearing' a series of '*ex tempore* conversation[s]' (Williams 1954, 21; Herman 1998, 24):

> The naturalists [...] insisted on representation, and accepted the limitations of normal expression. For those of them who were concerned merely with surface emotions, these limitations presented no difficulty: conversational resources for the discussion of food or money or bedrooms remained adequate. But the more important naturalist writers were fully serious artists, and wanted to be able to express the whole range of human experience, even while committed to the limitations of probable conversation. To meet this difficulty, several dramatic methods were employed. The most important, perhaps since it was used by three of the greatest dramatists – Ibsen, Strindberg, and Chekhov – was what came to be called 'symbolism'. The limitations of verbal expression were to be overcome by the use of visual devices that should bear a large part of the experience of the play.
>
> (Williams 1954, 23)

Williams makes a number of interesting assumptions in this passage. The idea that there are limits to 'normal' and 'verbal expression' suggests that language, and particularly register, is monolithic entities, and that there is no possibility of using different registers to express different emotions. The unproblematic way he interchangeably employs 'verbal' and 'normal' with 'expression' is also noteworthy, are we to take it that he regards verbal expression as the norm, or only in the context of drama? The meaning of 'normal' in this context are, in itself, problematic. It seems to be very closely allied to 'surface' emotions, and the discussion of mundane domestic aspects of life, rather than 'the whole range of human experience'. On a similar stylistic note, 'fully serious artist' seems to collocate with 'whole range of human experience', reminding us again of the Leavisite influence.[2] As noted in Chapter 1, very little attention is paid to the problematic status of 'articulacy' in discussions of drama and dialogue. Williams's description of differing attitudes to it here is useful for the discussion of drama in the proceeding chapters: his touching on 'symbolism' reminds us of the role semiotics has to play in the 1960s, and also how the political playwrights of the post-1968 generation adopt the idea of making the inarticulate articulate.

Given his defence of Naturalism in these early works, it seems inevitable that Williams should champion the kitchen-sink drama, and the 'vitality' and 'feeling' it stood for. In 1968 he summarised his 'own impression of the last six of seven years of English drama [...as] a period of extreme confusion and eclecticism, made more so by a genuine burst of vitality' (Williams in Russell Brown [ed.] 1968, 26). Later in the same article – having cited the work of Wesker, Kops and Behan as prime examples of this vitality – he makes the connection back to *feeling*: 'What came through, then, was not so much a new area of life, in the ordinary descriptive sense, as a new wave of feeling'. Here we see Williams's keywords (as opposed to *Keywords* (1976)) at work again: 'genuine' collocates with 'vitality'; 'ordinary' is pitted against 'feeling'. There is a clear distinction in Williams's prose between these attributes of 'genuine communication' and the dull surface patter of 'ordinary' life. The conduit metaphor is highly evident here: 'came through', 'wave'; and what comes through is *feelings* that are *genuine, vital*, full of life, the antithesis of 'orthodox middle-class drama' which 'is not about real people in real situations, but about conventional characters (superficial and flattering) in conventional situations (theatrical and unreal)' (Williams 1968a, 27).

By 1968, Williams had had the chance to develop his ideas of culture, community and communication sufficiently to include kitchen-sink drama – as seen in his reworking of *Drama from Ibsen to Eliot* (first published 1952), into *Drama from Ibsen to Brecht* (first published 1968) – but the book at the heart of this movement, in both date and sentiment, is *Culture and Society*, first published in 1958. In the Foreword, Williams states that the book is a continuation of an enquiry and reinterpretation of the tradition 'which the word "culture" describes in terms of the experience of our own generation' (Williams 1982, 11).

Theatrical context

In *1956 and All That* (1999), Dan Rebellato advances the idea that part of the New Left's project that kitchen-sink drama (wittingly or unwittingly) took up was to rectify what Eliot described as the 'dissociation of sensibility', the gap between thought and feeling. He describes how 'dissociation of sensibility' fed into the general idea of cultural malaise during the post-war period, which Leavis, and, later on, the New Left were trying to counteract by reconfiguring notions of culture:

> What Leavis and Eliot share is a certain historical view, a belief that at one point thought and word, feeling and expression, style and sensuousness were unified, before being torn asunder. Leavis' vision of life before this fall was of an 'organic society'. In *Culture and Environment* (1933) he and Denys Thompson imagine a life where culture was the expression of 'an art of life, a way of living, ordered and patterned, involving social arts, codes of intercourse and a responsive adjustment' [...]. Fantasising a historical sociology around Eliot's thesis, Leavis and Thompson imagine a time when word, thought, feeling and the body worked in harmony with each other and with their environment.
>
> (Rebellato 1999, 25)

In order to tackle the gap between thought and feeling, one had to be committed to the idea that one could express oneself in a way that could do justice to these feelings and thoughts, and the New Left believed this to be possible. In addition, as Rebellato points out, Leavis and Thompson had extrapolated this idea of a natural link between thought and feeling into the idea of an organic link between culture and community. For the New Left, the kitchen-sink drama seemed to fulfil these criteria. The work concerned itself with 'living' and needed a 'living' language in which to express it. This in turn necessitated rejecting the 'stale and dead' language of the previous generation of playwrights, in particular Terence Rattigan, who – as discussed in the previous chapter – was derided and ridiculed for the under-statedness of his characters' language.

The work of the English Stage Company (ESC) at the Royal Court dominates the history of post-war British theatre. Established in 1956 by George Devine – an established and respected actor, director and teacher – with a mission to create a 'writers' theatre' where playwrights could enjoy the 'right to fail' (i.e., to experiment with form and content without having to worry about the box-office), the theatre is often perceived as the home of the kitchen-sink play in the aftermath of *Look Back in Anger*. The typical kitchen-sink play features lower-class characters disillusioned with life in the brave new world their parents fought in the war for, they tend to despise the encroachment of mass culture and live in bed-sits or council flats. Those characters who have been to university have done so on a scholarship, or thanks to the Butler Education Act (e.g., Jimmy Porter in *Look Back in Anger*). If they are not graduates, they are, nonetheless, often incredibly well-read and articulate (e.g., Ronnie Kahn in *I'm Talking About Jerusalem* and *Chicken Soup with Barley*). They are never apathetic, unopinionated or content. Aside from the plays already mentioned, other classic kitchen-sink plays staged at the Court are John Arden's *Live Like Pigs*, which dramatises the upheaval caused by a travelling family's forced relocation to a council estate, and Ann Jellicoe's *The Knack*. The flag-flyer for this new form of theatre was *Encore* magazine, established in 1954, and given a new subtitle in 1956 as 'the voice of vital theatre' which reflected the highest accolade it could bestow on this new theatre. It was alive and bursting with energy where the drawing-room comedies of the 1940s and early 1950s were stale and deadly. It was necessary where the older forms were past it. Or so the hype would have it.

Encore did not restrict its enthusiasm to the work of the Royal Court. The Theatre Workshop company in Stratford, under the guidance of Joan Littlewood was also deemed to produce vital theatre; although the new plays produced there tended to deal with a very different class of character whose native intelligence was far superior to any experience of further education. The magazine was also supportive of the new European influences on the British scene: the plays of Beckett and Ionesco which proclaimed (or appeared to proclaim) the absurdity of existence;

and the work of Brecht which stripped away the comforting bourgeois notions of theatre as a form of entertainment and challenged audiences to rethink received truths about society. Each form had its champions, and very few critics proclaimed their approval of all three: absurd theatre, in particular, was often seen as the antithesis of the other two, despite being staged alongside them at the Royal Court. All three of these theatrical forms will be discussed at length in this chapter in terms of their linguistic reception and the extent to which the discourses which surrounded them perpetuated practices of theatrical and dramatic criticism.

The language of life: The new left and the new wave

> *Look Back* was to insinuate itself into theatrical perceptions, poisonously some might say, but it has survived and no one has yet found an antidote to what maybe its principal ingredient – vitality.
>
> (Osborne 1993, viii)

Osborne had the benefit of hindsight when he made this claim. Whether he was able to detect such vitality when he wrote the play is nigh on impossible to ascertain. What is certain is that many others detected it, and elevated it to keyword status. Just as Williams had picked 'culture' as the word through which the experiences of his generation could be interpreted, so 'vital' and its collocations came to define another generation (in the theatre at least). Rebellato traces the popularity of these key words in the work of practitioners and commentators of the New Wave theatre:

> 'Life' is the crucial word. It is part of a cluster of terms that are distributed through the works of the New Left and the New Wave: the variant forms, 'live', 'living', 'alive', the antonyms, 'dead', 'death', the synonyms, 'vital' and 'vitality', and the related term 'feeling'. In 1956, *Encore* changed its subtitle to *The Voice of Vital Theatre*, and promoted the term in articles like 'Vital Theatre?' and 'Vital Theatre: A Discussion'.[3] Tynan's review of *Look Back in Anger* saw it offering 'evident and blazing vitality' and found Porter 'simply and abundantly alive' (1964, 41). Williams praised the new movement for its vitality (1961, 26, 33).
>
> (Rebellato 1999, 21)

He goes on to note how often the themes occur in the plays themselves: Wesker's *Roots* trilogy and *Chips with Everything, Look Back in Anger* and *The Entertainer*, and Arden's *Serjeant Musgrave's Dance*, all praised by the critics for their direct contact with life. Jimmy Porter, alive with anger, rails at the complacency of his wife and housemate, which allows them to feel indifference while he is consumed with rage:

> No one can raise themselves out of their delicious sloth. You two will drive me round the bend soon – I know it, as sure as I'm sitting here. I know you're going to drive me mad. Oh heavens, how I long for a little ordinary human enthusiasm. Just enthusiasm – that's all. I want to hear a warm, thrilling voice cry out Hallelujah! (*He bangs his breast theatrically.*) Hallelujah! I'm alive! I've an idea. Why don't we have a little game? Let's pretend that we're human beings, and that we're actually alive.
>
> (Osborne 1957, 15)

The irony of this oft-quoted outburst is that the 'vitality' it displays is so reminiscent of the tantrums of Coward's glib, self-obsessed creations. The sardonic tone, vocabulary, particularly the extensive pre-modification of 'voice' and the breast beating are all incredibly theatrical. The pattern of this utterance is repeated later in the play when Jimmy scornfully describes a phrase from Alison's 'Dear John' letter to Helena (an actress). 'Deep, loving need! I never thought she was capable of being as phoney of that! What is that – a line from one of those plays you've been in?' (Osborne 1957, 73). Jimmy also reiterates Williams's distinction between articulating 'surface emotion' and felt 'experience' in his character assassination of Alison's brother Nigel, 'you've never heard so many well-bred commonplaces come from beneath the same bowler hat. The Platitude from Outer Space' (Osborne 1957, 20). The reason for Nigel's platitudinousness stems, inevitably, from the fact that he too is barely alive, 'His knowledge of life and ordinary human beings is so hazy' (Osborne 1957, 20). Archie Rice in *The Entertainer* is 'dead behind the eyes', beyond feeling, capable only of a simulacrum of feeling as obviously derivative as his act (in the same way that Orton's characters also 'parrot' feelings, in their case, not because they lack inner life, but because of their amorality) (Osborne 1961a, 72). Beatie in *Roots* fizzes with life in contrast to the other characters whose complacency, like Cliff and Alison's, leaves them unable to really think or *feel*. A stage direction early on in the play states: '*Throughout the play there is no sign of intense living from any of the characters* – BEATIE*'s bursts are the exception'* (Wesker 1995, 92). Eventually, Beatie's vitality allows her to find a voice of her own in which she can relay her own experiences, rather than 'parroting' Ronnie's: 'D'you hear that? D'you hear it? Did you listen to me? I'm talking. Jenny, Frankie, Mother – I'm not quoting no more' (Wesker 1995, 147).

The connection between 'life' and communication is paramount in the Wesker trilogy, and particularly in *Roots*. It is only by returning to her own community, by finding her 'roots' that Beatie acquires the courage and ability to voice her own feelings in a way that is relevant to her own experience (rather than those of her boyfriend and orator *par excellence*, Ronnie Khan). Her attempts to lecture her family, as Ronnie has lectured her, only create hostility and divisions within the community, for example, when she criticises her brother-in-law for joining the Territorial Army:

> **Jenny.** Blust gal, if you hevn't touched him on a sore spot. He lives for them Territorials he do – that's half his life.
> **Beatie** [*she is upset now*]. What's he afraid of talking for?
> **Jenny.** He ent afraid of talking Beatie – blust he can do that, gal.
> **Beatie.** But not talk, not really talk, not use bridges.
>
> (Wesker 1995, 94)

What is noticeable about this exchange is that Beatie makes the same distinction between 'really' talking and the antithesis of this (which is presumably just surface patter), as Williams makes between 'surface' emotions and 'the whole range of human experience' (Williams 1954, 23) discussed above. In addition to this, she employs the idea of communication both as a conduit metaphor, and as a means of reaching out and joining together, of forging community bonds through language.

Community and communication

In the eyes of the New Left, working-class life (as described by Hoggart and Williams) embodied the idea of community. Hoggart, in particular, extols the community aspects of working-class environments. In *The Uses of Literacy* (1957[1971]) he notes that because of the nature of their employment and happy-go-lucky attitude the socialisation of the working classes is characterised by either extreme spontaneity ('popping-in' for a cup of tea), or a high degree of organisation (weddings, bank holidays, charabanc trips):[4]

> Most working-class pleasures tend to be mass-pleasures, over-crowded and sprawling. Everyone wants to have fun at the same time, since most buzzers blow within an hour of each other. Special occasions – a wedding, a trip to the pantomime, a visit to the fair, a charabanc outing – assume this,
>
> (Hoggart 1971, 145)

Coincidentally, this extract comes from the chapter titled 'The Full and Rich Life' which details working-class financial priorities and entertainments (the 'pictures', visits to working men's clubs, and so on). In his first chapter, 'Landscape with Figures – A Setting', Hoggart paints a rosy picture of the neighbourliness of the working-class community: 'Home may be private, but the front door opens out of the living room onto the street, and when you go down the one step or use it as a seat on warm evening you become part of the life of the neighbourhood' (Hoggart 1971, 58). Later in the chapter he reaffirms, 'Life centres on the group of known streets, on their complex and active group life' (Hoggart 1971, 63). According to Hoggart, the strength of this 'group life' is what has saved the working-class way of life from being swept away by the iniquities of mass-culture. He asserts, for example, that mass-communication has had much less of an effect on working-class speech than anticipated, but it is this very anticipation of change which explains the New Left's hostility to mass-culture (Hoggart 1971, 27). As Rebellato explains, the decline of neighbourliness – represented in Wesker by the replacement of the Khan's basement flat (where anyone can pop by on their way home) with a council flat on an isolated estate, surrounded by strangers – was reflective of the loss of community spirit. Rebellato notes:

> the ominous tone Williams employs to imagine its complete demise: 'we live in almost overwhelming danger, at a peak of our apparent control', he writes; 'we need a common culture, not for the sake of an abstraction, but because we shall not survive without it' (1993, 336, 317). It is not just literary culture that is dependent on the preservation of a common culture; it is communication itself.
>
> (Rebellato 1999, 28)

It is not really communication, however, that is shown to be lacking in kitchen-sink plays. Jimmy and co are always ready to communicate their feelings. What they find difficult is reaching out to each other. The sense of community, of common culture evidenced in the Wesker trilogy, is hardly in evidence at all in other kitchen-sink works. The characters in *Look Back in Anger* are not on good terms with their neighbour and landlady Mrs Drury and Jimmy recalls previous neighbours in less than nostalgic terms:

> I had a flat underneath a couple of girls once. You heard every damned things those bastards did, all day and night. The most simple, everyday actions were a sort of assault on your sensibilities. I used to plead with them. I even got to screaming the most ingenious obscenities I could think of, up the stairs at them. But nothing, nothing, would move them.
>
> (Osborne 1957, 24)

In *A Taste of Honey* (1959), Jo and Geoff are at pains to stress their individuality, an individuality that makes them outsiders, without community. Arden's *Live Like Pigs* (1958) details the havoc that erupts on a council estate when a family of travellers are involuntarily re-housed on it. Beyond the New Wave, things look even bleaker. Pinter, Ionesco and Beckett concern themselves with the behaviour of individuals in isolation rather than in communion, and in many cases, their community has shrunk to the level of three or four people within the same building. The theatrical antidote to this was the work of Theatre Workshop at Stratford, east London where the idea of community represented both a way of running an ensemble and an engagement with a local audience.

Theatre workshop: Revolting cockneys

> It was a challenge, to express the inexpressible with a few well-worn sayings picked up from a previous generation – but feelings as profound and strange as yours or mine.
>
> (Littlewood 1994, 493)

The artistic director of Theatre Workshop was Joan Littlewood, a figure every bit as charismatic and single-minded in her pursuit of theatrical excellence as George Devine, but from a very different background and with a very different idea of excellence. Littlewood was born in south London into a working-class family in 1914, won a scholarship to a convent school and then another to Royal Academy of Dramatic Art

(RADA). She went on to work for the BBC in Manchester before joining the agit-prop group Theatre of Action where she met Jimmie Miller (later to become Ewan McColl). United by their desire to produce politically committed theatre for a working-class audience, they toured the North West acquiring actors, musicians and designers on the way. After the Second World War, when writer McColl and actor/producer Gerry Raffles rejoined the company, they renamed themselves the Theatre Workshop, settling at the Theatre Royal in 1953. With the exception of a presentation of *Uranium 235* – a play about the making of the atomic bomb – at the Embassy Theatre Swiss Cottage, the Workshop had little in the way of a public profile among the theatre establishment in London before the mid-1950s. The Embassy production had been arranged by Michael Redgrave and Sam Wanamaker and, as Littlewood notes, their reception was warm, but patronising:

> The profession gave us the warm applause they reserve for their own when we put on a matinee specially for them. Afterwards Lewis Casson came up on stage to thank us, praise the production, especially the movement, dance and mime, but he felt he couldn't be equally pleased with our vocal technique. I couldn't help thinking that he meant our accents. I'd never made any attempt to iron out local accents; if the vowels were distinctive, that was all right by me; class accents were adopted when the role called for them.
>
> (Littlewood 1994, 226)

As this comment suggests, the Theatre Workshop worked on very different principles to the Royal Court (with whom they were constantly compared). The company were committed to engagement with the local community. They took actors with little or no professional training, and concentrated on teaching them movement and improvisation rather than RP. In *Joan's Book*, Littlewood's account of her own 'peculiar history', she frequently attributes the reluctance of the Arts Council, local councils and charitable organisation to support the Workshop's work to this refusal to impose a 'standard' on the members of the group.[5] In common with the Royal Court, they aimed to present a wide repertoire of plays: new writing, classics, European plays, musicals and comedies. Unlike the Royal Court, the writer was not assumed to know best, and most of the successful new plays produced by the Workshop had been shaped as much by Littlewood and the company as by the authors who submitted the scripts.

The Workshop's early critical successes, or rather, plays that garnered critical attention, were classics: *Volpone, Richard III* and Brecht's *The Good Soldier Schweik* and *Mother Courage* (which, coincidentally, Littlewood had appeared in at the Barnstaple Festival that had brought together the men who would found the English Stage Company). Then in 1956, a week after *Look Back in Anger* opened, the Workshop produced *The Quare Fellow*, a play set in a prison on the eve of the hanging of one of the inmates. The play was written by Brendan Behan, a former member of the IRA whose 'authentic voice' was beyond question. This was followed by Henry Livings's *You Won't Always Be on Top* in 1957, the first of the company's cockney plays. The action is set on a building site, and in an extraordinary bid for realism, the actors all learned the trades of their characters and performed them during the course of the play. The programme note is careful to establish the authenticity of both the author and the actors' performances:

> The author has worked for a long time in the building trade and was a card steward of the National Federation of Building Trade Operatives.
>
> He writes of what he knows and his characters are men you can find on many small building jobs in the South of England.
>
> The company thank the real bricklayers and building workers at present in West Ham who have so carefully and generously watched and criticised and helped us to avoid some obvious gaffes.
>
> (V&A Production file for *You Won't Always Be on Top*)

It is difficult to assess what these declarations (the programme notes often contained them) were supposed to achieve. It was an abiding regret of both Littlewood and Raffles that the Workshop's success brought more 'theatre types' to the productions than ordinary East-enders. If the programme notes were aimed at the East-enders then they can be interpreted as a way of reassuring them that they were about to see a play written and endorsed by people like them. If they were aimed at the metropolitan theatre-going public then they seem to be advertising their superior claim to having captured voices and experiences as authentic as those staged at the Royal Court, if not better.

Littlewood described the play as 'no plot, no drama, just men going to work on a building site in the rain on a Monday morning and the story of their day': this lack of drama divided the critics (Littlewood 1994, 493). Tynan, predictably enough, wholly approved of its 'slice of life' style: 'the extraordinary thing about the production is that it makes ordinariness fascinating'. He goes on:

> Henry Livings's play lacks every kind of form and shape except the form and shape of life. It happens on a building site and shows us the men who work there. They are neither sentimentalised nor shoe-horned into propaganda; they are simply *shown*; and that in itself is a revolution [...] the acting is so starkly authentic that words become secondary, as they do in life.
>
> (Production file for *You Won't Always Be on Top*)

Other critics, including Hobson, were simply bored by the lack of action and failed to see any merit in the desultory talk of the men as they went about their business. Off-stage, the play caused considerable drama thanks to the unscripted asides and improvisations that found their way into every performance and so breached the Lord Chamberlain's regulations which stated that only the licensed script could be performed. Littlewood, Raffles, John Bury (the designer), Livings and Richard Harris (who acted in it) were all summonsed. Littlewood's description of 'our two coppers reading from their notes' at the hearing communicates both the rigidities of British society in the 1950s (reinforced by the Lord Chamberlain) and her own irreverent attitude towards it:

> It was good comedy stuff, a complete muddle. Brickies were given carpenters' lines, carpenters the brickies; 'mouthy mucker' had never had an 'f', and 'mush', 'gooper', 'run and jump' and 'fart' sounded rather endearing. You could take 'I'm going for a Tom Tit' whichever way you pleased. Henry himself was a Puritan. It was alleged that Dudley Sutton had made the dreaded V-sign, and Mickser [Richard Harris] had peed into the open trapdoor while impersonating Winston Churchill.
>
> (Littlewood 1994, 511)

The company were cleared of the charges and the experience did nothing to change the confrontational nature of their work. Indeed, many of their new plays seemed to present a calculated snub to the moral values the Lord Chamberlain's readers were trying to uphold: *A Taste of Honey* (1958) tackled homosexuality, unmarried mothers and mixed race relationships; Behan's *The Hostage* – described by one of the Lord Chamberlain's readers as 'a filthy play with nothing to recommend it' – the situation in Ireland (1958), and *Fings Ain't Wot They Used T'be* (1959) poked fun at the recently released Wolfenden Report recommendations on prostitution (LCP Corr. 1958/1359).

Fings took the realistic representation of cockney speech to new extremes with its fast paced backchat and songs about spielers (gambling dens), brasses (prostitutes), screwers (burglars) and Teddy Boys. Like *You Won't Always Be on Top*, *Fings* was written by a 'real' person, Frank Norman, with songs added by Lionel Bart, who would go on to be the master of the cockney lyric, writing *Oliver!* and *Blitz!* In the published script Littlewood once again lays claim to the authenticity of the experiences represented in the play, and reaffirms her commitment to an ordinary audience:

> In the theatre of those dear departed days when every actress had roses in her vowels, and a butler's suit was an essential part of an actor's equipment, the voice of the Cockney was one long blissful whine of servitude. No play was complete without its moronic maid or faithful batman – rich with that true cockney speech and humour learned in drama schools.
>
> This refined and treasured theatre could not attract nor touch the vulgar populace, our theatres were kept pure and innocent, with the charm of an aged Peter Pan.
>
> Frank Norman had never seen such plays, nor even been in a theatre, when he wrote *Fings Ain't Wot They Used T'be*. If he had he would probably have run for his life. His first venture into any theatre was at Stratford, with the first draft of his own play.
>
> (Norman 1960, 5)

The play is set in the Soho shpieler of Fred Cochran, once the toast of the 'manor' but now eclipsed by French Herbert and Meatface, crime bosses who are tougher, more ruthless and therefore more successful. All three pay protection money to Collins, the local police chief. Fred's mates are Tosher, a pimp ('ponce' in *Fings* parlance), Redhot, a 'screwer' who has just come out of prison, his girlfriend Lil, a prostitute, and Paddy, who runs the bar in the spieler. Their language is a mix of cockney rhyming slang and patter, now familiar to us through parodies of Cockney life. Tosher's entrance in Act I gives a representative flavour of the style of dialogue:

> **Tosher** *comes in. He is the ponce, wide boy, big mouth, coward, humorist, flash dresser, all in one.* **Rosey** *and* **Betty**, *his particular 'birds', are having a hard time on account of the new "Street Offences Act 1959".*

Tosher: Wotcher, me old son, and 'ow are we this bright and sunny morning?

Fred: None the better for seein' you – or am I? Gawd 'elp us, where did you get that peckham?

Tosher: Wot, the old peckham rye? I fort it was very tasteful

Rosey: 'E nicked it orf a barrow, I saw 'im.

Tosher: And 'ow's me little sweet pea this mornin? 'Allo darlin, 'allo Lil, d'you still love me? Come on, wriggle abaht a bit.

Lil: Get out of me way.

Fred: D'yer clock the Peckham, Lil?

Lil: Oh! My good gawd.

Tosher: Wot's the matter? Fort yer liked a bit of art and culcher?

(Norman 1960, 15)

The representation of cockney speech here is interesting for a number of reasons, not least because of the 'inconsistencies' in what is, effectively, an eye dialect. Tosher says 'wot' instead of 'what' even though there is no discernible difference in the pronunciation of the two in RP in this period. Norman is careful to use apostrophes where letters are 'dropped' or elided: '*ow* for *how*; *seein'* for *seeing*; '*im* for *him*, except in certain cases, where we see *darlin* for *darling* rather than *darlin'* and *mornin* for *morning*, rather than *mornin'*. There is no reason why he should have been consistent (assuming that it was Norman that transcribed the script anyway). Given that it was published after the production had been running for some time (whereas nowadays the text is usually published before the play opens), it seems Norman (and Littlewood) would be concerned to make sure the flavour of the language was transferred onto the printed page, rather than just assuming that future readers and actors would instinctively know how to speak Cockney.

The success of *Fings* was followed by another cockney musical, *Sparrers Can't Sing*, written by company member Stephen Lewis. In common with Livings and Norman, much was made of Lewis's ordinariness, both in press releases and in the programme note:

STEPHEN LEWIS

Thirty years old. Born in Poplar. Still lives in Stepney. Worked in the building trade as an electrician's mate.

Came to Theatre Workshop as an actor in 1958 for YOU WON'T ALWAYS BE ON TOP, a play about builders. Since then has acted on TV, in several other stage plays, and for the past year has been playing in THE HOSTAGE at Wyndham's Theatre.

This is his first play and was written in the dressing rooms of the theatres in which he was working.

Finished his schooling at twelve when his school was bombed out. A poet.

Of his attitude to theatre, he says: –

"The world as seen through the bottom of a pint pot is much more entertaining than usually seen through opera glasses, and less distorted".

> (VOA Production file for *Sparrers Can't Sing*)

Theatre Workshop strove to create a sense of community both in the theatre and with the local people. Littlewood, like Williams and Hoggart, had known the 'full and rich life' of a poor, close-knit community, as a child and when on the road around Manchester and the North West. Yet her drive to create and maintain this sense of community was also to be the destruction of the company. By the time of *Sparrers*, for some critics, Littlewood's 'authentic' Cockneys were beginning to look very similar to the stereotypical cockney she had set out to challenge. In the *Guardian* Peter Jenkins noted of *Sparrers*:

> This is no more a picture of Stepney than those Shaftesbury Avenue entertainments were true of life in ancestral homes. There is a danger, I fear, that the Theatre Royal, Stratford, E.15, will become encumbered with a traditional formula of entertainment as irksome as the one being shed so painfully and slowly in the West End.
>
> (V&A Production file for *Sparrers Can't Sing*)

A view corroborated by Robert Muller in the *Daily Mail*:

> Having recoiled from the sentimentalised working-class characters usually seen on the stage, she [Littlewood] seems to me to have taken a long jouney backwards and, travelling a full circle, arrived at her starting point.
>
> (V&A Production file for *Sparrers Can't Sing*)

Ironically, not only were Littlewood and her company accused of being complicit in the sentimentalising of the Cockney life, but the success of the plays only increased the pressure on them to produce more of the same. *Fings* and *Sparrers* both transferred to the West End, as had a number of other Workshop successes. West End producer Donald Albery had been giving the company seed money for some years on the understanding that successful shows transferred to his theatres. In a further twist, it is likely that more 'ordinary' people saw them there than ever did at Theatre Workshop.

Littlewood was always very quick to condemn Albery and other traditional producers for depleting her company, conveniently overlooking the fact that without their investment, it would have been very difficult to nurture the actors and writers that she did. The problem was not just in the time they spent in the West End, but that being in the West End brought them to the attention of talent scouts and agents who could lure them away from E.15. A number of her major finds went on to have extremely successful careers in film and television: Barbara Windsor, Roy Kinnear, Richard Harris, Yootha Joyce, Brian Murphy and Rita Tushingham among them. This in itself was a sign of the changing times, film and television, once the preserve of the immaculate of speech (and of dress – even television and radio announcers went on air in dinner jackets), was expanding its boundaries. Theatre was still lagging some way behind.

Like-life and life-like

As discussed in the preceding chapters and Introduction, every generation claims to be more life-like or realistic than its predecessor. In this period, however, the claim is made with renewed force simply because of the trappings of reality that accompanied the plays in this period. The shift in the class of the main characters, the change of setting, the appearance of the ironing board, kitchen sink and cooker – all these signifiers added weight to the idea that real life was being presented on stage for the first time. To conclude this section, I would like to consider how close to 'lifelike-ese' the new style of 'naturalistic' speech was that appeared on stage during the 1950s and 1960s. Much has been made of reception of the plays as a whole, but thus far, I have said very little about the extent to which the dialogue of these plays was seen to reflect vitality. This second wave of naturalism (if we count – as Williams does – Ibsen, Chekhov as representative of the first wave) has often been touted as the epitome of naturalism because of the class shift of its subjects. Realism was also supposedly inherent in acting methods, sets, costumes, and most of all in language: the language used by the characters, their accents, their colloquialisms, the unpretentious way in which the writers, actors and directors responsible spoke about their productions. Everything was suddenly far more life-like and a new language was needed to describe and reflect this: hence disillusionment with language on the one hand from practitioners of new wave, and fastidious horror on the other hand from those who liked their characters articulate and well-spoken. Browne notes that one of the problems facing the ESC when trying to put on new plays was that:

> the plays which were being submitted [...] continued to deal with a society that had passed away, in a language that was dead – the language of upper-class Kensington. (Indeed, one of the attractions of *Look Back in Anger*, apart from the its obvious thematic relevance to contemporary life, was its break from the so-called standard English – the English of the Edwardian drawing-room).
>
> (Browne 1975, 31)

This quotation is typical in its employment of the rhetoric of vitality discussed in this section, and for its inclusion of many of the 'keywords' of the New Wave; the moribundity of the old is juxtaposed against the liveliness of the new. Indeed here, as in many cases, it is not even necessary to make the comparison explicit, it is enough to comment on the deathliness of the old. It is also interesting to consider Browne's portrayal of 'standard-language' for a moment. As has been noted before, it is a commonplace of language commentary to compare new and old, and the fate of the 'realistic' nature of dramatic language is no exception. In the previous chapter we saw Somerset Maugham praising Coward for the realistic nature of his dialogue. Coward's polished style is subsequently vilified by the New Wave who hold up instead John Osborne as breaking the hegemonic stranglehold of the standard accent. By today's standards Osborne's characters are decidedly 'standard' in their use of English, they might swear and expostulate but they mostly speak in full sentences, avoid dialect words; even Cliff (whose Welshness is commented upon several times during the play) never falters from the standard, even by so much as a 'boyo' or 'y'ere' – the favourite indicators of Welshness from Shakespeare onwards. It is the word 'drawing-room' that is key to ideas of language here: the word and the object denote a certain class of character, and it is class that seems to be the over-determining factor in New Wave accounts of language, for when they talk about 'standard language' they seem to be referring almost entirely to accent. Part of their 'realistic' agenda was to have characters with regional accents on the stage who were not servants or walk-on Cockneys/yokels with hearts of gold. Regional accents were still unwelcome in most areas of public life, and actors tended to make a point of ridding themselves of such regionalisms as soon as possible. As Elsom notes, actors were usually taught

to speak 'neutrally' (i.e., received pronunciation) in order to widen their casting potential (and, as Gramsci and others would point out, in order to reinforce the hegemonic position of the standard accent and all it represented):

> They had been trained to talk like that in drama school and leading parts were written with such an accent in mind. An actor who could not get rid of a dialect was not unemployable, for there were always character parts. You could earn a living as a spiv (George Cole), a Lancashire lassie (Gracie Fields) or a Cockney char (Kathleen Harrison), but these were often cameos, and it could be a chastening experience just to walk on in Act 3 for the sake of a vowel sound. The BBC also favoured Home Counties diction and in 1952, it officially stated that no 'dialect' voices should read the national news (BBC Press Release, 23 Jan 1951).
>
> (Elsom 1992, 25)

It is illuminating to consider that only 4 years before the 'revolution', the BBC was implying that the stereotype it had reinforced through its restrictions on regional accents (the preserve of what Shellard describes as 'maids, bobbies and artisans' [Shellard 1999, 52]) had in fact become true, and therefore that a regional accent was an unsuitable one in which to read 'momentous events'. Admittedly, *Look Back in Anger* did nothing to challenge the dominance of RP (despite being set in 'the Midlands'), but other plays which form part of the New Wave had main characters who were distinctly non-standard and lived in places other than London. Beatie in *Roots* (1959), for example, speaks in Wesker's idea of a Norfolk dialect (as shown in an extract from the play earlier on in this discussion), and at the time, the play was praised for the authenticity with which Wesker has captured the peculiarities of Norfolk speech. *A Taste of Honey* is set in Manchester, and although the characters' speech is not written in dialect form, non-standard usage is fairly consistent, as it is in *Serjeant Musgrave's Dance* set in a Yorkshire colliery town. The dramatist most consistently praised for his 'realistic ear for speech' (as has already been discussed in previous chapters) was Pinter, whose inarticulate and cliché-loving characters became the template for later naturalistic drama (e.g., Ravenhill and Kane). Most importantly in terms of lifelike-ese, Delaney, Jellicoe, Wesker and Pinter achieved more effective results because their characters spoke something nearer to the restricted code than the elaborated one. If we substitute the other epithet for post-1956 drama, 'kitchen-sink', for New Wave, it reminds us that the new Naturalism/Realism was augmented orally/aurally as well as visually by the shift away from the drawing-room. The dense, multiplex, familiaristic community bonds which tie together the New Wave/kitchen-sink protagonists are the kind of bonds described by Bernstein in his theory of elaborated and restricted code (as discussed in Chapter 2).

These particularistic bonds do not, however, stop the New Wave denizens from showing-off to each other in extremely theatrical ways – one only has to think about Jimmy's rants, Archie's skits, Ronnie's posturing and Beattie's preaching – it is just that they do so (with the exception of Archie) in a much more earnest way than, say, Coward's characters. In this respect, the 'hostility to theatricality' to which Rebellato alludes manifests itself as a suspicion of the genuineness of hyper-articulate expression. Hyper-articulacy is in such close proximity to glibness that it is only seemly for characters to make the transition to articulacy when they have suffered for it. Hence Beattie finds a voice when she loses Ronnie and the taciturn Musgrave turns eloquent in order to denounce war, whereas Jimmy Porter's brother-in-law, 'the Platitude from Outer-Space' has been glib since birth because he has never really felt anything (Osborne 1957, 20).

'Anti-theatrical theatre'

As discussed above, the New Wave focus upon the need for a contemporary theatre which could address issues of public concern was highly compatible with the New Left's desire to rebuild communities, communication and the 'common life' of culture. The union of these two agendas implies – and in many cases is explicitly stated in a series of manifestos, statements and interviews – that New Wave theatre was to be, to some extent, 'improving', consciousness raising and thought provoking. The earnest desire to educate was, and often still is, seen at odds with the frivolous desire to entertain, an opposition that offers further explanation for the tension between the Young Turks and the Old Guard. Rebellato uses Derrida's critique of Speech Act Theory and his formulation of the notion of 'iterability' to articulate the change in attitude ushered in by the New Wave:[6]

> a hostility to theatricality underpins everything marked by 8 May 1956. If Foucault has provided the historiography [for this study], it is Jacques Derrida, whose textual theory places theatre in a chain of cultural concerns. In the controversy over Derrida's discussion of

J.L Austin's work one of the cruxes was the function of communication in the theatre, and, crucially, vice versa. A concern over
the hazards that theatricality can set for the theatre underpins the
political stance and theatrical practice of the New Wave.

(Rebellato 1999, 9)

As outlined in Chapter 2, Derrida's critique suggests that all speech, and
performatives in particular, only succeed in their functions if one is able
to recognise them for what they are through a process of authentication.
In other words, we identify a performative utterance by distinguishing
it from other types of utterance, not by recognising it as an original act
in itself. Iteration is the process of referral and authentication, the process by which one recognises an utterance and realises the context in
which it is being used. The rhetoric of the New Wave, and the keywords
with which it identified and marketed itself could only be constructed
through the process of iteration, the process in which a new 'vital language' was forged in reaction to the old 'dead' language of the previous
generation of playwrights.

This notion of 'citationality' can be carried over into the general post-
structuralist emphasis on reflexivity, in the case of drama, of drawing
attention to, or playing with, the notion of theatrical boundaries. Hence
the New Wave hostility to the work of Coward et al with its elaborate
plots and playful dialogue and the new emphasis on sincerity and genuineness and 'reality'. 'Citationality' is most obviously exploited in the
language games or 'canters' of Vladimir and Estragon in Beckett's *Waiting for Godot* and Stoppard's *Rosencrantz and Guildenstern Are Dead*.[7] The
games are predicated on each participant being able to recognise the
transference of context and the 'usual' meanings of the words used and
then playing upon their flexibility or meta-linguistically commentating
on their effect. Such frivolous use of language is a long way from the
exalted purposes the New Left and New Wave reserved it for, and as a
result, the difference between their styles has been somewhat overstated
in critical accounts.

'Nothing to express, no power to express, no desire to express' – The anti-vital Theatre of the Absurd[8]

This section examines the way in which Theatre of the Absurd functioned as the antithesis to New Wave values. New Wave emphasis on
the 'common life' of culture is countered by Absurd emphasis on isolation; vitality is countered by boredom; genuine expression is countered

by communication as play, or problem. This section also focuses on the way 'failure to communicate' became synonymous with Absurd drama, suggesting that the comedic aspects of this style of dialogue were overlooked because of the unfavourable contrast it presented with the earnest desire for communication in New Wave plays. The analysis highlights the fact that the linguistic strategies used in these plays are almost identical to that used in 'ordinary' conversation and in the New Wave plays analysed earlier on in the chapter, suggesting that perhaps the Absurd was as comfortable with lifelike-ese as the New Wave.

The first English performance of *Waiting for Godot* at the Arts Theatre in 1955 was Britain's first taste of what was to become known as Absurd drama, and for some critics (e.g., Lacey 1995) has a better claim to being the 'turning point' in post-war drama than *Look Back in Anger*. Its resolutely non-realist style, barren set and almost complete lack of action was far more of a challenge to the well-made play than Osborne's three-acter. Martin Esslin, who coined and defined the phrase in *Theatre of the Absurd*, repeatedly insists there is no such movement or genre as 'the Absurd', maintaining instead that certain writers and plays were pursuing common themes over a period of time. 'Loss of faith' in language and concomitant ideas of 'communication failure' have been portrayed and perceived as crucial markers of 'Absurd drama' ever since *Theatre of the Absurd* was published in 1962; the terms have also been used to characterise any kind of drama where the characters have difficulty articulating their feelings. Hence work as historically disparate as Sarah Kane's (1990s) and early Pinter (1960s) have been likened to the Absurd dramatists in their use of language simply for portraying a more 'realistic' representation of spontaneous speech.

The term 'Absurd' describes a style of non-realist drama in which the characters strive to exist in a world without certainty, in which God is dead and man is alone trying to make sense of the world. Esslin (along with George Steiner) sees this loss of certainty as symptomatic of the post-war, post-Holocaust disintegration of humanity. He cites Sartre and Camus as the original exponents of this philosophy, suggesting that their drama may be 'true' to the idea in terms of subject matter, but is undermined by its adherence to more traditional dramatic forms:

> the Theatre of the Absurd strives to express its sense of the sense-lessness of the human condition and the inadequacy of the rational approach by the open abandonment of rational devices and

discursive thought. While Sartre or Camus express the new content in the old convention, the Theatre of the Absurd goes a step further in trying to achieve a unity between its basic assumptions and the form in which these are expressed. In some senses, the *theatre* of Sartre and Camus is less adequate as an expression of the *philosophy* of Sartre and Camus – in artistic, as distinct from philosophic, terms – than the Theatre of the Absurd.

(Esslin 1980, 24)

In the light of this anxiety about the disintegration of humanity after the war, the New Left project can be seen as an attempt to repair the ravages effected by the war. One such attempt was the post-war Government's proposals regarding re-housing people on the new council estates (like the London County Council flats in which the Khans are re-housed in Wesker's *I'm Talking About Jerusalem*, or the Sawney's in Arden's *Live Like Pigs*), but they were regarded as strangling community feeling. Neighbours in bomb-damaged areas were often separated in the move to new estates, and in London sometimes moved out of London altogether and into East Anglia and Essex. Obviously then, there was a certain degree of tension between the Absurdists who seemed to advocate giving up any attempt at positive living, and the New Wave.

The charge of failure to communicate is easier to reinterpret in a less reductive manner. In Esslin's account, much of the evidence for this failure to communicate is based on a conflation of author and character, and author and reader. In the case of Beckett, famously close-mouthed about his work, the temptation to do this is overwhelming, and nearly always succumbed to in critical accounts. The possibilities of parody, of iteration, are almost always overlooked. For example, in Beckett's first play *Eleutheria* (not published until 1995) Beckett's protagonist Victor refuses to speak and the play is centred around discovering the reason for his metaphysical malaise. In true Beckettian style it is discovered that Victor has made his most coherent speech off-stage and to the servants; at this point another character loses his temper and parodies Victor's imagined speech and his audience's reaction:

I see it from here. Life, death, freedom, the whole kit and caboodle, and the disillusioned little laughs to show that they are not taken in by the big words and the bottomless silences and the paralytic's gestures to signal that that's not it, it's a different matter, an altogether different matter, what can you do, language isn't meant to express those things.

(Beckett 1995, 134)

The accuracy with which Beckett parodies the Absurdist quandary about language suggests his attitude towards it was perhaps more equivocal than is often supposed; however, Esslin (and other Beckett scholars) cannot resist the opportunity to match phrase to authorial intention, in the same way that Beckett's silence has led many academics to infer Beckett's attitudes from his reading habits. The most famous example of this is the oft-quoted fact that Beckett read Fritz Mauthner's *Critique of Language* to James Joyce when he was working as his amanuensis. Esslin describes Mauthner's *Critique* as 'one of the first works to point to the fallibility of language as a medium for the discovery and communication of metaphysical truths' (Esslin 1980, 34). It is then taken as axiomatic (by writers who followed Esslin, as well as Esslin himself, such as Kennedy 1975) that Beckett and Joyce wholly agreed with Mauthner's theories and proceeded to put them into practice. The reader is mapped onto the writer in much the same way as the character is mapped onto their creator. The humour in Beckett and Joyce's work is undervalued if the only response to this fact is that it must have convinced both of them that Mauthner's thesis was true. It seems plausible that the attitude to language evinced in their work may contain an element of parodying such highbrow theorising. It is not as if either were without a sense of humour, or capable of parodying philosophy – one only has to look at Lucky's speech in *Waiting for Godot* for an illustration, 'Given the existence as uttered forth in the public works of Puncher and Wattmann of a personal God quaquaquaqua with white beard quaquaquaqua' (Beckett 1990a, 42). It seems to me that this tendency to make one-to-one correlations embodies precisely what Absurdism was perceived to challenge; the continual need to find and attribute meaning.

Pinter suffered a similar fate when his work began to appear on stage during the late 1950s; in many press reviews he is described as an unsuccessful Ionesco (difficult to pull off, considering Ionesco's work was not exactly welcomed with open arms by the critics) and Esslin originally included him in the *Theatre of the Absurd*, although he subsequently revised his opinion. The fact that *The Birthday Party* (first performed 1958) was as much of a stranger to well-made conventions as *Waiting for Godot, Endgame, The Chairs* and *The Bald Prima Donna* with its unexplained happenings and its uncommunicative characters, made comparisons inevitable. For a press and public now fairly accustomed to plays in which characters did not speak 'properly' or 'sensibly', 'absurd' became a convenient shorthand.

In common with Ionesco, however, Pinter has always remained adamant that his plays are not about communication breakdown. As mentioned in the Introduction, in 'Writing for the Theatre', a speech given at the National Student Drama Festival in Bristol in 1962, he considers the reception of his work so far and addresses the notion of communication failure directly:

> We have heard many times that tired, grimy phrase: 'Failure of com-
> munication'... and this phrase has been fixed to my work quite
> consistently. I believe the contrary. I believe that we communicate
> only too well, in our silence, in what is unsaid, and that what takes
> place is a continual evasion, desperate rearguard attempts to keep
> ourselves to ourselves.
>
> (Pinter 1990a, xiii)

This response raises an often over-looked aspect of 'failure to com-municate', that any such failure tends to be volitional, rather than accidental, not the result of the increasingly moribund nature of lan-guage in the 20th and 21st centuries (note how the 'moribund' language of the Absurd can be set against the 'vital' language of the New Wave). Pinter (albeit unknowingly) is also partially describing the process of implicature here, one of the processes which tends to safeguard con-versation against non-volitional breakdown.[9] The fact that he acknowl-edges the myriad ways in which humans communicate outside of the telementary model of A transmits, B receives and decodes is another factor which was seldom taken into account in discussions of lan-guage until the advent of stylistic discourse analysis. Not surprisingly, since the inception of this branch of analysis, Pinter has been a pop-ular study choice because of the scope his work offers for exploring the pragmatic functions of language and the workings of language and power.

The 'Other' 1956 – The Berliner Ensemble visit London

Set against the New Wave emphasis on 'realism' and genuine feeling are the theories of Epic Theatre as proposed by Bertolt Brecht, particularly its anti-realist manifesto. In historical terms these two different meth-ods can be pleasingly juxtaposed by the fact that both methods were revealed in London in the same year. Having already examined in some detail the impact of the most famous theatrical event of 1956, I will now consider the *other* significant event of 1956, the Berliner Ensemble's visit to London. The Ensemble's work was enthusiastically received by influential theatre critic Kenneth Tynan and the staff at *Encore*, but (as Tynan acknowledges in his review), it did not impress the theatre-going public in general (nor, it must be reiterated, had much of the other 'groundbreaking' drama of the period).[10] Brecht's influence on modern drama and theatre can, albeit somewhat simplistically, be divided into several strands: dramaturgy, the relationship between theatre and state, politics and history. These different strands can be seen percolating British theatre at different rates, and for a variety of reasons. Prior to the Ensemble's visit to Britain Devine went to East Berlin to collaborate with Brecht on an English translation of *The Good Woman of Setzuan* (which the ESC had bought the English rights to in 1955). Given that Devine was nursing the fledgling ESC at this point, it is hardly surprising that the Ensemble's ethos of team-work, willingness to experiment and commitment to evolving a new style of theatre that would allow them to bring out the social and contemporary relevance of work from all eras, appealed to him. Another admirable facet of the Ensemble was its relationship to the State; it was a subsidised theatre, but not a lackey of, or to the State (something which struck a particular resonance with both Devine and that other famous and vociferous advocate of subsidised theatre, Kenneth Tynan). Devine's admiration can be overstated though, as Shellard is at pains to stress:

> It is disingenuous to claim, however, that Devine was to develop the Royal Court along the lines of Berliner Ensemble. Although he valued the collective endeavour, sense of purpose, shared convictions and desire to explore the non-illusionistic practices of the German company, Devine's vision of creating theatre that was modern and relevant was not predicated on a particular theory of theatre or guided by a codified system of beliefs.
>
> (Shellard 1999, 74)

However, it would be equally disingenuous to suggest that the Berliner Ensemble's example was not frequently cited in the battle to found a National Theatre, or in Devine's vision of an ensemble at the ESC, capable of challenging conventional mores through its embracing of non-naturalistic techniques which would further shatter the well-bred complacency of 'drawing-room drama' acting techniques. Robert Stephens's account of attempts to introduce the epic style into the ESC gives an indication of Devine's determination to change English theatre on every level, although his attempts in this area were not immediately a conspicuous success.[11]

The Ensemble's visit to London was to have a more far-reaching effect than Sloane Square, but outside the vanguard of the incipient new and vital theatre (and in this I obviously include Tynan's championship), the initial impression was a little more muted. Innes notes that, at the time, the political aspect of the company's work as evinced in the performance was lost on the majority of the audience:

> Since Brecht's writings were not yet available in translation, and few London spectators of the Berliner Ensemble productions understood German, the politics of his drama was obscured. As a result, its influence was primarily on production values and ways of playing.
>
> (Innes 1992, 122)

The language barrier was something that Brecht himself was acutely aware of. In the oft-quoted note on the Ensemble's noticeboard in Berlin, he stresses that much of the work normally done by speech and language in their productions will need to be re-deployed.

> For our London season we need to bear two things in mind. First: we shall be offering most of the audience a pure pantomime, a kind of silent film on the stage for they know no German. [...] Second: there is in England a long-standing fear that German art (literature, painting, music) must be terribly heavy, slow, laborious and pedestrian.
>
>   [...] The audience has to see that here are a number of artists working together as a collective (ensemble) in order to convey stories, ideas, virtuoso feats for the spectator by a common audience.
>
> (Willett 1981, 283)

This note is worth commenting on for a number of different reasons. First the Ensemble must foreground action over word, simply because the language used, the vocabulary, will be unintelligible to the majority who see the show; only speed and intonation will be able to provide any clue as to what sort of exchange is taking place: if voices are raised that would be interpreted as an argument, or a sign of rising passions. As a consequence of this, gestures must be exaggerated, or, more specifically, made to do some of the work of the dialogue. The second significant fact is Brecht's awareness that German art is considered ponderous, and could be contrasted most unfavourably with the prevailing trend on the English stage of light comedy, particularly as evinced by the Cowardian tradition of rapid delivery.[12] The third point is that Brecht is concerned to demonstrate the greatest achievement of his troupe: their ability to work as an ensemble; again, a great contrast to the English system of writing fat parts for one's lead actors.

In spite of this foregrounding of the performance aspects, and perhaps because the idea of ensemble acting was so alien, the impact and practice of epic theatre was slow to develop in Britain. In addition, as Innes points out, Brecht's interpretation was partly derived from the Elizabethans and Tyrone Guthrie had already used similar guiding principles in the previous decade for his productions of Shakespeare.[13] Also the style of theatre tended to be conflated with Brecht's politics.[14] This in turn suggests that those dramatists and theatre professionals who felt their work was devoid of politics or above politics, as well as those absolutely opposed to Marxism or leftist politics, would feel that Brechtian ideals of an Epic theatre could have nothing to offer them. It cannot be coincidence that the first dramatists to engage with Brechtian theories during this period were avowedly political writers and producers such as John Arden and Joan Littlewood, or that the only company to perform Brecht before the Ensemble's visit was the Unity Theatre. Brechtian dramaturgy was not separated from radical politics without hostile criticism until well into the next decade. In fact, it seems that not until Brook's experiments with Theatre of Cruelty in the 1960s was it acceptable to stage things non-naturalistically without having a didactic intention – usually a serious political point – to get across. It was with the next generation that all the various elements and implications of their (Brecht and the Berliner Ensemble) work appeared in English theatre. For example, a renewed push for generously subsidised theatre; political drama conceived in the epic style (e.g., Brenton, Churchill, Hare and Edgar) and attempts at plays examining history from the perspective of society; and epic style without the politics. Innes describes the latter as a:

> wide range of superficially Brechtian drama that appeared on the English stage at the same time [as Brenton, Hare, Barker etc]. This severed Epic techniques from the Marxist analysis of society that they were designed to express; and the effects can be seen in the plays of Robert Bolt, Joan Littlewood's Theatre Workshop and Peter Nichols, as well as those of Christopher Hampton.
>
> (Innes 1992, 122)

The main objections to the work of Bolt, Hampton (and in Lacey and Tynan's case) Osborne's *Luther* is that the historical setting became more like a gimmick than an opportunity to draw attention to the inexorable path of history and the lessons that can be learnt from it (as the Marxist historical materialist tradition dictates). Lacey notes an additional effect of the Berliner Ensemble's visit was to set up a critical paradigm against which plays and productions set in another historical era could be measured.[15] Tynan, already a Brecht aficionado by this point, was able to criticise Bolt's *A Man for All Seasons* in comparison to Brecht's *Galileo*:

> Mr Bolt is primarily absorbed in the state of More's conscience, not in the state of More's England or More's Europe. . . . Brecht, on the other hand, though he gives us an intimate study of Galileo's conscience, takes pains to relate it at every turn to Galileo's world and to the universe at large.
>
> (Tynan 1984, 287–288)

It is interesting to note that Tynan uses a very different criterion for assessing Epic Theatre than those he applies to the New Wave. Tynan praises *Look Back in Anger* precisely because it gives us an 'intimate study' of Jimmy Porter, yet here an ostensibly 'Brechtian' play is criticised for doing the same thing, rather than reflecting the state of the country at large. Tynan's legendary pomposity can also be found in his reviews of the Absurd, a genre with which he seems to have had an uneasy relationship, and which he is much quicker to compare unfavourably to the Epic techniques.

The next generation of playwrights, as Innes has noted, were to unite the political content with revolutionary form much more successfully, and realism came under a different kind of attack from Epic techniques and Peter Brook's Theatre of Cruelty season and experiments with physical theatre. As I argue in the next chapter, the result of this is that the visual is foregrounded over the verbal in many plays, and in many of the others, lifelike-ese is eventually rejected in favour of a passionate articulacy designed to awaken the conscience and consciousness of the audience.

5
1964–1975: Revolution On and Off Stage

Theatre critic Harold Hobson summed up this period as one in which:

> restraint of verbal expression ceased; instead of being a necessity, it became a handicap to a player to have a standard English accent; the commercial theatre, hitherto the mainstay of the drama, wilted because many dramatists first offered their plays to the National Theatre, and much of the middle-class public began to stay away from the playhouse because they missed the old, comfortable, reassuring, nicely spoken, well dressed entertainments they had been accustomed to see.
>
> (Hobson 1984, 200)

His comment alludes to some of the key events of the era: the increasing appearance of non-standard speech and non-RP accents on stage; the success of the newly established Royal Shakespeare (RSC) and National Theatre (NT) companies; and the experimental theatre which flourished after the end of theatre censorship. Theatre expanded in every direction in this period embracing the political, the highly visual and the non verbal as well as continuing to produce variations on the kitchen-sink theme and the traditional well-made play. In order to examine disjunctures and continuities in attitudes to language in the theatre this chapter draws out three dominant threads: 'life-like'/realist theatre, theatre as a means of galvanising (rather than merely reflecting) society and theatre as spectacle.

Historical context

The myth of the 'Swinging Sixities' is a pervasive one: 'free love', 'the white heat of technology', Woodstock – all these phrases are invoked

either to recall a time of uninhibited social and sexual experimenta-
tion, or to suggest that this moral laxity was the undoing of British
society. In reality, 1964–1970 was an eventful period characterised first
by what Roy Jenkins called 'the liberal hour', then by the backlash
against the 'permissive society', but many of the freedoms gained were
starting points rather than climaxes – particularly where the legali-
sation of homosexuality and abortion were concerned. Certainly the
abolition of capital punishment (1965) and pre-censorship of theatre
(1968) were momentous events, but so were the Russian invasion of
Czechoslovakia and student riots and the protests against Vietnam (the
other side of the 'peace and love' coin). For the purposes of this study,
the most important factor was the increasing visibility of 'ordinary people' in privileged positions in society. Harold Wilson, who became the
Labour Prime Minister in 1964, epitomised this new breed. As John Seed
points out:

> while Macmillan and Home [the previous Conservative Prime Min-
> isters] posed as Edwardian gentlemen on their grouse moors in
> plus-fours, Wilson was a pipe smoking northerner, a self-proclaimed
> supporter of Huddersfield Town with traces of a Yorkshire accent.
>
> (Seed 1992, 29)

A former grammar school boy and proud of his provincial roots, Wilson
famously asserted that he preferred beer to champagne and tinned
salmon to smoked. His main interest was in manufacturing, technology and trade and in restoring Britain's economy, but he also presided
over the exponential increase of the cultural industries (not that the
word even existed) and the part they played in the rehabilitation of
Britain's fortunes and world status. The Beatles, the Rolling Stones, pho-
tographers David Bailey and Terence Donovan, boutiques like Biba and
Mary Quant's Bazaar all helped put Britain, or rather 'Swinging London',
on the map.[1] At the beginning of Wilson's period of office, the angry
young men of the previous decade had little to be angry about: the
year 1964 saw the appointment of the first Minister of the Arts, Jennie
Lee, and the shift of funding the arts from the Treasury to the department of Education and Science. Labour followed the Conservatives in
continuing to increase arts funding: the performing arts were particular
beneficiaries of this, including the building of a number of new venues
(15 between 1958 and 1970) and the funding of new companies. The
end of the Lord Chamberlain's reign as theatre censor in 1968, along

with increased funding and a generation brought up on the kitchen-sink drama of the 1950s, led to a boom in theatre companies engaged in a range of different styles. The Robbins Report of 1963 laid the foundations for the opening up of higher education: recognising that it should be the province of anyone who merited it and recommending the establishment of 16 universities (the building of six new ones and the upgrading of ten colleges of advanced technology). Those interested in broadening their minds without entering higher education were able to take advantage of the improvement in public library services introduced under the Public Libraries and Museums Act 1964. In addition to this, new printing technology made it possible for 'serious' publishers and academic presses to launch paperback imprints and almost anyone to launch a magazine.

However, by the end of Wilson's period in office, there was plenty to be angry about. His perceived procrastination over Vietnam; his indecisiveness about the devaluation of the pound (which had crippled Britain economically); his support of the abolition of grammar schools (an advantage he had so conspicuously benefited from); and above all, his inability to tell the truth and face difficult situations created a dissatisfied and now highly (and widely) articulate electorate. When Edward Heath was elected Prime Minister in 1970, ushering in 27 years of Conservative rule, he was faced with a growing and articulate body of 'minorities' (in terms of race, gender and sexuality) and workers demanding equal rights and by the time he ceded office to Margaret Thatcher in 1975, the British economy was once more in the doldrums, and the country was once more in a restless mood.

Linguistic context

> I doubt if there are any rational people to whom the word 'fuck' would be particularly diabolical, revolting, or totally forbidden.
> Tynan, speaking on BBC3, 1965

Theatre critic Kenneth Tynan was the first person to use the word 'fuck' on British television, and, contrary to the opinion he professed, it proved shocking and revolting to a large proportion of the British public, as indeed he had known it would. The swinging sixties were just not *that* liberal: Mary Whitehouse had set up the 'Clean Up TV' campaign the year before, hardly a good indicator of a country at ease with sex, swearing and nudity. But television (and radio) did play a crucial part in the receding ubiquity of standard English and 'neutral' accents on and off stage: partly because of its role in allowing viewers and listeners to see and hear a range of regional voices, and providing access to high quality commentary on arts and politics, but also because of its role in showcasing new drama. When Terence Rattigan remarked that all Joe Orton's characters 'expressed themselves as if they were brought up on television', he meant it regretfully, because it showed a society 'diminished by telly technology' (Rattigan quoted in Lahr 1980, 184). But for most people, television offered access to a range of art forms and opinions they would not necessarily have come across in everyday life. The BBC initially did so in a paternalistic way, and at the beginning of its life, even hoped to improve the speech of the general public by setting good example, but by the mid-1960s, things were changing, not least because of the rise of commercial television. As Mugglestone notes:

> The new informality of the ITV and commercial networks contrasted sharply with what came to be seen, negatively, as the excessive 'pluminess' of the traditional BBC, a feature which in itself strongly urged the imperatives of democratisation in a variety of ways. Pluralism necessarily became the norm, leading, as Colin MacCabe has commented in his study of television in the 1960s, 'to an even greater diversity of accents and speech patterns and an ever more fragmented national culture'.[2]

> (Mugglestone 2003, 274)

The stigmatisation of non-RP speakers waned as it became apparent that it was possible to be educated, articulate and even witty, and have a regional accent, or use dialect words. From Richard Hoggart's impassioned defence of *Lady Chatterley's Lover* to the Beatles, non-RP speakers were an increasingly visible majority, so much so, that by 1977, the BBC even went so far as to declare in the Annan Report that 'we welcome regional accents' (Crystal 2006, 186).[3] The 1970s saw the gradual waning of commentary about lifelike-ese on the stage. As television drama became the primary means by which British society saw itself portrayed in all its class, regional, and increasingly ethnic, variety, critics and pundits became accustomed to hearing a range of accents and dialects.

In linguistics, the study of spoken English was underway helped immeasurably by the appearance of easily portable tape-recorders that allowed linguists to record 'real' speech (conversations, interviews and reading tests). In 1960 Randolph Quirk had begun collecting samples of real speech for his Survey of English Usage in order to describe the grammar of all the major varieties of spoken and written English. Yet, as Crystal notes, as linguists 'got their act' together, the teaching of grammar in England 'quietly died' (Crystal 2006, 203). He cites 1965, the year in which English Language was withdrawn from O'Level and CSE examination boards as the final nail in the coffin. For the following two decades, there was no formal teaching of grammar in English schools.

Two key factors in the more realistic representation of speech on stage are the consequences of educational reforms and the abolition of the Lord Chamberlain's role as censor in 1968. Firstly, the cessation of the Lord Chamberlain's powers of censorship broadened the scope of *what* could be discussed on stage; secondly, there were no longer any restrictions on *how* things could be discussed. Under the Lord Chamberlain, scenes of, or references to, adultery, homosexuality, blasphemy, 'invidious' representations of living people, or unflattering references to the monarchy and/or politicians, and swearing were refused the right of performance until the offending scenes/references were removed. Until 1968, theatres circumvented these restrictions either through ingenious innuendo (e.g., Orton) or by staging the plays on a 'club' basis (the Lord Chamberlain having no power to censor private performances), as with Bond's *Saved* and a host of other plays. In terms of language, although the freedom to swear obviously offered an opportunity for characters to express more than mild annoyance in slightly more realistic terms, some critics saw this freedom in disproportionately marked class terms. Kerensky's response, for example, attests to the fact that the idea of 'authentic working class language' was still as confused over issues of lexis in 1977 (when Kenrensky's book was published) as it had been in the 1926 when Newbolt compiled *The Teaching of English in England*:

> Before that time [i.e. the end of censorship], the actual language spoken by people in real life, especially by people without middle-class inhibitions, could not be spoken on the stage. Everyday 'four-letter' swear words were banned.
>
> (Kerensky 1977, xix)

Amusing as the (no doubt accidental) implication is that people without middle class inhibitions swear like the proverbial trooper (while their commanding officers, we must suppose, continue to speak like Rattigan's Arthur Winslow or Sir William Collyer), Kerensky's comment prefigures the moral crusaders of the 1980s (particularly Tebbit and Whitehouse) and their equation of 'bad' language with 'bad' morals. Kerensky also reports an interview with Trevor Griffiths in which Griffiths admits he would have found it impossible to keep within the Lord Chamberlain's bounds of good taste, adding that:

> Olivier told him he was the first writer to have the word 'cunt' spoken on the stage of the National Theatre, though, Olivier added, 'the actors have said it under their breath often enough'. 'I absolutely insist on using the language that would actually be spoken by my characters', [said Griffiths].
>
> (Kerensky 1977, 205)

Again, we see the reductive logic which suggests nothing about the change in social and cultural conditions which was making swearing more socially acceptable. The fact that the public school educated, soon to be peer of the realm, Olivier peppered his letters to Peter Hall with some imaginative uses of the 'f-word', and Oxford educated Tynan actually uttered the word on national television in 1965, is overlooked or excused on 'artistic' grounds (Kathleen Tynan 1988, 236).[4]

The second key factor that allowed for greater authenticity in working-class speech on stage lies in the fact that many of the actors who appeared in these plays were from the new generation of working-class children who had been given the opportunity to train as actors (thanks in part to the 1944 Butler Education Act, as well as the Robbins Report). As Lacey points out:

> By the mid-60s there was a significantly larger proportion of actors of working class origin in the profession, which Michael Sanderson has related to the increase in local authority grants for drama schools, the increased pool of potential recruits from the universities, and the new opportunities created by social realism in both the theatre and television (Sanderson 1984: 293).[5] The result was a pool of actors who could respond to the demands of the new plays and, in doing so, shift the perameters [*sic*] around what was considered 'real' and 'authentic'.
>
> (Lacey 1995, 67)

Terence Stamp was one of these actors, and one of the few of his generation who elected to keep his own Cockney accent and regard RP as yet another one of the accents they taught at drama school: 'rather than speaking "proper", I would treat Standard English roles as a dialect' (Stamp 1988, quoted in Mugglestone 2003, 274). Kenneth Cranham was another, and his remark about his status as one Joe Orton's favourite actors bears witness to the idea that authenticity off-stage could help to portray authenticity on stage: 'I was very right for Orton's plays physically. I'm also genuinely working-class London, which he liked too' (quoted in Lahr (ed.) 1986, 47). Cranham's background signalled to Orton that the actor would be able to identify with the background Orton's characters try so hard to disguise, as well as with the aspirations they so vehemently proclaim. As Ed tells Sloane shortly after asking him if he wears 'leather...next to the skin': 'You may as well know I set a great store by morals. Too much of this casual bunking up these days', the decency expressed by the formal register of the first sentence is hilariously undermined by the informality of the second (Orton 1995a, 87). However, it is important not to over-emphasise the recession of modified RP in the acting profession at this period: the actors who retained a distinct regional accent are still in a minority. Ian Richardson, born and trained in Scotland; Ian McKellen from Lancashire; Jonathan Pryce from Wales; Anthony Sher and Janet Suzmann from South Africa; and Judi Dench from York all speak modified RP.[6] All of these actors have combined classical and modern roles with great success, giving credence to the prevailing notion that, in this period, the theatrical establishment had difficulty in coming to terms with the idea of Shakespeare, or Chekhov or Ibsen being played with anything other than a neutral accent – unless it was a rustic, or 'character' part.

Theatrical context

Television, along with social and educational reforms, and the skirmishes between linguistic researchers and language minders habituated theatregoers to hearing non-standard English without necessarily drawing the reductive conclusions which characterised the reception of, for example, *Roots* or, *Saved* (discussed later in this chapter).[7] Whereas the linguistic style of works like these is now accepted without comment (or, as is sometimes the case with *Roots*, ridiculed because of its distance from lifelike-ese), the language of other, similarly criticised, playwrights has undergone a more positive re-evaluation. Pinter's early work is a case in point. Initially his style of dialogue was criticised as opaque and 'low', yet by the late 1970s critics and the public had become accustomed to it and the style had been assimilated into the dramatic linguistic repertoire. This acclimatisation to non-standard usages is evident in the reviews of the first production of *The Homecoming* (1965). The dysfluent and hesitant speech style Pinter made so famous was quickly accepted as part of the 'Pinteresque' experience, and if not exactly welcomed, it was no longer regarded as bordering on communication breakdown. Bernard Levin, writing in the *Daily Mail*, notes: 'The first act of the two displays all his dazzling dramatic legerdemain, his ability to trans-mute the smallest of small talk into dialogue, quivering with sinister, half-caught meanings' (Levin in Elsom 1981, 158). Herbert Kretzmer in the *Daily Express* is less flattering, but equally acute at spotting the dramatic impulse behind the dialogue. 'We have all learnt to recognise these Pintermimes a mile off – with those long, unblinking pauses, the aura of something horrific behind the humdrum action, the sense of suppressed violence beneath the banal utterance' (Kretzmer quoted in Elsom 1981, 160). What was once shocking in terms of language has become naturalised.

At the same time as one form of theatre was becoming more natural-istic in terms of speech, another form was questioning the supremacy of the written word. As Elsom, a theatre-critic of many years standing, noted, until the mid-1960s:

> British acting, in general, had always been associated with a some-what cerebral approach to the art – very good on the spoken delivery of lines, able to convey nuances of words and precise in its natu-ralism, but not athletic or physical. Two productions from 1964, *The Royal Hunt of the Sun* and Peter Brook's *The Marat/Sade*, helped change this reputation, so that for the next ten years, there were many British productions which explored the visual and tactile qualities of the stage.
>
> (Elsom 1981, 144)

The Royal Hunt of the Sun and *Marat/Sade* represent the emergence of a type of 'total' theatre in which every aspect of theatre was synthesised – costume, scenery, movement, speech and music – and in which lan-guage is an element within the theatrical experience rather than the dominant component, and as such, offered respite for language minders concerned by 'life-like-ese'.

Peter Brook, director of the *Marat/Sade* and the Theatre of Cruelty sea-son at London Academy of Dramatic Art (LAMDA), came to prominence with *Love's Labour's Lost* at the Shakespeare Memorial Theatre in Strat-ford in 1944. The production was strong on visual imagery (scenery and costumes were based on the work of Watteau), and although not universally well-received, established Brook as an interesting young talent.[8] He went on to work in opera and mainstream West End theatre as well as with the RSC, and continued to develop his own theories of theatrical practice and engagement. In 1962, when Brook renewed his link with Stratford (now the home of the newly christened Royal Shakespeare Company) Brook's interest in the visual impact of theatre and spontaneity had moved from the lushness of *Love's Labour's Lost* to an entirely different aesthetic, later exemplified by his famous 'white-box' version of *A Midsummer Night's Dream* at Stratford in 1970. Brook's style during the 1960s, beginning with The Theatre of Cruelty Season at the RSC in 1964, was based on Artaud's *Theatre and Its Double*, and followed Artaud's prescription for putting striking and violent images on the stage. In *The Empty Space* (1968) Brook reviewed the three dominant trends in theatre from the previous episteme – kitchen-sink, Epic and Absurd – and proselytised on behalf of their successor, the Holy Theatre:

> What he [Artaud] wanted in his search for holiness was absolute: he wanted a theatre that would be a hallowed place, he wanted that theatre served by a band of dedicated actors and directors who would create out of their own natures an unending succession of violent stage images, bringing about such powerful immediate explosions of human matter that no one would ever again revert to a theatre of anecdote and talk.
>
> (Brook 1968, 59–60)

Brook's staging of Peter Weiss's *The Persecution and Assassination of Marat as Performed by the Inmates of the Asylum of Charenton under the Direction of the Marquis de Sade* (abbreviated to *Marat/Sade*) at the RSC in 1964 certainly fulfiled this requirement with its gruesome depictions and descriptions of the public executions and other atrocities in revolutionary France. The subject of the mime in 'Song and Mime of Corday's Arrival in Paris' is *'the piercing and the bursting of the fat belly of the priest. The condemned man leans across the execution block. His hands are sawn off'*. The mime continues into the next scene, titled, aptly enough, 'Conversation Concerning Life and Death', *'The hands of the victim fall off. Howls. The executioner starts sawing off his head'*, the mime culminates in the priest's head falling off and being used as a football by the patients of the asylum (Weiss 1965, 29–30). Brook and the critics who attended the play all commented on the success of Weiss's play as a piece of 'total theatre', glossed by Brook as 'that time-honoured notion of getting all the elements of the stage to serve the play', but the power of the piece is more tellingly described by the critics (Brook in Weiss 1965, 6). *The Times* reported that:

> on a first showing one is far less impressed by the intellectual line of the play than its impact on the visceral level which, in Peter Brook's production, is tremendous. The use of music (by Richard Peaselee) mirrors the grotesque figures of the actors with harsh bell and organ sonorities, and sets bloodthirsty events in the idiom of Lully.
>
> (Elsom 1981, 151)

Bernard Levin in the *Daily Mail* commented:

> Its breadth, its totality, its breathtakingly rapid and varied use of every imaginable technique, dramatic device, stage-picture, form of movement, speech and song, make it as close as this imperfect world is ever likely to get to the *Gesamthunstwerk* of which Richard Wagner dreamed, in which every element, every force that the theatre could provide would fuse in one overwhelming experience.
>
> (Elsom 1981, 153–154)

The Royal Hunt of the Sun, performed by the newly formed National Theatre Company at Chichester in 1964, incorporates mime, music and a series of striking tableaux which Dexter realised would give the NT a chance to demonstrate its strengths. The play depicts the colonisation of the Incas by the Spanish, encompassing battle scenes, sacrifices, torture and mutilation, a procession of gold and the climbing of the Andes. In the Author's Notes to the play, Shaffer praises Michael Annals's 'superb' set which 'so brilliantly succeeded in solving the visual problems of the play'. The dominant image of the play is the 12 feet wide sun constructed from golden petals:

> When closed, these interlocked to form a great medallion on which was incised the emblem of the Conquistadors; when opened they formed the rays of a giant golden sun, emblem of the Incas. Each petal had an inlay of gold magnetised to it: when these inlays were pulled out (in Act II, Scene vi) the great black frame remaining symbolised magnificently the desecration of Peru. The centre of this sun formed an acting area above the stage, which was used in Act I to show Atahuallpa in majesty, and in Act II served for his prison and subsequently for the treasure chamber. This simple but amazing set

was for me totally satisfying on all levels: scenically, aesthetically, and symbolically.

(Shaffer 1966, xviii)

This remarkably striking set, the mimes, the musical score and Robert Stephens's strange high-pitched intonation designed to convey his otherness (and the fact that he is supposed to be speaking a different language) gave the play more arresting visual and emotional qualities than the usual 'theatre of anecdote and talk' could easily achieve. The 'Mime of the Great Massacre' gives an indication of the careful balancing of theatrical elements composing the spectacle:

> *To a savage music, wave upon wave of Indians are slaughtered and rise again to protect their lord who stands bewildered in their midst. It is all in vain. Relentlessly the Spanish soldiers hew their way through the ranks of feathered attendants towards their quarry. They surround him.* **Salinas** *snatches the crown off his head and tosses it up to* **Pizzarro**, *who catches it and to a great shout crowns himself. All the Indians cry out in horror. The drum hammers on relentlessly while* **Atahuallpa** *is led off at sword point by the whole band of Spaniards. At the same time, dragged from the middle of the sun by the howling Indians, a vast bloodstained cloth bellies out over the stage. All rush off; their screams fill the theatre. The lights fade out slowly on the rippling cloth of blood.*

(Shaffer 1966, 38)

The cloth of blood remains onstage for the next three scenes, reminding the audience of the massacre and the inevitable decimation of the Incas. This theme of decimation is continued from then on by the gold processions and 'The "Rape of the Sun"' alluded to by Shaffer above. As we see the stage literally and symbolically stripped of the people and gold which symbolises the Inca empire, the fate of the sun god Atahuallpa becomes all too inevitable. Unmoved by threats of execution because he believes his father the Sun will resurrect him, Atahuallpa faces his death with a heartbreaking degree of confidence. Such was the emotional impact of the play that when 'the beam of morning light failed to stir him [Atahuallpa], the dismay on the part of the audience was palpable' (Shellard 1999, 110).

Both Brook and Shaffer challenged the theatrical norms of the time through their attempts to decentre language. As Shaffer commented, the 'visual action is to me as much a part of the play as the dialogue' (Shaffer 1966, 199–200). Both were instrumental in relocating language within the entirety of the theatrical sign system, as one of a number of signifying practices which go to make up a performance, rather than the main event itself. Such reordering inevitably involves an interrogation of the meaning of language, as Brook shows in *The Empty Space*:

> Is there another language, just as exacting for the author as a language of words? Is there a language of actions, a language of sounds – a language of word-as-part-of-movement, of word-as-lie, word-as-parody, of word-as-rubbish, of word-as-contradiction, of word-shock or word-cry? If we talk of the more-than-literal, if poetry means that which crams more and penetrates deeper – is this where it lies?
>
> (Brook 1968, 55)

As in his summary of Artaud, Brook was determined to move away from the theatre of 'anecdote and talk', and later experiments with *Orghast at Persepolis*, *The Conference of the Birds*, and ultimately the peripatetic 'Rough Theatre' Brook and the International Centre for Theatre Research took to Africa and India in order to discover 'if communication is possible between people from many different parts of the world' (Brook 1999, 180). Brook is using the word 'communication' primarily to refer to non-verbal signifying practices. His theatre offered a very different challenge to the senses than the naturalistic plays discussed below, but the legacy of this work has had as great an impact on British theatre as the naturalistic tradition.

Drawn from life: Bond and Orton

> You've only got to be sitting on a bus and you'll hear the most stylised lines. People think I write fantasy, but I don't; some things may be exaggerated or distorted in the same way that painters distort and layer things, but they're realistic figures. They're perfectly recognisable.
>
> (Lahr 1995, 9)

The ultra and sometimes hyper-naturalistic dialogue of Orton, early Pinter and early Bond, with its repetitions, clichés and (particularly in the case of Bond) emphasis on a restricted code was a move forward in terms of 'life-like' language. The main difference between Wesker and Osborne's early attempts at 'lifelike-ese', and the more convincing renderings of Bond, Pinter and Orton is that the characters of the latter are denied the extensive vocabulary and rhetorical skills so memorably showcased by Jimmy Porter, Ronnie Khan and Beatie Bryant. The difference between Orton and Bond's early characters is that Orton's work towards speaking stylishly, to elevating themselves above the mundane, whereas Bond's are impervious to the notion of 'improving' their speech in this way. This subsection explores in more detail the way in which Bernstein's restricted code can be applied to dramatic dialogue normally denigrated for its lack of articulacy. In particular I will be examining the way in which the reception of the dialogue in Bond's *Saved* corresponds to Bernstein's findings about the perception of speakers of restricted code, while Orton's plays show his characters appropriating their elaborated code from the mass media. That such articulacy should be conferred on Orton's characters from 'the newer mass art' is a nice irony given Hoggart's fears that it would turn the working classes into a bunch of monosyllabic uncommunicative morons.

First performed at the Royal Court in 1965, *Saved* is frequently cited in accounts of post-war British drama because of its role, in conjunction with Osborne's *A Patriot for Me*, in bringing about the end of theatre censorship. The torturing and stoning to death of a baby in its pram caused a furore in the media, but is not relevant to this account; rather it is the language of the play's characters, and the reception of this language which earns it a place here. As outlined in Chapter 2, Bernstein's experience of teaching young working-class men in London during the 1950s led him to a life's work formulating a model of speech as communication which would move away from the deficit model (i.e., that working-class language deviated from the norm in undesirable ways). To summarise, restricted speech is something everyone uses for certain types of communication, specifically, ritualistic types of conversation, and/or between family and very close friends (literally in contexts that need little or no elaborating on, e.g., making tea, discussing close family and friends). Restricted speech is characterised by simple syntactic structure and ease of lexical prediction (which explains the ritualistic element) and is highly context dependent. Elaborated speech is typically confined to those sections of society with more education and/or the sort of occupations which require abstract reasoning; it is context independent and has low degrees of syntactic and lexical prediction because it draws on a larger vocabulary. The speech of the characters in *Saved*, in common with Pinter's early characters, shares many of the properties characteristic of a restricted code. Innes's assessment of *Saved* picks up on how easily assumptions about restricted code users are made: 'the reductionism of stunted, basic dialogue [...] gave the impression of unredeemable factuality, the apparent gratuitousness of the violence obscured the intended social criticism' (Innes 1992, 164).

Language, and communication in general, has a very low priority in *Saved*. Harry and Mary, the 'stable' couple of the play, are locked in a war of attrition in which verbal conflict plays a very limited part. In an exchange thin on rhetorical flourishes Len questions Pam about the silent stalemate that constitutes her parents' relationship:

> **Len.** Ow'd they manage?
> **Pam.** When?
> **Len.** They write notes or somethin'?
> **Pam.** No
> **Len.** 'Ow's that?
> **Pam.** No need.
> **Len.** They must.
> **Pam.** No.
> **Len.** Why?
> **Pam.** Nothin' t'say. 'E puts 'er money over the fire every Friday, an' thass all there is. Talk about somethin' else.
> **Len.** Wass she say about 'im?
> **Pam.** Nothin'.

> (Bond 1977b, 35)

The characters in the play seem to use language only for ritualistic functions like posturing, telling dirty jokes and singing lewd songs:

> She was only a goalkeeper's daughter
> She married a player called Jack
> It was great when 'e played centre forward
> But 'e liked to slip round to the back.

> (Bond 1977b, 111–112)

In common with both Pinter and Wesker, the dialogue prompted highly polarised responses, Penelope Gilliat, writing in the *Observer*, acknowledges the planned nature of seemingly inarticulate dramatic discourse:

> though the vernacular language may make the play look like a 'slice of life', a phrase that is used to mean a very inferior slab of theatrical fruitcake, the truth is that the prose is skilfully stylised. It uses a hard,

curt unit of dialogue, a statement of panic masquerading as an attack, hardly ever more than five or six syllables to a line. People don't elaborate; they stab in the dark, the dagger turns into rubber or a wisp of fog.

(Gilliat in Elsom 1981, 178)

Herbert Kretzmer in the *Daily Express*, on the other hand, like Norman Tebbit in the great grammar debate, cannot, or will not, distinguish between 'sloppy speech' and 'sloppy morals': 'It is peopled by characters who, almost without exception, are foul-mouthed and dirty-minded and barely to be judged on any human level at all' (Kretzmer in Elsom 1981, 180). Kretzmer's comment is echoed by Kerensky who sums the play up as: 'concerned with unmotivated and badly educated people who have nothing to occupy themselves with except mindless violence and sex' (Kerensky 1977, 19).[9] The consistent feature of these reviews is that they assume an inability to communicate on any 'meaningful' level. Such an assumption is consistent with Bernstein's findings about the particularistic nature of the restricted code, the characters feel no need for 'meaningful' interaction as they have nothing they feel is meaningful to impart. This is what makes them seem devoid of morality. Pete running over a child is not seen as something which should be agonised over, just as something to report to the lads. The characters move in a closed society, and have no need to ever elaborate on their behaviour and practices, there are no strangers appearing in their rooms as in Pinter, and therefore no need to concern themselves with the kind of philosophical or lexical conundrums that beset Pinter's characters.[10] They are alienated from 'Society', as Lacey, discussing *The Pope's Wedding* and *Saved*, notes:

This kind of staccato, apparently inexpressive dialogue appears at first sight very much like Pinter's, but the effect over the play as a whole is not so much to concretise the experience of 'non-communication' as to provide a tangible sense of the limitations on the characters' control over their environment.

(Lacey 1995, 150)

I would go further and suggest that the characters have little desire to control their environment. The rhetoric of the New Wave and New Left about class mobility and access to education has no place here. *Saved* takes place in a very different economic climate to the depressionary period of *Look Back in Anger* and the Wesker trilogy. All the male characters are in work, there is no revolutionary, or quasi-revolutionary figure to inspire them to 'want more', no 'brave causes' that concern them; they seem content to remain in their bleak surroundings, despite Len and Harry's faint threats about moving on. Even the itinerant protagonists of *Waiting for Godot* weighed down with the *ennui* of existence in such a meaningless universe manage more ambition in their desire to amuse themselves and to change their circumstances. The end of *Saved* recalls *Godot*; having previously discussed the possibility of leaving, the next scene sees the characters resuming their normal activities, Pam and Mary read the *Radio Times*, Harry busies himself with his pools coupon and Len fixes the chair. All these actions are freighted with significance, all echoes of previous sites of conflict in the play: the scene in which Pam accuses Len of hiding her *Radio Times*, and the scene in which Harry comes in for his pools coupon and discovers Len and Mary in what he assumes to be a compromising position which in turn leads to a row during which the chair gets broken. In 'The First Author's Note to *Saved*', Bond describes this scene as:

> a silent social stalemate, but if the spectator thinks this is pessimistic that is because he has not learned to clutch at straws. Clutching at straws is the only realistic thing to do. The alternative, apart from the self-indulgence of pessimism, is fatuous optimism based on a superficiality of both feeling and observation.
>
> (Bond 1977, 309)

Bond may refute charges of pessimism, but his characters just as surely refute the New Left ideals of strength in community, confirming Hoggart's worse fears by seeking solace in television and pop music rather than in doorstep communing. William Gaskill, artistic director of the Royal Court, and the director of *Saved*, further recalls this New Wave agenda by conjuring the magic word 'vitality', in his observation about the Lord Chamberlain's powers:

> The Lord Chamberlain [...] was the old-fashioned, harmless and stupid English gentleman (though it must be said, advised by bishops), but he was limiting not just the scope of what could be shown on the stage, but the strength and vitality of the language.
>
> (Gaskill 1988, 68)

It is ironic that Gaskill should use the word 'vital' to describe the language of a play in which most exchanges end in stalemate or disinterest. Len tries to communicate but no one is really interested, not even Pam at the beginning of their courtship. He makes all the conversational openers which she sometimes responds to, but in the most minimal way possible:

> **Len.** Suit yourself. You don't mind if I take me shoes off? (*He kicks them off*). No one 'ome?
> **Pam.** No
> **Len.** Live on yer tod?
> **Pam.** No.
> **Len.** O.
> *Pause. He sits back on the couch.*
> Yer all right? Come over 'ere
> **Pam.** In a minit
> **Len.** Wass yer name?
> **Pam.** Yer ain' arf nosey.
>
> (Bond 1977b, 22)

It does not seem such an unreasonable question, given that they are just about to have sex, but Pam is unflatteringly uninterested. Len might have come into read the meter judging by her responses. There is not a vital – in the New Wave sense of the word – bone in her body. Bond's characters might be content to exist in silence, or in shouted exchanges, but Orton's equally 'low-life' characters, in common with Winnie in *Happy Days* (1962), cannot manage without company and communication. If we compare Len and Pam's encounter with Mr Sloane's initial visit to Kath's house, the latter positively crackles with soul-baring:

> **Kath.** I should change them curtains. Those are our winter ones. The summer ones are more of a chintz. (*Laughs.*) The walls need re-doing. The Dadda has trouble with his eyes. I can't ask him to do any work involving ladders. It stands to reason.
> *Pause*
> **Sloane.** I can't give you a decision right away.
> **Kath.** I don't want to rush you. (*Pause.*) What do you think? I'd be happy to have you.
> *Silence.*
> **Sloane.** Are you married?
> **Kath** (*pause*). I was. I had a boy ... killed in very sad circumstances. It broke my heart at the time. I got over it though. You do, don't you?
>
> (Orton 1995a, 65)

Kath and Sloane construct an intimate atmosphere on a cursory inspec-
tion of the house. Len and Pam are just about to have sex, and Pam
feels no compulsion to reveal relevant facts about herself, let alone construct any sense of intimacy. Orton's characters display their own kind
of vitality derived from a disregarding of societal and moral norms and
much of the comedy in his plays derives from the careful lip-service his
characters pay to these norms in their attempts to appear respectable.
For the most part they attempt to convey this respectability through
their language, a hybrid of elaborated and restricted speech types. For
example, when Kath pleads with Ed to be allowed to have Sloane for a
lodger:

> **Kath** (*off*). Mr Sloane! Would you step down here for a minute? My
> brother would like to meet you. (*Re-enters.*) He's trustworthy. Visits
> his parents once a month. Asked me to go with him. You couldn't
> object to a visit to a graveyard? The sight of the tombs would deter
> any looseness.
>
> (Orton 1995a, 83)

The characters in *Saved* may spend a lot of their time watching television, or planning to watch television with the help of the *Radio
Times*, but Orton's characters have internalised the language, along with
a selection of choice phrases from the print media. Rattigan's comment about the telly-literacy of Orton's dialogue (quoted above) refers
to the disconcerting way in which Orton's characters shift abruptly
from a formal to informal register or vice versa, creating a collage of
different speech styles. This collage style is perhaps the most noted
feature of Orton's dialogue. Sheridan Morley describes *Entertaining
Sloane* as a play 'written almost entirely in mid-sixties Colour Supplement jargon' (Morley 1983, 19); Bull and Gray comment on the
News of the World style of salacious prudery (along the lines of 'our
reporter made his excuses and left') which peppers even the most
mundane conversation (Bull and Gray 1981, 89), as well as the elaborate descriptions of consumables advertised in women's magazines
(e.g., the 'brushed nylon' t-shirt Ed promises Sloane); and John Lahr
describes the characters' registers as redolent of 'the stilted luscious-
ness of B-movies' (Lahr 1995, 7). Orton continually mocks aspirations to 'bettering' oneself, and language is a particularly rich seam
of such aspirations. From Mike in *The Ruffian on the Stair* describing himself as 'a powerfully attractive figure' to the woman that he
lives with, as if reading a Barbara Cartland novel aloud, to Kath

telling her father to 'See your oculist at once' which could be taken directly from the prim tone of a public information film were it not followed by 'Go to bed. I'll bring you a drinkie' (Orton 1995a, 92). Bull and Gray note a particular instance of this in *The Ruffian on the Stair*, during the breakfast scene between Joyce and Mike, where Joyce clamours for a compliment about her cooking of Mike's breakfast:

> The query 'did it go down well?' strikes an accurate note of lower middle-class pseudo-gentility; as Nancy Mitford would put it, it is non-U, a term which might be inscribed over the door of the Orton inferno. The placing is not one of class. 'The eggs are perfect now I have the timer. Have you noticed' has the aggressively joyful domesticity of a TV commercial, a note reinforced by the 'Gollies', which suggest not only the brand of marmalade Joyce buys but also the exact quality of emptiness her life possesses.
>
> (Bull and Gray 1981, 86)

As the authors point out, Joyce's repeated questioning is reminiscent of the breakfast scene between Meg and Stanley in *The Birthday Party*, the difference being that Meg confines herself to 'Are they nice?', as opposed to Joyce's more elaborated 'did it go down well?' (Pinter 1990a, 4). Orton's characters appropriate these elaborated registers not only to give the impression that they live the luxurious life outlined in colour supplements and advertisements, but also to demonstrate that their morals are on a par with the virtuous denizens of those pages.[11] As noted above in the case of *Entertaining Mr Sloane*, knowledge of the correct moral position is produced as if voicing it has a performative effect. To say it is to make it happen.

The only people who make no pretence of upright morality are the middle-class Prentices from *What the Butler Saw*. Mrs Prentice's only reaction to finding her husband in a dress is to comment: 'Have you taken up transvestism? I'd no idea our marriage teetered on the edge of fashion' (Orton 1995a, 373). Orton's characters are articulate, but they are articulate in a way that is consonant with their class and educational background. Their elaborate turns of phrase ('Give me your word you're not vaginalatrous?') are betrayed by the common non-standard features they display in speech, particularly 'incorrect' grammar, for example: 'Good job I come when I did', 'He was killed instantaneous', 'that new stove cooks excellent' (Orton 1995a, 51, 83, 88, 130). Pinter and Orton have often been paired on the grounds of their 'comedies of menace', but there is also a similarity in the nature of their dialogue, which appears similarly natural, but stylised, because of this tendency to pepper their conversation with such memorable phrases. Pinter's early work tends towards inarticulacy (lacking the words) which is interpreted as a class indicator. In his later work, in particular *No Man's Land* (1975), inarticulacy is exchanged for dysfluency (lack of ability to string the words together) and a tendency to cast around for what sounds like a suitable expression – much more reminiscent of Orton.

Regional voices

The rise of television, pop music and the global exports of Swinging London helped to legitimise regional and non-standard speech, and the Beatles' combination of accent and wit was a particularly potent contribution. At the same time, the Arts Council of Great Britain began funding regional theatre companies and regional buildings in earnest: the Victoria in Stoke-on-Trent in 1962, the Everyman in Liverpool opened 1964, the Royal Exchange in Manchester in 1968 and the Crucible in Sheffield in 1971. Liverpool and Stoke both committed to reflecting local life and supporting local writing. Peter Terson (born in Newcastle and living, at the time, in Worcestershire) was an early beneficiary of the Arts Council's playwright's bursary scheme and wrote a number of plays exploring life in the Midlands and North East for the Victoria Theatre. The correspondence in the Lord Chamberlain's collection relating to Terson's *The Mighty Reservoy* and *A Night to Make the Angels Weep* (both 1964) demonstrates the extent to which the establishment was struggling with the increasing liberalisation of theatrical practice and exploration, and the playwrights and producers involved. Peter Cheeseman, the director of the Victoria Theatre, recalls convincing the Lord Chamberlain's functionaries that 'knackers were a form of north country castanets' rather than a slang term for male genitalia in order to keep a running joke about Dezzell playing on his knackers in the script.[12] The notes on the Reader's Report bear this out, and also give a flavour of the Lord Chamberlain's office's expectations of Cheeseman and Terson in advance of their visit:

> We saw the producer and author today. Both quite reasonable people. [...] As regards their letter of 6.6.64 they assure us that 'knackers' in Northumberland are 'castanets' that originally this character

was to be a double-jointed man who could play noises on his knucklebones – for casting reasons they've had to substitute the castanets.

(LCP Corr: 1964/4247)

However, the Lord Chamberlain's readers were not so easy to pacify over Terson's second play of that year, *The Mighty Reservoy*, which they described as 'a dreary mixture of simple symbolism and the two four letter words', and they demanded extensive cuts:

i.i Shit (five times)
2. ditto
3. shit and cunt
4. shit (twice) and fucking
5. Jesus and cunt and shit and fuck
6. Shit and buggered and jesus
7. Buggered and shit and Christ and jesus
9. [sic] Christ (twice) and half-frigging and Jesus
10. Shit
11 bugger and Christ (twice) and Jesus and buggered
12. buggers and Christ
15. bugger (twice)
19. shit and jesus (twice)
22 Christ
26 christ
29. shit (twice)

II.1 fucking
2. Jesus (twice) and maiden's water and Christ
3. Christ (three times)

II.4 Fecking (equals fucking)
7. Christ
9 Fucking
10 Sweet fuck all
12 fucker and fuck and fucked and Christ
13 Christ (twice) and bugger and buggered and fucking and fuck and knacker and pissed. Not sure about pissed but will draw attention to it
14. fuck
15 fucked
17 pissed and alter the marked lines

18 bollox
19 stuff them
22 shit
23 shithouse and stuff them
24 pissed (twice) and buggers
25 friggin' and buggers
32 buggers
34 shit

III.1 shit and pissed up
2. shit
3. alter the marked lines and piss
7. shit
8. pissed
10. fucking

IV.2 bugger
7 shit (four times)

Otherwise,
RECOMMENDED FOR LICENCE.

(LCP Corr: 1964/4421)

Underneath this, examiner of plays Charles Heriot has rather plaintively written: 'May I again enquire whether these people could have a letter telling them to clean up their texts before submitted them [*sic*]: they surely must know that we can't allow most of this?' The censor's misgivings were not shared by Benedict Nightingale in the *Guardian* who described Terson as:

> Formidably gifted. He can write dialogue with natural, but varied, exciting rhythms, bright language that is neither affected nor hackneyed; dialogue with some superficial resemblances to Pinter, but tougher and altogether less mannered.
>
> (*Guardian*, 30 September 1964)

Being likened to Pinter was high praise indeed in terms of a description of life-like language, and increasingly, this life-like language included swearing. The Lord Chamberlain's readers and examiners of plays were well aware of this and were in the difficult position of having to carry on upholding the old standards while hoping that the government would free them from the indignity of bandying words about dirty words.

Heriot, for example, had been both an actor and a producer before joining the Lord Chamberlain's office in 1937, and he was not the only
member of staff with theatrical experience and enthusiasm. In 1968,
after several years of lobbying, the Lord Chamberlain's office was finally
relieved of the burden, leading to a general freeing up of subject matter
and language.[13]

The Might Reservoy and *A Night to Make the Angels Weep* played to
mostly regional audiences, as did many plays which originated in
regional theatres. Very few regional productions transferred to London,
and few national newspaper critics travelled to the regions to regularly
review shows, so the regional language varieties and accents used in
the shows were, in a sense, playing to the converted.[14] This was not
the case with David Storey's *The Changing Room* (1971), a play about
semi-professional rugby league players in Yorkshire, first performed at
the Royal Court in London. Set in the home team's changing room
before, during and after the match, the play featured nudity, swearing, pronounced regional accents and dialect words, and the reviews
were overwhelmingly positive, focusing on the sense of community
that existed among the team. The fetishisation which occurs in the
reception of this play is not based on language and communication, but on class. The fact that the men are engaged in something
alien to the majority of the audience transforms the ordinary business of preparing for a match, half-time and dressing afterwards into
an entirely different kind of artistic object: Harold Hobson invoked
poetry:

> Behind the ribbing, and the swearing, and the showing off, the piece
> is permeated by a Wordsworthian spirit. You can, if you listen, hear
> through it 'the still sad music of humanity'.
>
> (*Sunday Times*, 14 November 1971)

While J.C. Trewin compared it to both film and, by implication,
painting:

> Its dialogue may be firmly demotic, yet in the context its repetitions,
> the insistence on one epithet – 'bloody' is sovereign – son cease to
> worry. The author, without obvious effort, has turned life into drama.
> It is not just a mass-observation document, an edited camera record:
> it is Storey's Match.
>
> (*Illustrated London News*)

Writing in *The Lady*, Trewin was more restrained:

> The dialogue, firmly demotic and realist is not maybe for a sensitive playgoer, though our ears are becoming tuned to it nowadays. Mr Storey is offering entire realism at a period in the theatre when it is possible to do so; and though I would not recommend the play for a family occasion – these things must be considered – it is certainly a piece for collectors.
>
> (*The Lady*)

John Barber, critic for the *Daily Telegraph*, commented on the 'fascination in watching homely men at work at a difficult job'; while Irving Wardle praised Storey's 'assumption [...] that ordinary life is interesting enough in itself without being distorted to meet the requirements of plot, character, or editorial comment' (*The Times*, 10 November 1971). In some senses, these favourable reviews are not really surprising: at this point Anderson had made his name as a film director with *If* and *This Sporting Life* (written by Storey), and Storey was well known as a novelist. Along with fellow Royal Court director Tony Richardson, Anderson had helped usher more realistic and more regional voices into the cinema. Regional voices, as discussed earlier, were increasingly present on television, and television was now part of British life; but if we compare the reception of *The Changing Room* with *Roots* it shows just how quickly language minders had become accustomed to hearing regional voices on stage. No one complains that they cannot understand characters in *The Changing Room* even though they use more dialect words than those in *Roots*. For example, 'laking' ('laik' being a Yorkshire dialect term for 'playing'); 'thysen' and 'thy' (you and your); 'mesen' (myself, me); and 'aye' and 'nay' for yes and no, as well as orthographical representations of pronunciations, such as 'winder' for 'window'. There may be other factors attached to this: some dialects (and accents) are stigmatised more than others; Storey's rugby players are seen preparing for action or recovering from it, while Beatie and her family are seen preparing meals or relaxing; it will also be coloured by the perceptions of individual reviewers, but the shift in perception is still profound.

Society under scrutiny

Where Bond (in *Saved* and *The Pope's Wedding*) had explored the limitations of inarticulacy, and questioned the idealism of the Wesker trilogy's consciousness raising through articulacy, the political playwrights of the

1970s give their protagonists a 'fund of language' with which to explore and articulate their disillusionment in the hope of promulgating revolution. The preferred method for David Hare combined elements of naturalism and agitprop. As Innes explains:

> A photographic reproduction of individual behaviour (to which Naturalism leads), is the opposite of the two-dimensional class figures (characteristic of Agitprop). In one, the factors that determine how people act are psychological and environmental. In the other they are economic or historical necessity. And each style distorts reality. The primarily personal emphasis of the first rule out the objective overview necessary for dealing with the political issues, while the ideological focus of the second ignores the subjective reactions of the participants. The solution is a 'synthesis... that of the surface perception of Naturalism and the social analysis that underlies Agitprop plays'.
>
> (Innes 1992, 182)

This distinction between naturalism and agitprop-style caricature can be seen in the way in which non-standard English is represented onstage by political playwrights in the 1960 and 1970s. Where Wesker and Bond attempted naturalistic detail in the speech of their characters, Brenton, Hare and Edgar cover a spectrum from semi-naturalism through to caricature. To relate this distinction back to Innes's observation about political drama, Hare, Brenton and Edgar (discussed in the next chapter) disregarded the realism of inarticulate or dysfluent characters in favour of highly articulate protagonists who could serve as mouthpieces for their messages, but retain a semblance of accent or idiom in order to provide a realistic flavour. Caryl Churchill's early work also falls into this category – although she generally displays more awareness of the power dynamics of interaction – reminding us that the working practices of Joint Stock had a decisive impact on the extent to which ordinary characters become temporarily articulate, because of the company's emphasis on research and source material. In common with Brenton, Hare and Edgar, Churchill's characters are never lost for words, but the explicit analysis of language and power suggests this is because the people she is writing about are already in a marginalised position and need someone to speak on their behalf, so they might as well have someone speaking articulately.

If new writers and directors of the 1960s rejected the 'well-made play' format that had largely continued to dominate the New Wave stage, one prominent writer of the 1970s also questioned the New Wave

doctrines of vitality and community. David Hare's plays, as John Bull noted back in 1984, are often categorised as 'well-made' with the unfortunate consequence that the political commentary contained within them is overlooked by critics: 'by stressing their wit and polish, at the expense of attention to what it is that the characters are so articulate about' (Bull 1984, 61). However, articulacy is not necessarily a blessing for Hare's characters, but rather a means by which they can express and appreciate their moral vacuity and disappointment in society. Yet this does not mean that inarticulacy is valorised either; instead the characters in the early plays (from *Slag* up to *Licking Hitler*) seem to be trapped by their articulacy into knowing but not really feeling, comparable perhaps to Hare's description of the failure of satire to raise consciousness in Britain. Proposing that 'satire is based on ignorance', Hare suggests that the failure of political comedy to galvanise the audience through revelations that Eden was high on Benzedrine during Suez, or that 'Churchill dribbled and farted in Cabinet for two years after a debilitating stroke, and nobody dared to remove him' is because the audience are no longer surprised by such revelations:

> after his railing, the satirist may find that the audience replies, 'Well, we do know now; and we don't believe it will ever change. And knowing may well not affect what we think.'
>
> (Hare 1992a, 3)

The characters in these early plays eloquently express their disillusionment with the Labour government of 1964 and the ideals of community promoted by the New Left in the previous decade but seem unable to come up with a workable alternative. Articulacy no longer paves the way to 'a positive utopia, to revolution' as it did in Brecht, it just leads to more introspection and pessimism, further removing people from the ideal of community.

As well as poking fun at the extremes of the Women's Liberation movement and radical socialism, *Slag* (1970) offers a very bleak view of the progression of the New Left ideals. The three female teachers, isolated and divided in their attempt to build a utopian community at Brackenhurst school, end up in a farcical situation in which the Head (Ann) rugby tackles the militantly feminist and political Jo after she tries to leave the school. The third teacher, Elise, comments:

> **Elise**. I thought this was meant to be the ideal community.
> **Joanne**. If we are to be grouped together for some social purpose . . .

Elise. Social theory.
Joanne. But this is a repressive...
Ann. You are hardly likely to get any farther than anyone before you.
Joanne. Masculine...
Elise. Not on those legs!
Joanne. Does no one listen to anything I say?
Elise. No.
Joanne. I feel victimised.
Ann. This school...
Joanne. Don't bother to go on.
Ann. This school...
Joanne. Don't bother to go on.
Ann. This school...
Joanne. I don't want to hear. We don't want to hear.
Ann. This school...
Joanne. Don't finish that sentence.
Ann. This school...
Joanne. I won't let you.
Ann. This school...
Joanne. You're not to.
Ann. This school...
(*Pause. Surprise*)
This school has some standards to keep up. And I will murder to
maintain them.

(Hare 1992a, 42)

The ideals of community and cooperation advanced by Hoggart and
Williams (discussed in the previous chapter) are shown here as tools of
repression. The only way in which the community at Brackenhurst can
continue is if the head forcibly detains the other two members. Beatie
Bryant's plea that we must all listen to each other is literally shouted
down, to be replaced by the dogmatic repetition of 'This school' and various interruptions from Joanne. The New Left's emphasis on education
is similarly ridiculed by the extreme programme on offer at Brackenhurst and the lack of success the women have in attracting and retaining
pupils:

Elise. We're appalling schoolteachers.
Ann. Come, come.
Joanne. Are you going to teach?

Elise. No.
Joanne. I think I will, then.
(*Exit* **Joanne**)
Ann. I won't have that said.
Elise. Why have we only got eight pupils then?

(Hare 1992b, 21)

Joanne's own curriculum, which includes teaching masturbation, dialectics and Marxist economic theory, is even more extreme in its parody of all things leftwing. The parody reaches its high point in a scene re-enacting the ideal of the 'full and rich life' of the working class when Joanne discovers that Elise is apparently from a poor Northern family:

> **Joanne**. Oh Elise I never guessed you were working class. Why's your name Elise?
> **Elise**. They mis-spelt Elsie on the birth certificate.
> **Joanne**. And when you were young was it all day trips to Bingley and Huddersfield and Salford and Leeds? Is that how it really was? I see it so clearly. Did your parents fuck loudly in the upstairs rooms?
> **Elise**. The only person who fucked was my sister. She married early and they came to live with us in the room next door to me. And at nights before I really knew what was happening she used to cry out suddenly when she reached her orgasm – 'Eh, by gum.'
> **Joanne**. How splendid!

(Hare 1992b, 49)

Girlish delight at discovering a genuine working-class person (which of course Elise is not) is followed by passionate validation of Elise's sister's authentically colloquial expression of pleasure/surprise at the moment of orgasm.

The Great Exhibition (1972) concentrates in even greater detail on the gap between eloquence and sincerity. The subject of the play is Labour MP Charlie Hammett and his withdrawal from his constituency and his party as a result of his disaffection with the new breed of Labour men. According to Kerensky, Hare described the play as a 'deliberate parody of all Royal Court-type plays, and explained that it's about people who suffer with a capital S, mainly from lack of self-knowledge' (Kerensky 1977, 177). Hammett fears his Sunderland constituency because, as he tells the Home Secretary: 'It's a long way and when you get there it's a dump. And the people resent me because I'm not working-class' (Hare 1992c, 106), and he in turn seems to despise the Left's emphasis on the working class as the only authentic people, or the only people worth listening to. His wife, Maud (a casting director), reinforces these anti-New Left jibes, as well as swiping at the self-absorbed nature of the theatre and its workers:

> **Maud**. I thought through you I'd meet some *real* people. I mean real people. But in Sunderland they were rather aggressively real. They made a fetish of it. And you used to stand there shifting foot to foot, worrying about your accent, and how can I get these people to respect me? You weren't getting terribly close. Pints of black and tan jammed in our hands didn't fool anybody. The week-end felt like a penance for the life we lived elsewhere.
>
> (Hare 1992c, 119)

Her account of these trips to a 'genuine' community as a penance rather than a glorious voyage of self-discovery seems once again to be mocking the revolutionary zeal with which Hoggart had described these communities. Hammett owns his eloquence as a curse, he tells the Home Secretary: 'I can't talk about what I believe in. I can talk about anything else. Eloquence should be reserved for things that don't matter.' and because of this he seems unable to feel anything (Hare 1992c, 108). He explains his feelings of dislocation to Catriona, an old friend of Maud's who, it transpires, is trying to recruit him into the Conservative party precisely because of his insincerity:

> **Hammett**. The ground I've trodden on for ten years has shifted away and I'm conscious of talking in the air. I can't even mouth the word 'revolution' any longer. It sounds so limp and secondhand. Those of us who believed that the world would get better have been brought up short. The thing gets worse not just because of what happens, but because the weight of knowledge of what ought to happen gets greater. As things get more impossible they also get more obvious. As our needs get simpler, they get more unlikely to be fulfilled.
>
> (Hare 1992a, 130)

Hare's characters continue to express their disillusionment with both the Left and the Right for the next 30 years: from Susan's private disappointment in *Plenty* to George's public disappointment in *The Absence of War*, slick rationalisation is never enough. Hare's former Portable colleague and sometime collaborator Howard Brenton moves on from the rejection of rationalisation to demonstrate a harsher reality in which direct action offers an alternative, but not necessarily a solution to this disillusionment.

6
1976–1989: Staging the Nation

This chapter focuses on the ways in which the opening up of society was reflected on stage between 1976 and 1989. As theatre was increasingly able to function as a 'rapid response unit' to current affairs after the end of censorship, writers were able put an ever widening demographic on the stage with more and more verisimilitude, because the pool of writers and actors had also widened. The plays I have chosen as case studies here reflect the 'regionalisation' of English drama: *Road, Educating Rita* and *The Arbor*; the obsession with a new economic breed: *Serious Money* and *Revengers' Comedies*; and large-scale attempts to represent the whole of society on stage: *Destiny* and *Epsom Downs*.

Historical context

It is impossible to write about language and theatre in the 1980s without mentioning Thatcherism and the conditions which aided Margaret Thatcher's election, notably the industrial disputes leading up to the 'Winter of Discontent' in 1979 which gave her a clear mandate to tame the unions and 'modernise' the public sector. Urban and industrial unrest continued to escalate as the Conservatives put their policies into practice: riots in Brixton, Southall, Toxteth and Moss Side in 1981, the miners' strike in 1984, and in 1986, the abolition of metropolitan councils (including the left-led Greater London Council and Merseyside council). The new era of enterprise and the 'rationalisation' of heavy industry contributed to rising unemployment (more than 3 million at its peak). Cuts to state welfare and attempts to make all public sector providers profitable created a social underclass living on or below the poverty line in increasingly dilapidated council housing with no prospect of work or an improvement in their circumstances. As the north of England became poorer, the south became richer, helped by increasingly buoyant property prices and the deregulation of the City of London which introduced a new breed of super-earners to the UK. The divide between rich and poor was no longer, however, evident in how people spoke, and the changes in the City of London provide a microcosmic study of this.

The City functioned like an extended gentlemen's club, employing Oxbridge men and public school boys in the merchant banks and on the Stock Exchange. As a result of the abolition of exchange controls in 1979 international banking firms were able to set up offices in London and bring with them a newer and more aggressive way of doing business. In 1982, the London International Financial Futures Exchange (LIFFE) was established. LIFFE dealers worked on the floor, buying and selling stock to each other at the behest of bond dealers; it was a new style of working and the speed, noise and aggression were beyond the experience of the largely public school City traders. The people who did have a gift for it were young working-class men and women from the East End and Essex who came to be nicknamed 'barrow boys' and who acquired great personal wealth while retaining their native accents and dialects.[1] Accent was no longer a reliable marker of wealth and social influence in business, but a standard accent and persuasive tone continued to be a useful asset in a parliamentary career, as Thatcher's decision to lose her Lincolnshire accent (albeit back in the 1950s) and take voice lessons attest.

Theatrical context

By 1976 alternative theatre (helped in many cases by funding from the Arts Council) had firmly established itself as a major player on the British theatre scene, and, in doing so, had revitalised touring theatre (which had last flourish when CEMA-sponsored tours of Welsh mining villages during the Second World War). Regional theatres also continued to flourish; some, like the Liverpool Everyman, put their creative energy into fostering new and local writing talent, providing opportunities for Alan Bleasdale, Willy Russell, Chris Bond and John McGrath. Others, like the Victoria Theatre, Stoke on Trent, continued to engage with the local community through documentary plays. The Arts Council was continuing to fund the building of new theatres in the regions and the arts scene was, on the whole, buoyant and creative. The Conservative government that came to power in 1979 would gradually halt this benign funding reign. For them, subsidy was another adjunct to the Welfare State that they so despised, and under their rule, theatres and theatre companies would cease to operate, or operate in restricted circumstances imposed not only by cuts in subsidy but by being forced to look for sponsorship and 'investment' from commercial firms which then affected their repertoire. As Wu notes,

> For left-leaning writers of the time, that decade, [the 1980s] can only have been traumatic. The great project of the 1960s, with which they been brought up, was a socialist one. It had been stalled by the multiple incompetencies of the Labour government of 1974–79, but the more optimistic among them must have believed that the Thatcher government of 1979 was a blip. It wasn't. It marked the end of an experiment begun by the Labour government of 1945. That generated crisis in the arts generally.
>
> (Wu 2000, 6)

This crisis manifested itself in a number of ways. Large subsidised companies such as the National Theatre and Royal Shakespeare Company (RSC) and regional producing houses were forced to commission and programme commercially successful plays which could have extended runs and even West End transfers. This inevitably led to a restricted repertoire of popular classical revivals (Shakespeare and Chekhov), adaptations of novels (particularly Dickens), commissions from established and successful writers (notably Stoppard, Ayckbourn, Hare, Edgar and Russell) and an increasing number of musicals in an attempt to follow the RSC's success with *Les Miserables*. This was one of the new genre of historical musicals in which characters were able to communicate their feelings via song and without the inconvenience of trying to express naturalistically what it was like to live in an increasingly divided Britain (although it was permissible to explore the theme of living in a divided society from a historical distance, as in *Les Miserables* (1985) and *Evita* (1978)). During the 1980s the Conservative government undermined the 'arms-length' principle of funding, and theatre workers became increasingly politicised, and increasingly convinced that they were being targeted for expressing their dissatisfaction with both arts policy and the way in which society was developing. Many writers were similarly galvanised given a new series of targets to aim at: urban deprivation and the effects of unemployment as depicted in *Road* (1986); an increasingly right-wing press as portrayed in *Pravda*; the growing cult of money illustrated by Churchill in *Top Girls* (1982) and *Serious*

Money (1987); and the conflict and confusion among both left and right explored by Edgar in *Destiny* (1976) and *Maydays* (1983).

The case studies in this chapter are of plays which examine the ways in which playwrights articulated their responses to the changing social and political climate, and the linguistic strategies they employ to do this. As we saw in the last chapter, many playwrights tend to favour articulate characters who act as a vehicle for their messages; for political playwrights, this articulacy has an added dimension when they confer articulacy on the traditionally 'unheard' or inarticulate in order to allow their situation to speak to a wider constituency. On these occasions, the conduit metaphor moves from being a way of theorising communication, to a way of theorising political drama. When they began to work in the mainstream, and on the main stages, Brenton, Hare, Edgar and Churchill all stated that they had done so in order to reach a greater number of people, and in order to do so they adopted the most 'transparent' mode of language available to them: that of the elaborated code.

Staging the state of the nation: Language and the public sphere

The two plays examined here, David Edgar's *Destiny* and Brenton's *Epsom Downs*, capture a particular moment in British theatre history when certain playwrights attempted 'state of the nation' plays that focused on a broad canvas of society from the ruling classes down to the working classes. For both authors, in common with many fringe practitioners, there was a growing sense in the 1970s that political drama was preaching to the converted, and that when it wasn't doing this, it was losing its audience entirely. Edgar, who began his career with General Will, recalls performing *Rent* for the National Union of Public Employees in Bangor: 'we started with eighty people and ended up with two. After that, whenever I suggested a line which included a word of more than three syllables, people would say, how would that go down in Bangor?' (Edgar in Trussler 1981, 162).

Politics: *Destiny* (1976)

Destiny traces the political trajectory of a group of British soldiers from Indian Independence in 1947 to 1970s Britain, and, in particular, the journey of the patriotic league of a West Midlands town towards fascism. A key scene is a public meeting to debate whether the patriotic league should join Nation Forward (equivalent to the National Front), the point being that people become attracted to fascism regardless of class and wealth, because of the way in which it appears tailored to their individual suffering. As Edgar explains, the people at the meeting:

> the unemployed worker, the older worker threatened by technological change, the middle class woman with her savings being destroyed, the polytechnic lecturer, his lower-middle class property oriented wife, who brings in the technical worker, and so on, all being brought together by the philosophy of fascism, by the character Maxwell, who takes of all their different little worries and despairs and neatly fits them together into a conspiracy theory of history – wham, bang, fascism.
>
> (Edgar in Trussler 1981, 169)

Maxwell's particular skill lies in co-opting the rhetoric most relevant to each of the characters' ideological position and marketing Nation Forward as the party that best understands these viewpoints. Mrs Turner, for example, described as *'an elderly gentleperson'*, voices the classic conservative complaint about the degeneration of morals and values and the Empire (a rhetoric that would gain even greater ground in the 1980s with Norman Tebbit). As befits a 'gentleperson', Mrs Turner uses a highly elaborated speech code (I have excised the interruptions from her speech to give a sense of its fluency and the way in which it epitomises Tebbitism):

> **Mrs Howard.** Mr Chairman, I have been a member of the Conservative Party for 40 years. That's what I wish to say [...] It would be complete anathema for me to support or vote for any other party [...] However. I am afraid that the Party is not what it once was. It has become craven. Once it represented all the finest values of the middle classes. Now gangrenous [...] Values sneered at. Sniggered over. In the Party. Young Conservatives, who often seem more socialist than the socialists themselves. They look embarrassed when you talk about the Empire, or self-help, or discipline. They snigger and talk about the Common Market. Sneer and talk about a wind of change [...] I'm sure it's infiltrated. From the left. The cryptos. Pale-pinks. Sure of it.
>
> (Edgar 1987, 352)

The syntax of Mrs Turner's speech is straightforward: short, punchy sentences which convey the impression of thinking on the move, but also carry rhetorical force. Her vocabulary and recourse to abstract metaphors is highly characteristic of elaborated speech styles (anathema, craven, gangrenous, infiltrated). She also employs the rhetorical trick of repeating key words in alliterative pairings (sneered, snigger). In contrast, Tony (an unemployed furniture porter unaccustomed to public speaking) struggles to express elaborated ideas in his own more restricted code, with neither the practised fluency nor the vocabulary to make his point in a slick manner. However, it is important to point out, this does not *prevent* him from making his point:

> **Tony**. I think, what the last speaker was saying. You know, I mean, you're middle class, and you lost your business, didn't you. I hope you don't mind me saying, but I mean it was the same, big firm taking over … And take me. I'm on the dole, in'I? Like you were saying. It just does seem to me, what class you are … same kind of …
>
> (*He's run out.* **Maxwell** *stands.* **Tony** *sits, relieved*
>
> (Edgar 1987, 354)

Tony's hedges (you know, I mean), pauses and inability to articulate his point is reinforced by the fact that Maxwell, the practised public speaker, follows him with his 'wham, bang, fascism' speech:

> **Maxwell**. If I could perhaps come in there. Well, my friends, I said I thought I'd learn a thing or two from you, and by God I was right. We've heard about subversion in the colleges. From Mrs Howard about the Tory Party. And from Mr (*Checks notes*) Attwood on the local industry. But it's my view that the last speaker really grasped the point. That what we have in common is greater by far, than what divides us. I'm sure, for instance, that Mrs Howard does not oppose trade unions as such, but only their perversion for political ends. I am convinced that Mr Attwood does not oppose honest profit, but speculative profiteering. Of course, we disagree on many issues. But more, much more, unites us than divides us.
>
> (Edgar 1987, 354)

Maxwell's speech is masterly in the way in which it puts words in the mouths of the speakers, and, in particular, in Tony's case, how he transforms a faltering outline of an idea into the smooth 'what we have in common is greater by far than what divides us' – the inversion of 'greater' and 'far' signalling a proverbial feel, rather than the more prosaic 'far greater'. Maxwell is also careful to employ politeness strategies ignored by the others at the meeting who continually interrupt and shout each other down. Even though it is clear that Tony's turn has lapsed, Maxwell still signals his intention to enter the discussion with a strategy designed to minimise the imposition with two hedges: 'if I *could perhaps* come in there' (my emphasis). *Destiny* highlights how susceptible people are to interpellation via their own rhetoric. In one telling scene, Maxwell and another Nation Forward official, Cleaver, argue about the content of a speech written for Turner (the local NF candidate):

Cleaver. [. . .] (*He reads:*) 'Nation Forward believes that the cause of our present crisis is not the legitimate wage demands of British workers, but the domination of our economy by a tiny clique of international capitalists – the very people who deliberately import cheap foreign labour and cheap foreign goods to undercut our wages and throw us on the dole.'
Pause.
Maxwell. Well?
Cleaver. Drop the wog-bashing and it could be Tribune, David.
Maxwell. So what do you want? Wicked union holding the country to ransom? Eastbourne über alles? Cos that's what Turner –
Cleaver. (*angry, stabbing at the typescript*). Where, amongst all this jolly stuff on the thieves' den of the Stock Exchange, is the support of free productive industry? Where, amid all this merry rhetoric about the plight of the ordinary working folk, is the need to isolate the Commie wreckers? Where, in the midst of all this happy talk of democratic structures and meaningful participation, is the hint, no more, the hint that all men are not equal and that some were born to lead and others only fit to follow?
Maxwell. Richard, we can reprint Mein Kampf if it'll make you –

(Edgar 1987, 364)

Although Edgar does sprinkle the play with some dialect phrases for his lower middle class and working-class characters (NF candidate Denis Turner frequently refers to people as 'bab', occasionally says 'ar' instead of yes), accent is the primary indicator of social class, and tends to be used in a coarser, more agitprop style. The factory workers are described as having 'West Midlands' or 'Brummie' accents which clearly separates them from the unmarked speech of the other characters (literally unmarked, Edgar writes in stage directions when an accent is called for). Interestingly, the only Cockney accent in the play is given to the fleeting character who represents the new breed of Conservative: Selsdon Man. Monty, the Jewish businessman who raises Turner's rent and puts him out of business, is a caricature Cockney: he repeatedly calls Turner 'love' or 'old love', and responds to Turner's 'Bastard' with 'No, not bastard, Selsdon man' (339). Strictly speaking, Selsdon (in Croydon) is too far from the sound of Bow Bells to qualify as truly Cockney, but the symbolism is clear.[2]

Edgar's awareness of language and class is used to specific purposes in *Destiny* (1976), and his determination to convey important and complex political points explains the generally elaborated nature of his characters' speech. In addition, as Innes points out, it is written in such an elaborated code precisely because of the audience the playwright was seeking to interpellate. Edgar himself has acknowledged that his early agitprop plays tended to be overly complex in relation to the intended audience (factory workers, union representatives, etc.) and in *Destiny* rather than alter the language, he focused on a different audience:

> the need to provide an insight into personal motives was reinforced by the targeted audience – the middle-class theatre-goers most susceptible to right-wing extremism. This meant creating 'characters that the audience could relate to and in a way that they could confront themselves'. Hence Edgar considered that the transfer of the RSC production to a West End theatre (where it was seen by 20, 000 people) had more significance than the television showing of the play, which reached a far larger, but more socially diverse audience.
>
> (Innes 1992, 183)

Staging the nation's great day out: *Epsom Downs*

In contrast, Brenton's *Epsom Downs* seems a more egalitarian entertainment – as befits a play about the Epsom Derby 'for thousands it is a good day out' – political statements appear as joking banter, asides, and the occasional speeches of a disgruntled communist stable boy or a drunken Labour peer, rather than the rather formal speeches of *Destiny* (Brenton 1986, 277). While Hare, and even Edgar, continued to work in a broadly naturalist, well-made tradition, Brenton rejected these conventions, refusing any constraints on his wish to produce political theatre. Where Edgar and Hare focused predominantly on middle class audiences, Brenton is concerned with the young and working class. In his Preface to *Plays One*, he explains that:

The great socialist leaders wake in their cells in South Africa, in South America, as do the cadres in Soweto and Nicaragua, confident that history is moving as surely as the planet moves. But millions do not have that vision, confidence and heroism, and some are traumatised by defeat. It is they whom I want to write about – the young, uneducated workers in *Weapons of Happiness*; Judy, the abused divorcee in *Sore Throats*; the young couple in *Epsom Downs* with their children, at their wits end about making ends meet [...] For me, people like these are the salt of the earth. I try to dramatise them coming to life, gaining visions, confidence and courage in their own way. If the Left convinces and wins people like them, the British Revolution will be unstoppable.

(Brenton 1986, xiv–xv)

With such a mission in mind, inarticulate characters can be nothing but a disservice to the cause, and in *Epsom Downs* this desire to speak to and for the people gives every aspect of the play a voice: even the horses, course and betting stakes are capable of articulate speech. The Horse's register is that of the opinionated expert – as well it might be – 'The mentality of a race horse can be compared to the mentality of a bird. Nervous, quick, shy and rather stupid' (Brenton 1986, 305). The play is set at the Epsom Derby, described by Superintendent Blue ('the crowd control overlord') in Hoggartian overtones as: 'The Cockney's holiday. Half a million cheeky chappies on the grass stuffin "emselves with Brown Ale and ham sandwiches. It has a lot of old world charm" ' (Brenton 1986, 262).[3] The Derby represents an excellent opportunity for demonstrating that 'all human life is here', as characters walk across the downs and the track. Like Edgar, although Brenton does give the different social strata of his plays different idioms, there is no real attempt at 'life-like speech'; instead he uses a 'lite' version to demonstrate the spectrum of social classes. However, these representations are by no means unsubtle; Primrose the Gypsy Girl, for example, is slightly more standard than her mum Minty:

Primrose. Oh Ma'am, what you doing?
Minty. I bain't talking to you Girl. You don't know how dangerous that is, to go lying there shameless, all arms. When your Pa gets out the nick, won't he give you a wallop.
Primrose. Oh Ma'am, let me lug that battery for you.

(Brenton 1986, 271–272)

Primrose may use the odd slang word (lug), but Minty has non-standard lexicogrammatical features as well (bain't, token, you'se, and so on) perhaps in an effort by Brenton to convey her 'otherness' as against her daughter's assimilation. In the next class up, the repentant sinners, Mr Tillotson and Miss Motrom, move easily between their formal 'chapel' register and their normal mode of speech:

> **Miss Motrom**. The congregation at the Mission are all with us, in Christ.
> **Mr Tillotson**. Yeah? Where are they then? Other Missions'll be here. Come lunchtime the punters won't be able to move for missions. Thick the praises to the Lord will be.
> **Miss Motrom**. It was felt –
> **Mr Tillotson**. It was felt it was Jim Tillotson's idea. Come down here. Bear witness at The Derby. So it was given the holier-than-thou cold shoulder. And none of them turned up. Fucking about –
>
> (Brenton 1986, 277)

The register-switching in this scene is comic, but also displays the thinness of the linguistic veneer of holiness Tillotson is using. At the top of the social pile, the horse owners speak fairly standard Loamshire:

> **Smooth Woman**. But we must meet before Ascot. If only for tea and cakes?
> **Sweet Woman**. Not before Ascot. Perhaps in September? My diary is a traffic jam.
> **Smooth Woman**. One's life does flow over. (*She looks at the HORSE.*) When I look at a race horse, I always think of footballers' legs. So lean and tight.
>
> (Brenton 1986, 307)

Class is conveyed here not so much through the language itself (although referring to oneself as 'one' in an informal context is a heavy clue as to social status), but the content of their utterances. People whose social diaries are governed by Ascot and the Derby tend to inhabit the upper echelons of society, and tend to be largely confined to the plays of a much earlier era. The effect of broad caricature is inevitable in a play with such a huge cast of characters, but the crucial point is that everyone, from Minty upwards, gets a voice, a chance to be heard and this was crucial to a generation who had been so influenced by the Royal Court tradition.

The 1980s: New words; new world order

The fundamental changes that Thatcherism would bring about were not, of course, immediately apparent when Thatcher first took office, nor in the first years of the 1980s. By the time she left office in 1989, however, the effect of her reign was visible everywhere, particularly in language. Thatcherism manifested itself not only in the continued and dogmatic re-association of 'proper' English with 'proper' behaviour and the repercussions this would have on the teaching of English language, but also in the number of new words, and new connotations of old words. In *Investigating English Discourse*, which charts the attempts of linguists to influence the government's new guidelines on language teaching, Ronald Carter gives a list of 'eighties words', which he notes, 'did not appear in British English, at least with the meanings accrued during that decade, before the 1980s'. On the list are

Enterprise zone/initiative   insider-dealing

Fax	compassion fatigue
Interface	golden hello
Theme park	brat pack
Street cred	loony left
Wets	heritage business
Handbagging	polyunsaturates
On yer bike	lean cuisine
Wicked	bad
ECU	north south divide
Militant tendency	'quality time'
Ozone-friendly	niche-marketing
Reagonomics	'care in the community'
Greenhouse effect	community service
Flexible friend	community charge

(Carter 1997, 5)

Unsurprisingly, the themes that these new words and usages reflect – business and money, community, lifestyle and environment – are also the preoccupations of many plays in the 1980s. *Top Girls* (1982), *A Small Family Business* (1985), *Serious Money* (1987) and *Revengers' Comedies* all focus on business; *The Arbor* (1980), *Educating Rita* (1980) and *Road* (1986) examine 'community'; and *Lettice and Lovage* (1987) pays homage to the 'heritage industry'. As the decade progressed, theatre (and the other arts) increasingly found themselves having to justify their existence (and plead for funds) on the basis of their contribution to the heritage industry and/or their local community. By the end of the decade, the leaders of subsidised theatres had become as fluent in business speak as the characters satirised in the plays they staged. Richard Eyre's diaries from his time as artistic director of the National Theatre reflect this dilemma, and Eyre's mastery of the new discourse:

> Board meeting. We discuss the purpose of the NT and its future. I describe the aim of the NT to provide of continuity of 'investment', employment and theatrical tradition, at ticket prices which aren't punitively expensive, and to present what couldn't or wouldn't be done in the commercial theatre in both content and style.
>
> (Eyre 2003, 87)

The language of commerce: *Revengers' Comedies* and *Serious Money*

Alan Ayckbourn's *Revengers' Comedies* bears out Carter's thesis about the infiltration of Thatcherite discourse into the language of the person in the street. Ayckbourn's work, more frequently produced than any other living playwright, provides an excellent theatrical barometer of the way in which the concerns of free market enterprise filtered into the language and consciousness of the 'everyday' folk. Churchill's take on the world of high finance, *Serious Money* was a huge success, packing out the Royal Court with traders and city boys and proving to the startled author and director how much the subjects of the play enjoyed seeing their world represented on stage. The plays operate on very different stylistic plains: Ayckbourn's a slice of naturalism, albeit originally played in the round, Churchill's written in a combination of verse, song and demotic speech, and episodic in structure.

The Revengers' Comedies (1989) mixes the 'honourable' world of the rural, land-owning upper classes with the world of big business. The play begins when two would-be suicides meet on Albert Bridge. Middle-ranking businessman Henry Bell rescues the upper-class Karen Knightly and they share the motives behind their attempts to end their lives. Both give fairly typical accounts: Karen has been thwarted in love, Henry has been made redundant:

Karen: Where did you work?

Henry: Lembridge Tennit. If that means anything.

Karen: Can't say it does. What line are they in?

Henry: Everything, really. From biscuits to bicycles. You'd know the brand names.

Karen: Oh, I see. One of those. Multinationals.

Henry: Multi. Multi. Multi.

Karen: Polluting the rivers, poisoning the atmosphere and secretly funding right-wing revolutionaries.

Henry: Those are the chaps.

Karen: Why did they fire you?

Henry: Oh. All the jargon. Redefining the job profile. Rationalising the department. Restructuring the management team. Which essentially meant either get promoted or – get out. And, innocent that I was, so certain that I'd been doing a good job, I sat there fully expecting to be promoted.

Karen: Being good is never enough in itself.

(Ayckbourn 1991, 12)

Even though Henry seems a thoroughly decent man, he placidly acknowledges the environmental and political devastation wreaked by his employers as if this were an inevitable concomitant of business. As in *Serious Money*, the 'jargon' used to justify his redundanacy was, by this point, increasingly familiar to British audiences who had witnessed these phrases (and others like them) being cited for the closure and/or privatisation of coal mines, steel works, car factories and utilities. Henry's decency is partially signalled by his ability and willingness to see through this jargon to the reality of big business in the 1980s: 'You've also got to be working the system. Chatting up the right people. Buying the drinks that matter' (Ayckbourn 1991, 12). Henry's successor, Bruce Tick, has absorbed these rules, but not – his different patter to clients, colleagues and underlings, suggests – entirely successfully. A running joke during his appearances is his failure to remember people's names. He tries to observe the principle of making a personal connection by continually using the name of his interlocutor and asking after other people in their office/life, but can never get the name right, and so appears more self absorbed and unfeeling than if he avoided names altogether. Combined with Ayckbourn's description of him at his first entrance, Bruce's language conveys everything we need to know about him: he is sexist, self-important and entirely without a sense of irony or self awareness:

> (**Bruce Tick**, *an overweight, mid-thirties, dynamic executive, comes whirling out of his inner sanctum.*)

> Bruce   (*Yelling to no one in particular*)...three billion profit at the last quarter you'd think we could afford someone to answer the bloody phones...(*Answers phone.*) Hallo...Bruce Tick speaking...Tell me all...Hallo, sweetie...Good morning to you...(*Listens*)...uh-huh.... Uh-huh...

> (*As he speaks, he gives **Karen** and **Lydia** the briefest of glances, failing to note who they are at all.*)

> (*To them*) Sorry, beautifuls, won't keep you a moment. (*Into the phone*) Yes, my sweet. Yes...yes...Well, rest assured it will be with you tomorrow morning. At the latest. This is my first day, I have barely unpacked the briefcase and the place is like early-closing day on the *Marie Celeste*...Yes, yes, right. Will do, sweetie. Love to Helga...Hilda, rather...Yes, will do. Bye.

> (*He slams his hand down on the phone and immediately punches up an internal number*)

> Lydia: Mr Tick...?
> Bruce: (*To the phone*) I don't believe this...(*As he punches another number, to* **LYDIA**.) Just one moment, I'll be right with you, my sweet...(*Into phone*) Rachel, I have been trying since nine, I cannot get a reply from Mrs Bulley's office. I think she has finally taken an overdose of formaldehyde and pickled herself. Would you be a sweetie pie and stick your head out of your office and tell that twelve ply plank of an assistant of hers that I want a secretary *now*, not tomorrow. I don't care if its stocking seams are crooked and it looks like the rear end of a turnip, I need someone now. OK? Thank you so much, my sweet. Nothing personal. My love to Derek when you see him...Dennis, rather...Will do.

> (*He puts down the phone*).

(Ayckbourn 1991, 58)

Of course, Lydia is Mrs Bulley's plank of an assistant and Karen his new secretary and in an attempt to cover his embarrassment and establish his rightful supremacy he switches his register from that of an indulgent colleague to the powerful and decisive boss:

Bruce: Well now, Miss... I suppose we'd better start by getting each other's names. I'm Bruce Tick. Call me Bruce. And you're –

Karen: Karen Knightly. Call me Karen...

Bruce: (*A little confused by her pronunciation*) Kieron?

Karen: No, Karen.

Bruce: Oh, *Karen.*

Karen: (*Giggling*) Kieron's a boy's name.

Bruce: (*Laughing*) Yes, of course it is... (*Under his breath*) Jesus. (*Briskly*) Right. Now, Karen. I don't know you. You don't yet know me. We're both new here. This is my first day. This is yours. We're going to have to a certain amount of learning as we go, all right? Thinking on our tootsies, OK?

Karen: Yes, Bruce.

Bruce: Now, there's a few things you ought to know about me straight away. I work hard and I play hard. All right?

Karen: Yes, Bruce.

Bruce: I don't like half-measures, pissing about or pussyfooting around, all right?

Karen: You believe in calling a spade a spade, Bruce?

Bruce: A what?

Karen: A spade.

Bruce: Oh, a spade, yes. I'm hard but fair. All right? You support me, Kieron, you give that hundred and five percent I'm asking for and I promise you, you will have a ball, baby. But you let me down, Kieron and... (*He brings his hand down on her desk*)... OK. You know what I mean? (*He repeats the gesture*)

Karen: Oh yes, I do, Bruce.

(*She repeats the gesture*).

(Ayckbourn 1991, 59–60)

As Allen has pointed out *The Revengers' Comedies* is atypical Ayckbourn in terms of depth of characterisation and structure (Allen 2004, 131–132). Fleeting characters like Bruce are drawn in a series of crude gestures, in this case, through parodying the jargon of business executives. Employing a raft of clichés (work hard, play hard, hard but fair, spade a spade) allows Aykbourn to convey Bruce's character in a nutshell and the phone device allows him to show this empty jargon at work in a variety of situations. The satire on bizspeak continues throughout the play: first when Karen rings Henry to tell him that she has been promoted:

> What do you think of that? I've got a new boss. Up four floors, two grades and a thousand a year. [...] I'm a mobiley upward special secretarial temp. I'm a MUSST, Henry Bell. An absolute MUSST.

(Ayckbourn 1991, 105)

Henry, by contrast, is a straight speaker, as demonstrated in the scene where he explains to Marcus Lipscott why J.W. Lipscott's is making such heavy losses:

> **Marcus:** The firm's in a spot of trouble, is that it?
> **Henry:** I'd say a fairly big spot.
> **Marcus:** Yes?
> **Henry:** Desperately big.
> **Marcus:** Yes. (*He worries.*) I was hoping that the – whatjercallit – general upsurge in trade that's been apparently happening of late – might have carried us with it ... But we seem, as a firm, to have been left a bit high and dry ... Very disappointingly.
> **Henry:** The thing is, you see – it would appear to me that your basic problem – please, this is just one man's opinion –
> **Marcus:** No, carry on. Carry on ...
> **Henry:** Your basic problem is that you're producing something – much more expensively than anyone else is producing it ...
> **Marcus:** Ah well, there are sound reasons for that, of course ...
> **Henry:** And on top of that, you're not really producing enough of them ...
> **Marcus:** (*Recognising the truth in this*) Yes, yes ... That's an excellent point.
> **Henry:** And, if that wasn't enough, nobody seems to want them anyway.
> **Marcus:** I think you've just put your finger on it. This is just the sort of talk I wanted to hear ...
> **Henry:** So, as far as I can see, the only reason you haven't been declared bankrupt is that the Inland Revenue and the Customs and Excise are in nearly as much chaos at present as you are.
> **Marcus:** (*Thumping the furniture*) I said it, you see, I said this – almost these exact same words – at our last board meeting. We need substantial capital investment. We need to modernise the plant, drastically reduce the cost per unit and on top of that –

Henry: – make sure you're producing something that people want.

(Ayckbourn 1991, 187–188)

Language is also the means of comedy, as the developing emotions between Imogen and Henry are shown, not through the kind of eloquent display that might characterise a Stoppardian encounter, but through a much more realistic and bumbling exchange:

Henry: I – I wanted to say – I wanted to tell you ... I really did want to tell you ... to say how ...
Imogen: You don't have to say ...
Henry: No, I wanted to say just ...
Imogen: I know what you wanted to say ...
Henry: You do?
Imogen: And you don't need to say it. Really.
Henry: It's just I ...
Imogen: All I wanted to say, from my side, is that I wanted to say that too.
Henry: You did?
Imogen: Yes, I did.
Henry: That's wonderful.
Imogen: No, it's not wonderful at all. It's terrible.
Henry: Terrible?
Imogen: What are we going to do? It's awful. I never thought this would happen to me. It's appalling.

(Ayckbourn 1991, 76)

The humour in this exchange derives in part from the fact that even though the conversation centres on wanting to 'say' something, the pair manage the whole conversation without actually saying what it is they want to say. The additional fillip for the audience is that when Imogen disagrees with Henry – 'it's not wonderful at all. It's terrible' – there is a split second where it seems possible that they haven't understood each other at all, that in fact they have been speaking at cross purposes. When the conversation continues, it becomes apparent that this isn't the case, but by this point, Imogen's sentiments are as resolutely unromantic as the setting for the discussion (the piggery):

Henry: I don't think falling in love is appalling.
Imogen: I went to bed last night hoping I'd sleep it off. You know, like a cold. Only I didn't. When I woke up this morning it was

even worse. But you see, I don't want to fall in love. Don't you understand? Not with you. Not with anyone. I just want to get on with my life and feed the pigs and – grow old. If you must know, I'm very miserable. And I blame you entirely. It's nothing personal.

(Ayckbourn 1991, 76)

In *Serious Money*, Churchill merged the overlapping dialogue that commentators found so noteworthy in *Top Girls* with rhyming couplets, real accounts of life in the City of London and the jargon that goes with the job. In an interview she explained that the prime motivation for the verse scenes was to move the dialogue away from a purely naturalistic style:

I think it was partly the slightly documentary nature of the material, or what I feared might be the dryness of the material (although actually it isn't dry at all), and thinking it would give it a theatrical edge…More important, it was a way of driving the play incredibly fast which seems very right for it.

(Biographical File, Caryl Churchill, V&A
Theatre & Performance collection)

The play examines the changes that the deregulation and the Big Bang wrought on the City: the change in social class of the traders, dealers and brokers and the concomitant change in business practices and networking. The clash of class and cultures is evident in Frosby's monologue:

The stock exchange was a village street.
You strolled about and met your friends.
Now we never seem to meet.
I don't get asked much at weekends.
Everyone had a special name.
We really had a sense of humour.
And everybody played the game.
You learned a thing or two from rumour.
Since Big Bang the floor is bare,
They deal in offices on screens.
But if the chap's not really there
You can't be certain what he means.

> I've been asked to retire early.
> The firm's not doing awfully well.
> I quite enjoy the hurly burly.
> Sitting alone at home is hell.

I can't forgive Greville. He's gone with that Yankee bank buying its way in, that Yak, Whack, whatsisname, Zac, trying to keep up with his children. His son Jake's one of these so-called marketmakers. Some of us have been making markets for thirty years. And his daughter Scilla works with those barrow boys in LIFFE you'd expect to see on a street corner selling Christmas paper and cheap watches, they earn more than I do, they won't last.

(Churchill 1990, 215)

Betrayed by his own class (Greville) and increasingly redundant in a world that has moved on to 'barrow boys', Frosby reports Jake to the Department of Trade and Industry (DTI) for insider trading (no different to his own learning 'a thing or two from rumour') and sets in motion the downfall of all the other dealers and brokers in the play. One of the most striking things about the differing language of the characters in the play, and between the old guard and the new city boys is that the latter tend to speak plainly and avoid the euphemisms and fudging that characterise Frosby's discourse ('the firm's not doing awfully well'). The new generation are openly aggressive and the opposite of 'gentlemanly'. In the case of Scilla's colleagues in LIFFE, their lower social class is demonstrated not just by their ungentlemanly behaviour, swearing and lewd jokes ('Why's a clitoris like a Filofax? Every cunt's got one'), but by their 'ungrammatical' speech ('Jake's the only public schoolboy what can really deal' (Churchill 1990, 215). Yet they are as fluent in their own brand of financial talk as Greville, Frosby and their other social superiors, who tend to be bankers, corporate raiders or stock brokers.

The registers used by the bankers, raider and arbitrageur are more familiar to British audiences. Corman the corporate raider presents a healthy company as a failing one:

> Albion is obviously deficient
> In management. Old-fashioned and paternal.
> These figures stink. I can make it earn a lot
> more for its shareholders, who are
> The owners after all. It will be far

Better run, streamlined, rationalised,
When it forms part of Corman Enterprise.
(And anyway I want it).

(Churchill 1990, 225)

As surreal as the play seems in these isolated excerpts, it is clear that the very people it set out to satirise recognised the underlying truth of the business practices depicted and the thrills they confer. In an interview about the impact of Thatcherism Howard Brenton recollects that whenever he went to the Royal Court:

> It was full of traders and brokers. The champagne bottles were rolling around in the bar.
> They probably didn't understand it, did they?
> I thought they understood it all too well. They understood that it was a critique. And the sight of them being shits – I think they loved it, loved it! [...] if you want to understand that phenomenon in the Eighties then *Serious Money* is the play to look up – as much as any essay, I'd have thought.

(Wu 2000, 37)

The traders were as impervious to criticism as Thatcher was – as Andrew Marr notes, she interpreted 'Iron Lady' as an unwitting compliment, not because she was oblivious to the implied criticism, but because she was pleased that the Soviets regarded her in this light. What the reaction to *Serious Money* does demonstrate is that the theatre of the Left's anxiety that they could not mount an effective protest at an increasingly capitalist society was not unfounded. In *Theatre in a Cool Climate*, Vera Gottlieb notes the extent to which Thatcherism seemed to silence its detractors:

> There is now a kind of collapse of the language of opposition. Perhaps since Thatcher virtually took over some of the language – words like radical, like revolutionary. Words that we thought belonged on one side suddenly were being used in a different way. [...] Language hijacked by the 'other side', and I think this may have put a number of artists in a difficult position because there seems to be a loss of language, a vacuum, for articulating opposition.

(Gottlieb and Chambers 1999, 21)

Carter's observation on the language of the 1980s bears this out; he uses 'community' as an example of a word which has had its meaning renegotiated:

the word 'community' is changing before our very eyes in the 1980s and 1990s. From a basic sixties and seventies meaning which referred to an organic social group, to the eighties meaning wrested from the left wing by the right wing and established as referring to the approved practices of the state (community service, care in the community), the word now appears to be undergoing a reversal of this meaning, prompted no doubt by the cancellation of local taxes, somewhat inappropriately named the 'community' charge.

(Carter 1997, 6)

In *The Arbor* and *Road*, the communities which Hoggart had once lauded – working class and tight knit – were now bound together only by misfortune and a mistrust of authority; the nostalgic view of working-class life as hard but fair could not have been more effectively refuted than by these two plays.

'Community': *The Arbor* and *Road*

The Arbor caused something of a sensation when it was first performed at the Royal Court: it was written by Andrea Dunbar, an 18 year old who had never been to the theatre, and was a largely autobiographical account of living on a council estate near Bradford, and thus provided the Court with a truly 'authentic' unmediated working-class voice. The main character, Girl, is 15, lives on estate near Bradford called Brafferton Arbor and is called Andrea Dunbar. Her speech, and that of her family and friends, is typical of the restricted code found in dense social networks. Grammar typical of spoken rather than written English was already becoming a common feature of theatrical dialogue, and in this play, when combined with the repetition of the same, or similar phrases, it adds considerably to the evocation of the claustrophobic and monotonous nature of life on the Arbor.

The play begins with the Girl and her boyfriend at a friend's house. Boy walks her home and they discover that her mother has locked her out. After some debate, they go to the Boy's house and he tries to persuade her to have sex:

Boy: Go on. You're rotten.
Girl: No I'm not.
Boy: You are, or you'd let me have it.
Girl: Some lasses I know would jump at owt like that but I'm not just any lass. Anyway I'm not stupid. If I ended up pregnant, I'd get killed.

Boy: Well I won't get you pregnant.
Girl: Well you just might.
Boy: I won't.
Girl: No. I'd better not. You just might.
Boy: If I said I won't then I won't.
They both stay as they were. He lying on his bed, she sitting, for about quarter of an hour – neither of them speaking.
Boy: Are you or aren't you?
Boy: Come on. Hurry up. Are you or aren't you?
Girl: No. I've made up my mind up. I don't like the idea.
Boy: Oh come on! Don't be tight.
Girl: I will.
Boy: Come on.
Girl: No. Go and ask somebody else.
Boy: I don't want nobody else. I want you.
Girl: Well, you'll have to get somebody else 'cause you're not getting owt off me. I've told you.

(Dunbar 1980, 4)

The scene has a lack of urgency to it – even more so if the 15 minutes of silence asked for in the stage direction is observed. The repetitive nature of their exchanges gives it a monotonous feel, almost as if this happens every time they see each other. It is interesting to note that Dunbar uses minimal punctuation, simply breaking up the phrases into speakable units rather than attempting to obey the rules of grammar. The very short sentences almost suggest boredom: neither boy nor girl can be bothered to make a more spirited case for their desire. Her determination makes her sudden capitulation even more surprising. Up until this point she has refused him because she fears becoming pregnant, then when he offers to use a condom, she replies:

not on me you won't.
Boy: Why not?
Girl: Because you won't.
Boy: Go on. If we use one you won't get pregnant then. It's better to be safe than sorry, isn't it?
Girl: I don't care. You're not using one of them on me.
Boy: Go on.
Girl: No
Boy: Well without one then.

Girl: (*Pause*) Okay.
That night the GIRL became pregnant.

(Dunbar 1980, 5)

Girl is not always so quiet, in the scene in which her family find out she is pregnant, she gives as good as she gets. The extract below reveals the family as the stuff of *Daily Mail* dreams: foul-mouthed and dysfunctional with a wife battering alcoholic father providing a role model for his vast family (eight children aged 6–18):

Father: Who is the dirty bastard?
Girl: I'm not telling you who it is.
Sister: I bet it's a dirty fuckin' old man.
Mother: Will you shut your fucking mouth.
Sister: You must be proud of her, the dirty slag, she's nowt else.
Girl: You've no room to fuckin' talk, you go with anybody.
Sister: All we fuckin' want to know is who the father of it is.
Mother: Surely you must know that I'm only concerned about you. You are my daughter you know.
Father: She's no fuckin' daughter of mine.
Sister: She's nowt else but a slag if you ask me.
Girl: Oh go fuck off will you.
Mother: I can't fuckin' undertand you two, you're both as fuckin' bad, yet you'll sit there and pull each other down.

(Dunbar 1980, 6)

Mother's extraordinary change of register 'surely you must know' confirms that even council estate dwellers have recourse to more than one register. Her appeal to Girl suggests either that she has deliberately chosen such a dramatic shift to indicate her sincerity, or she is 'double-voicing' – appropriating another register as a joke.

The play's critical reception was mixed, but praise for Dunbar's rendering of likelike-ese was expressed in almost every review. *Time Out* noted that 'the author's is an authentic working-class voice, but she also captures the speech of the other classes with a deft, sometimes satirical brilliance' (Production file for *The Arbor*). This satirical brilliance is at the forefront of Dubar's depiction of the kindly teacher at the school for unmarried mothers, and of the headmaster of her own school when he explains why she must move:

Headmaster: It's necessary you see. I'm afraid we can't keep you here for reasons I have no doubt you will understand. For instance you may well suffer at the hands of some of your more ignorant among your schoolmates. They might call you names and generally make life difficult and unpleasant for you. So it is thought better, in cases like yours that you leave. But at the same time it is important that you don't get too far behind with your school work...

Girl: Yes I know.

Headmaster: ...and so you are temporarily transferred to a special school. Have arrangements been made, do you know, for you to go into the mother and baby home?

(Dunbar 1980, 9)

Conscious of the unpleasantness of his task, the Headmaster employs a range of politeness strategies to try and ease the rejection. Given Girl's home-life, his worrying about her being called names and having her life made unpleasant at school is supremely ironic. It is also consistent with the mockery of 'do-gooder' teachers/social workers/nurses and GPs promoted by the Conservative party and the media during the 1980s.

If *The Arbor* ends with a chink of hope, *Road* offers no such comfort. The play was produced after the Conservative government secured another term in office and charts life on a typical 'road in a small Lancashire town' where most of the inhabitants are unemployed or struggling to support families on one wage. Like *Epsom Downs, Road* tries to give voice to a whole community, and a range of linguistic registers. It also demonstrates the linguistic creativity of a section of society usually portrayed as prosaic, and in complete contrast to *The Arbor*, shows people giving vent to their feelings and playing with language in an attempt to either relieve the gloom or to help them understand it. Scullery, a middle aged man, acts as a guide to life in 'the road', showing the audience scenes in various 'houses'. Significantly, he seems to have no home of his own, or at least we never visit it or see it. The play was conceived and originally played as a promenade performance in which the audience followed Scullery round different 'houses'; in the theatre, and this interactive element is mirrored in Scullery's welcome:

Scullery: Wid' your night yous chose to come and see us. Wid' our night as usual we's all gettin' ready and turning out for a drink. THIS IS OUR ROAD! But tonight it's your road an' all! Don't feel awkward wi' us, make yourselves at home. You'll meet 'all-sorts' down here, I'm telling you love. An 'owt can happen tonight. He might get a bird. She might ha' a fight, she might. Let's shove off down t'Road

and find out! We'll go down house by house. Hold tight! Here we go!
Come on.

(Cartwright 1989, 3)

His speech, along with the broken road sign – 'the name has been
ripped off, leaving a sharp, twisted, jagged edge, only the word "Road"
is visible' – gives the audience a clear indication of what to expect. His
non-standard grammar, 'yous' 'wes' and general informality is mixed
with a touch of old-fashioned showmanship in the form of direct
address to the audience – 'hold tight! Here we go!' – evoking the spirit of
working men's clubs and fairground rides. However, the friendliness and
warmth Scullery's welcome engenders is not typical of life in *Road*, as
the early scene demonstrates. Louise and her brother continually insult
each other 'fuck facey, fuck facey. Fuck facey fuck facey. Fuck off. Fuck
off' (Cartwright 1989, 5). Brenda and her daughter Carol are no better,
bickering over money:

Carol: No, you mouldy old slag.
Brenda: Yes, you young pig.
Carol: Cow!
Brenda: Sick!
Carol: Oh God, you're crude. How could I have let you bring me up.
Fling me up more like. I was flung through the years.

(Cartwright 1989, 7)

Carol's shift into a more lyrical register is consistent with many of the
other characters in *Road*. They move easily between lifelike-ese and a
mildly poetic register, much as people do in conversation with close
friends and family.[4] This is particularly apparent in the last scene in
which Carol and Louise go home with Eddie and Brink and endure the
awkwardness of a typical pick-up. Then, after listening to Eddie's only
record, 'Try a Little Tenderness', they all become liberated by the music
and perform their own riffs:

Eddie: Bzzzzzzzzzzzzzzzzzzzzzz. Raaaaaaaaaaaaaaa. Blast off! Waytt
Earp, Wild Bill Hicock, Jesse James, Buffalo Bill, Billy the Kid,
Maverick, Jim Bowie, Geronimo, Butch Cassidy, Davy Crockett, Doc
Holliday. Eddie, Eddie, Eddie the here. This is it, you let owt out,
show what's below, let go, throw, glow, burn your Giro. I got me
suit, I got me image, suit, image, (*He sings*) 'Who could ask for
anything more?' Me! England's in pieces. England's an old twat in

the sea. England's cruel. My town's scuffed out. My people's pale. Pale face. (*He pulls a pretend gun*) Bang bang bang. It's a shoot out with the sheriff. EDDIE, EDDIE, EDDIE, the hero. Don't weaken, or you're Dole and Done, Dole and Done, never weaken, show yourself sharp, so sharp you cut. Head up. Eyes hard. Walk like Robert Mitcchum. (*He draws and shoots*) Bang, bang, bang, bang, bang, bang, bang. I'm going to lie out now and burn for all I'm worth. (*He stops, lies down*).

Silence. The girls' faces are wide open, stunned and drunk.

Brink: That's what you do, you drink, you listen to Otis, you get to the bottom of things and let rip.

Louise (*in wonder*): What for?

Brink: To stop going mad.

(Cartwright 1989, 53)

Eddie's outbreak borrows from the techniques of poetry and pop lyrics, starting with basic patterning, then moving on to interpret the rhetorical question 'who could ask for anything more?' (from 'I got rhythm') literally, and in doing so exposing the lie promoted in the song that poverty is fine as long as there is music. With one record between them, even the music is rationed, and all four know that the release it brings them is only temporary. Inspired by Eddie and Brink, Carol follows their example:

Carol: Can I say anything? Can I? I'll say this then, BIG BUST. BIG BUST ON ME BODY. BIG BRA BURSTING BUST. MEN LOOK. How's that? CRACK CRACK CRACK the whip on'em. Crackoh crack, cut men for their sins. POVERTY. Poverty wants me. He's in my hair and clothes. He comes dust on me knickers. I can't scrape him off. Everythin's soiled you know, our house, me mum, the bath. I'm sick. Now't nice around men. Nowt's nice. NOWT'S NICE. Where's finery? Fucked off! Where's soft? Gone hard! I want to walk on the mild side. I want to be clean. Cleaned. Spray me wi' somethin' sweet, spray me away. (*Stated*) Carol has nowt.

(Cartwright 1989, 54)

The juxtaposition of frenzied rhyming with the stated 'Carol has nowt' brings us up short. These are not the orgiastic ramblings of young people high on the music, they are people pushed to the edge of sanity by deprivation and hopelessness. Louise's contribution ends on a different note: 'anyway I never spoken such speech in my life and I'm glad I have. If I keep shouting somehow a somehow I might escape' (Cartwright 1989, 54). Then they begin an incantation which continues to the end of the play 'somehow a somehow, might escape' (Cartwright 1989, 55). But it seems very unlikely they ever will.

The play was well received by critics. *City Limits* commented, 'What prevents this play from becoming just another trite northern soap is the sharp poetic dialogue which rends [*sic*] the simplest of situations a sharp edge of disillusion', while the *Sunday Telegraph* praised:

> The skill with which Mr Cartwright depicts the stunted, impoverished lives, full of regrets for the past and dreams for the future, of the inhabitants of one small road in one small Lancashire town; and secondly – and even more remarkably – in his creation for these people of a poetic demotic, the North Country equivalent of that created by Synge for his peasants.
>
> (*London Theatre Record* 1986, Vol. 5, 313)

Praise for capturing the 'authenticity' of everyday talk was now more common than complaints about not being able to understand what was being said. Theatre and theatre criticism had come a long way in the last two decades.

The language of learning: *Educating Rita*

If there is a question mark over Carol, Eddie, Brink and Louise's escape from their situation in *Road*, the question in *Educating Rita* is whether or not escaping one's surroundings can bring happiness. The play is the story of Liverpool hairdresser, Rita (her real name is Susan but she has renamed herself after the writer of her favourite novel), and her path to intellectual betterment via the Open University and her drunken tutor, Frank. In the course of the play her linguistic repertoire broadens along with her cultural one, but, in a new twist on the Pygmalion theme, crucially, she is able to retain her bidialectalism and the qualities associated with it, in the same way as she is able to retain her skills as a hairdresser. After she has transformed herself, outgrowing Frank on the way, she returns to thank him, and give him a haircut – the only thing she feels she can offer him. These qualities are bluntness, straightforwardness and 'honesty' in her critical judgements and language as 'Rita', while as the educated 'Susan' she is more articulate but less 'honest' in her speech and opinions. The conflict at the heart of the play is not simply about whether a working-class hairdresser can get an education, but

192 The Changing Language of Modern English Drama 1945–2005

whether they can get an education, retain their 'authentic' sensibilities and pass between the two worlds. Rita's appraisal of working-class life is reminiscent, in parts, of Hoggart's. She is critical of both liberal middle class impressions of working class, and the working classes' own attitude to its ways of life and traditions. In an early tutorial, she tells Frank that she's read about the 'working-class culture thing' but never seen it, that 'everyone pissed, or on the Valium, tryin' to get from one day to the next' is not culture, that they have become spoiled by increased affluence:

> Rita: [...] there's no meanin'. They tell y' stories about the past, y'know, the war, or when they were fightin' for food an' clothin' an' houses. Their eyes light up as they tell y', because there was some meanin' to it. But the thing is now, I mean now that most of them have got some sort of house an' there's food an' money around, they know they're better off but, honest, they know they've got nothin' as well.
>
> (Russell 1986, 194)

She returns to this theme in a later tutorial in order to try and explain to Frank why she lost her nerve arriving for his dinner party and bolted back to her family:

> Rita: I'm all right with you, here in this room; but when I saw those people you were with I couldn't come in. I would have seized up. Because I'm a freak. I can't talk to the people I live with any more. An' I can't talk to the likes of them on Saturday, or them out there [the students], because I can't learn the language. I'm a half-caste. I went back to the pub where Denny was, an' me mother, an' our Sandra, an' her mates. I'd decided I wasn't comin' here again.
>
> Frank *turns to face her.*
>
> Rita: I went into the pub an' they were all singin', all of them singin' some song they'd learnt from the juke-box. An' I stopped in that pub an' thought, just what the frig am I trying to do? Why don't I just pack it in an' stay with them, an' join in the singin?
>
> Frank: And why don't you?
>
> Rita (*angrily*): You think I can, don't you? Just because you pass a pub doorway an' hear the singin' you think we're all O.K, that we're survivin', with the spirit intact. Well I did join in with the singin', I didn't ask any questions, I just went along with it. But when I looked round me mother had stopped singin', an' she was cryin',

but no one could get it out of her why she was cryin'. Everyone just
said that she was pissed an' we should take her home. So we did,
an' on the way I asked her why. I said, 'Why are y' cryin, Mother?'
She said, 'Because – because we could sing better songs than those'.
Ten minutes later, Denny has her laughing and singing again, pre-
tending she hadn't said it. But she had. And that's why I came back.
And that's why I'm staying.

(Russell 1986, 208)

Naturally enough, the comedy in the play is derived from the cultural
clashes between student and tutor. The opening scene of the play shows
Frank is his office on the phone to his girlfriend explaining that he
won't be home for dinner because 'I've got this Open University student
coming' and that:

I probably shall go the pub afterwards, I shall need to go to the
pub afterwards, I shall need to wash away the memory of some silly
woman's attempts to get into the mind of Henry James or whoever it
is we're supposed to study on this course. [...] Look if you're trying to
induce some feeling of guilt in me over the prospect of a burnt dinner
you should have prepared something other than lamb and ratatouille... Because, darling, I like my lamb done to the point of abuse
and even I know that ratatouille cannot be burned... Darling, you
could incinerate ratatouille and still it wouldn't burn... What do you
mean am I determined to go to the pub? I don't need determination
to get me into a pub.

(Russell 1986, 169–170)

His speech on the phone is full of indications of his status as a speaker of
standard English. His speech is closer to written English than spoken. He
uses lots of modals *shall* go the pub, *shall* need to go the pub and peppers
his conversation with rhetorical flourishes in repeating words, '*shall go*',
'*shall* need to *go*', and 'determined to go to the pub?' 'Don't need determination to go the pub' all in order to communicate his dread of the
impending tutorial. His speech is also characterised by lots of Latinate
vocabulary (induce, incinerate, prospect, ratatouille) and word ordering
more often associated with written language rather than spoken: 'you
should have prepared something *other than* ratatouille.' On a more prosaic level, the very fact that he eats ratatouille marks him out as middle
class. His conversation is finally interrupted by a series of knocks at the

door, yet no one appears, despite him repeatedly shouting coming in. Eventually:

> *The door swings open revealing* **Rita**.
> **Rita** (*from the doorway*): I'm comin' in, aren't I? It's that stupid bleedin' handle on the door. You wanna get it fixed!
> (*She comes into the room*).
> **Frank**: (*staring, slightly confused*): Erm – yes, I suppose I always mean to…
> **Rita** (*going to the chaor by the desk and dumping her bag*): Well that's no good always meanin' to, is it? Y'should get on with it; one of these days you'll be shoutin' 'Come in' an' it'll go on forever because the poor sod on the other side won't be able to get in. An you won't be able to get out.
> **Frank** *stares at* RITA *who stands by the desk*.
> **Frank**: You are?
> **Rita**: What am I?
> **Frank**: Pardon?
> **Rita**: What?
> **Frank** (*looking for the admission papers*): Now you are?
> **Rita**: I'm a what?

(Russell 1986, 170)

The contrast between his verbosity and indirect way of saying he won't come home for dinner, and Rita's direct style sets the tone of the play. The final exchange between them here 'you are?' 'what am I?' lends itself to two separate interpretations. Either Rita is challenging Frank's use by taking his question seriously and ignoring the maxim of relevance, or she simply does not understand the overtly formal tone he uses and its meaning in that particular context. Either one successfully establishes the gulf between them. As does the 'What'/'pardon' distinction.

When the play first opened, many critics made the association with *Pygmalion* and *Roots*, yet very little comment was passed about Rita's broad Liverpool accent. Instead, the critics who mention the play's regionalism, criticise Russell's 'blowzy Liverpudlian line' (Coveney in the *Financial Times*) and 'Liverpool Corn' (Billington in the *Guardian*). Only Eric Shorter, writing in the *Daily Telegraph*, falls into the trap of conflating Scouse with illiteracy, describing Rita as 'an eager but illiterate of the northern working classes'. Rita is anything but illiterate, devouring Harold Robbins and other 'pulp' fiction before she begins the course. It may seem a small, and pedantic, point to make, but Shorter's description does serve as a reminder of the swiftness with which non-standard speech is associated with illiteracy. In *The Fight for English: How the Language Pundits Ate, Shot and Left* (2006), David Crystal's account of grammar teaching in the 20th century provides an insight into why Shorter and other critics of a certain age make this mistake. They are passing judgement on a generation 'who were educated in that barren period – a 40-year wilderness which lasted roughly from 1960–2000. Most of them had little or no training in the formal properties of language' (Crystal 2006, 155). Rita is a product of this 'lost generation' (as am I). The scene in which Rita tries to talk 'properly' demonstrates another cherished strand of the language myth, that:

> RITA (*talking in a peculiar voice*): Hello, Frank.
> FRANK (*without looking up*): hello Rita, you're late.
> RITA: I know, Frank, I'm terribly sorry. It was unavoidable.
> FRANK: Was it really? What's wrong with your voice?
> RITA: Nothing is wrong with it, Frank. I have merely decided to talk properly. As Trish says there is not a lot of point discussing beautiful literature in an ugly voice.
>
> (Russell 1986, 217)

Rita, or more properly Trish's assertion, has, in the context of this play, and Frank's progressive attitudes, morphed into a comic attitude, outmoded and stuffy. Yet, in real life, this is precisely the opinion that prominent language minders were to breathe new life into during the debates about the new National Curriculum (discussed in the next chapter).

7
1990–2000: Talk Is Cheap

By calling this chapter 'Talk Is Cheap' I am foregrounding a number of things: the way in which the revolution in telecoms and information technology opened up the world and the global economy during the 1990s; the way in which 'therapy' culture took off and encouraged people to 'get in touch with' and 'talk about' their feelings; and the way in which the ordinary business of talking was re-packaged as 'communication' and a set of related skills. The World Wide Web went from being a way scientists across the globe could communicate and share data by computer, to a global system, in the space of a few years. Mobile phones went from being the privileged communication tool of the few to the default device of the many in a similar time space. Companies saved on wages and office space by opening up 'call centres' to deal with customers and the centres were increasingly based outside the UK (often in India); transactions that had only a decade before been carried out locally (buying insurance, paying bills, dealing with the bank) were now done at arms length.[1] Richard Hoggart's vision of a community where everyone knew each other and helped each other out was replaced by the idea of a global community in which people formed relationships with each other without ever having to meet.

Moreover, the changes in industry and technology that led to the demand for global networking made communication a commodifiable skill, as Deborah Cameron has observed in *Good to Talk? Living and Working in a Communication Culture*. She defines a communication culture as one that:

> is particularly self-conscious and reflexive about communication, and that generates large quantities of metadiscourse about it. For the

members of such a culture it is axiomatically 'good to talk' – but at the same time it is natural to make judgements about which kinds of talk are good and which are less good. People aspire, or think they ought to aspire, to communicate 'better'; and they are highly receptive to expert advice.

(Cameron 2002, vii)

Interestingly in this context, 'expert' seldom means 'linguist' (as the Great Grammar debate demonstrated), rather psychologists, psychotherapists, business consultants, journalists and even illusionists (e.g., Paul McKenna and his neurolinguistic programming courses) are the primary generators and arbiters of this discourse.[2] This expert advice ranges from everything from how to get a better job or relationship through to teaching 'communication skills' in school, colleges and universities. Communication also became the buzz-word of the new Labour government: where previous Prime Ministers had Press Secretaries, Tony Blair had a Director of Communications and Strategy.

The fetishisation of communication on stage has kept pace with these socio-cultural and technological developments. Mark Ravenhill's *Shopping and Fucking* (1997) depicts a generation who are not only telly-literate, but therapy literate too, and when they need to make a quick buck, his characters set themselves up as phone-sex operatives to pay off their debt: a literal example of commodifying their communication skills. Ravenhill's *Some Explicit Polaroid's* (1999) employs overlapping dialogue and adds to it the continual babble of ansaphones, techno-music and Internet exchanges all competing for the characters' attentions. The extent to which the technology aids communication is a moot point, particularly in the case of Nadia's ansaphone which either plays messages from friends she never manages to speak to – '*Hi. Me returning our call returning my call returning your call returning my call./Et cetera. And so on. Ad infinitum. So. Call me.*' – or relays threatening messages from an ex-boyfriend (Ravenhill 2001b, 248). Patrick Marber's *Closer* (1997) goes further, not only incorporating email sex but, in the first production at the National Theatre, actually displaying the emails on a screen suspended above the actors (Marber 2000). He exploits what was then a relatively new mode of communication to full dramatic effect (a new twist on the ventriloquising motif used in *Cyrano de Bergerac*, *Much Ado About Nothing* and many other plays). Dan (maliciously) pretends to be Anna, arranges a date with Larry after

their virtual sex session and sends him a 'virtual' rose as a token of
his love:

(Marber 2000, 25)

Unaware that they have been set up, Anna 'bumps' into Larry at the
Aquarium, and Dan's scheme is exposed:

> **Larry.** *Why*? Why would he pretend to be you?
> **Anna.** He likes me.
> **Larry.** Funny way of showing it, can't he send you flowers? (*Larry
> produces a crumpled rose from his coat pocket. He hands it to Anna*) Here.
> **Anna.** …Thanks… (*Anna looks at the rose, then at Larry.*) Wonderful
> thing, the Internet.

(Marber 2000, 28)

The screens in the theatre allow the audience to see the words as they
appear on the page of the play-text, adding a new dimension to non-
standard language usage as the e-mails are written in the shorthand now
more commonly referred to as 'txt' language, for example 'RU4 real?'
(Marber 2000, 24).

The historical context: 'Cool Britannia'?

The history of Britain in the 1990s is often presented as beginning in
1997, the year that Labour finally returned to power after a 27-year hia-
tus. The year 1997 is also the year that Diana, Princess of Wales, died
in a car-crash, provoking a hugely public, and entirely uncharacteris-
tic, display of grief from the British public, and that *Vanity Fair* put Liam
Gallagher and Patsy Kensit in bed under a Union Jack duvet on the front
cover with the strapline: 'London Swings! Again!' The issue featured
the Young British Artists, designer Alexander McQueen and members
of Blur (Oasis's biggest rivals at the time). This period saw the rise of
'Cool Britannia', a reinvention of the swinging sixties in which Britain

once again had a thriving arts scene and a young and (relatively) sexy Prime Minister. The seductive nature of this message makes it easy to forget that up until 1997, the 1990s was a fairly bleak decade. The economy was slow to recover from the previous decade's recession for all the government's talk of the 'green shoots of recovery' and it is the period in which Britain wholly gave itself over to market-values.[3] The Conservative government's project of dismantling the Welfare State and privatising utility companies, which had begun under Thatcher, was continued by John Major when he succeeded her as Prime Minister in 1990. Local government and agencies were systematically disempowered: central government had taken control of the school curriculum in 1988 and introduced league tables and performance targets in the 1990s; healthcare provision was divided into trusts run along business models with the associated performance management system, and even the police force found themselves being measured. All this had linguistic implications too. As Carter notes:

> in a society whose discourses are impregnated with the semantics of monetarist economics, [...] even the language of the curriculum reflects the language of the dominant culture. For example, the accountancy metaphors we now live by reveal the underlying ideology that learning has to be more measurable, that teachers, lecturers, schools and universities should compete in a market to produce an annual output, that the output satisfies (possibly at a given percentile level) externally controlled tests and that league tables of performance indicators can then be drawn up, rather in the manner of an annual balance sheet, with clear accounts of profit and loss.
>
> (Carter 1997, 6)

The privatisation of the railways began and Major introduced a 'Citizens Charter' aimed at making local services accountable to its 'customers' – a newly ubiquitous word in the public sector which applied to people formerly known as passengers, tenants and patients. All these shifts provided rich fodder for the playwrights discussed in this chapter, not least because it seemed as if they, like the Labour party, would be condemned to permanent opposition. The 1992 election, which Labour, and the country, seemed to think was a foregone conclusion, turned out be the occasion on which the Conservatives won more votes than any other party in history and the biggest percentage lead since 1945: it seemed improbable that Labour would ever lead the country again.[4] So when

Tony Blair led Labour to victory in 1997, it really was the beginning of a new era: hence the potency of the 'Cool Britannia' narrative.

This narrative necessarily positions Britain as global force in politics and culture, but the global history of the decade was determined by incidents which had their origins in the previous decades and would reverberate for decades to come. The fall of the Berlin Wall in 1989 transformed the landscape of Europe literally and metaphorically as Soviet-supported Eastern European states grasped the opportunities of the west. The Yugoslavian wars, Kosovo, the reconfiguration of Czechoslovakia and the break-up of the Soviet Union and European Communism affected the whole world, and produced an extraordinary range of dramatic and cultural responses and new euphemisms ('ethic cleansing'; 'detention centre'; 'human shield'). Iraq's invasion of Kuwait in 1991 led to the first Gulf War and prompted what Michael Billington has described as 'an obsession with the Iraqi dictator [Saddam Hussein] that was to have lasting repercussions for both American and British politics' (Billington 2007, 324). At the end of the century, Britain began its own partial break-up with the devolution of areas of policy and legislation to Scotland and Wales in 1999, and plans to extend this to Northern Ireland. In the space of a decade the landscape had shifted enormously.

The linguistic context

If theatrical language minding has become a thing of the past, language minding – in particular anxiety about non-standard language – in other aspects of public life was still alive and well. Nineties' language minding continued to focus on the 'Great Grammar Crusade' – the debates about if, and how, English language including grammar should be taught in schools. As in the previous chapter, Carter's *Investigating English Discourse* (1997) continues to be a key reference point (alongside Cameron's *Verbal Hygiene*). Carter was Director of the Language in the National Curriculum (LINC) between 1982 and 1992, and oversaw the production of a pack of training materials designed for teachers to increase their own knowledge, and awareness, of investigating the way in which English language was used. In broad terms the positions can be summarised as follows. The government wished to reintroduce the formal teaching of grammar in schools believing that it would encourage students to speak better, write better and understand the importance of 'standards' (and all the concomitant associations of 'standard' and 'correctness' discussed earlier in the book). Teachers of English were concerned that a return to formal grammar teaching would stifle individual creativity of expression and perhaps discourage people from the study and enjoyment of English. Linguists were in favour of a much wider programme of study – Knowledge About Language (KAL) – which would treat written and spoken language equally but differently and would encourage students to analyse language in use and to learn grammar discursively rather than through the study of decontextualised examples. The result of these differences of opinion was that the government refused to publish the teacher training LINC pack designed to teach KAL, and refused permission for the pack to be published commercially.[5]

As the government strove to return to a 1940s style of grammar teaching (and perhaps wished for a 1940s electorate to govern who were largely uncritical of the idea of 'proper English', 'proper behaviour' and 'proper manners'), Britain in the 1990s became increasingly cosmopolitan and multi-cultural. The Queen's English was rarely heard on the street, on the stage or on the screen, and the Queen herself was moving further away from the 1940s RP she had spoken all her life. There were even suggestions that her accent was moving towards the new 'estuary' accent which 'suddenly' appeared in the 1990s, although in reality of course, nothing happens all of a sudden in language development, as Crystal observes:

> Estuary had been around for years before its name arrived. By the 1970s, accents showing a mixture of RP and Cockney were becoming noticeable. They were motivated by an upmarket movement of originally Cockney speakers and a downmarket trend towards 'ordinary' (as opposed to 'posh') speech by the middle class. By the 1990s, attitudes towards the new accent had begun to change. People started calling it 'warm', 'customer-friendly', and 'down to earth'. Then an amazing thing happened. RP began to attract some negative evaluations. People started calling it 'posh' and 'distant'. It was a remarkable turnaround.
>
> (Crystal 2006, 183–184)

FCUK rules ok?

In spite of the insouciance with which Kenneth Tynan had dismissed the power of 'fuck' power to shock in the 1960s, three decades later, the 'f-word' still retained its provocative power.[6] The case of *Shopping and Fucking* is an interesting example of the way in which in-yer-face theatre challenged the limits of what society deemed acceptable, not only, or even primarily, in terms of subject matter. The play was notorious from the minute the production company, Out of Joint, were advised that they would be breaching the 1889 Indecent Advertisements Act if they advertised the play with its full title because 'fuck' is banned from public display. As a result, the production company and the Royal Court (who were presenting the play) had to go through a remarkable and farcical subterfuge: on posters, programmes, the printed play-text, listings and outside the theatre, the play was advertised as *Shopping and F∗∗∗ing*.[7] The box-office staff referred to the show as 'Shopping and Effing' – the full title was only revealed after customers had bought their ticket – and the Court's new e-mail system rejected all messages that used 'fucking'. David Blunkett, then education secretary, condemned the play for its foul language and called it a waste of money (without ever seeing it). The British public, it seemed, were still not ready for 'fucking' to make its public debut.

The theatrical context

In the same way that 'Cool Britannia' has tended to dominate the history of the 1990s in general, so 'Cruel Britannia' and 'in-yer-face' have dominated the story of theatre in the 1990s. This is largely to do with the alacrity with which the press and the theatre industry seized on the idea of a new phenomenon to market. For most of the 1990s money was tight, theatres and companies folded in the wake of cuts to subsidy and drama was perceived to be in crisis, permanently wounded by the success of the blockbuster musical. There were very few new playwrights coming through (companies and theatres couldn't afford to risk untested talent), and the plays produced by the established playwrights tended not to break new ground in terms of form or subject matter. Hare produced his 'state of the nation trilogy' (*Racing Demon, Murmuring Judges* and *The Absence of War*) at the National and Edgar produced a series of plays about the state of the world (*The Shape of the Table* and *Pentecost*), but for the most part, as John Bull suggests, there was a shift away from wider social themes and panoramas of post-1968 theatre back to the naturalistic 'room' of the New Wave play: a move dictated by falling budgets as well as a dominant aesthetic (Bull 1994). And 'in-yer-face' theatre returned to the room with a vengeance: exploring the lives of groups of friends with no money to go out, no jobs and few prospects. Aleks Sierz, who coined the phrase 'in-yer-face' theatre, articulates another way in which these new plays seemed to break with tradition (while of course continuing to use the discourse developed for describing new writing in the Fifties):

> What strikes the reader about nineties writing is its vitality and imme-diacy; both of which recall and mimic real speech, but without being documentary or realistic. Compared to previous new waves, the dia-logue is faster, the exchanges sharper, the expressions of emotion more direct and extreme, and the language more highly coloured. Plays have rarely been so thrillingly alive. By contrast, much political theatre and the issue plays of the 70s and 80s are – with a few excep-tions – wordy, worthy and woolly. In them, people speak as if they were broadcasting; their language is middle-classless and bookish; their speeches large and baggy and rhetorical.
>
> (Sierz 2001, 244)

Even the non-standard spelling of 'yer' reflects the extent to which its characters have embraced lifelike-ese. As befits the 'movement' which heralded the third renaissance of British theatre, the provocative and sexually explicit content of in-yer-face plays constituted an attack on the well-made play of the previous decades in which sex, violence and bad language were supposedly hidden behind the net curtains of subur-bia. As usual, the reports of the storming of the West End citadel were somewhat exaggerated; the veiled improprieties of Ayckbourn and Ben-nett were not so much exchanged for a frankness in which profanities are accepted as inevitable, rather they coexisted alongside them in the same way that Coward and Rattigan continued to coexist alongside the New Wave and Stoppard and Friel coexisted alongside the political play-wrights of the 1970s. The interesting thing about 'in-yer-face' in relation to theatrical language minding is that it has acted as a kind of rerun of the 1960s in that once again, spectacle is foregrounded over language. In *Blasted* (1995), for example, the swearing contributed to its celebrated epithet (courtesy of *Daily Mail* critic Jack Tinker) as 'a disgusting feast of filth' but it was the physical actions on stage: rape, fellatio and baby-eating which caused the furore (*Theatre Record* 1995, Vol. 14.1). In the case of *Blasted*, the linguistic stereotype merely reinforces the dramatic one: men who eat babies are bound to swear like troopers, use racist and sexist language, have a regional accent (Kane's stage direction describ-ing Ian notes that he is '*45, Welsh born but lived in Leeds much of his life and has picked up the accent*' (Kane 2001, 3)). But after *Blasted*, theatrical language minding effectively ceased.

An aside: Politeness theory and in-yer-face theatre

The 'in-yer-face' strand of 1990s British theatre repays examination via the methodologies of politeness theory: the very title of the movement invokes notions of face theory, and titles like *Shopping and Fucking*, *Fucking Games*, *Sleeping Around* and *Penetrator* all indicate the extent to which these plays were presented, and received, as a challenge to both the positive and negative face of the audience, their sensibilities and their idea of a 'good night out'. Martin McDonagh, born in south London to Irish parents, provided the in-yer-face version of Irish ruralism in a series of plays now known as 'The Leenane trilogy': *The Beauty Queen of Leenane* (1996), *A Skull in Connemara* (1997) and *The Lonesome West* (1997).

In *The Lonesome West* excessive politeness becomes a sadistic competition: the illocutionary acts of forgiving and apologising are given the perlocutionary force of insults. The play revolves around two brothers, Coleman and Valene, whose father has just died. Their relationship, always volatile, declines alarmingly without him there to keep the peace (the task now falls to the nice but ineffectual priest Father Welsh). Their unrepentant and seemingly inexhaustible ways of insulting each other finally lead Welsh to commit suicide, and in his suicide note he pleads with Coleman and Valene to love each other again. The scene analysed below follows their return from Welsh's funeral, and at first, their attempts to fulfil his dying wish seem genuine, however, after an initial mistake reminds them of the tortures they inflicted on each other as children, their cooperative mood begins to evaporate. Coleman's first apology seems sincere but Valene's is close to being an outright insult:

(1)VALENE: I do apologise for dropping stones on you so.
(2)(*Pause.*) For your brain never did recover from them injuries, did it, Coleman?
(3)COLEMAN: *stares at Valene a second, then smiles.* VALENE *smiles also.*
(4)VALENE: This is a great oul game, this is, apologising.
(5)Father Welsh wasn't too far wrong.

(McDonagh 1997, 53)

In (1) Valene performs the illocutionary act of apologising, but by indirectly insulting Coleman in (2) (you are still brain damaged, and therefore stupid), he reduces the air of goodwill and thus detracts from the effectiveness of his apology. Moreover, the deliberate way in which he performs the insult is emphasised by the pause. In terms of signification, the pause could either indicate that he wants Coleman to believe that (1) is the end of his turn, so that Coleman accepts the apology as a genuine one, before having it snatched back again; or merely that he is pausing for effect, so that (2) cannot be construed as having slipped out accidentally. Coleman's stare (3) indicates awareness that his patience and temper are being tested while the smile indicates that he has decided to overlook the implied insult. Valene's smile could be one of triumph at having insulted his brother without repercussion, or an indication of his relief at having got away with it. By not rising to the bait immediately, Coleman adds a further dimension to the apologising game; now the participants must not only indirectly insult each other, or outdo each other through their confessions and apologies, they must also magnanimously forgive each transgression. As a result, their confessions must become progressively more outrageous in order to goad the other into cracking first. 'Stepping back' becomes as great a virtue as apologising, as demonstrated when Coleman exacts revenge for Valene's insult:

> (1)**Coleman**: Who'd go marrying you, sure? Even that no-lipped girl in Norway'd turn you down.
> (2)**Valene** (*pause. Angrily.*): See, I'm stepping back now...I'm stepping back, like Father Walsh [*sic*] said and I'm forgiving ya, insulting me.
> (3)**Coleman** (*sincerely*): Oh...oh, I'm sorry now Valene. I'm sorry now. It just slipped out on me without thinking.
> (4)**Valene**: No harm done so, if only an accident it was.
> (5)**Coleman**: It *was* an accident.
> (6)Although remember how you did insult me there earlier, saying I was brain-damaged as a gasur,
> (8)and I didn't even pull you up on it.
> (9)**Valene**: I apologise for saying you was brain-damaged as a gasur so.
> (10)**Coleman**: No apology was necessary, Valene,
> (11)and I have saved you the last vol-au-venteen on top of it.

> (McDonagh 1997, 55)

Coleman's insult (1) is a direct threat to Valene's positive face with no redressive action, and as such Valene feels that he is entitled to draw attention to his own generosity of spirit (2), and ability to respect a dead man's wish (3). The sincerity of Coleman's tone when he apologises, plus his redressive action in claiming that it was an accident (4) means Valene must forgive him if he is playing the game. He makes his forgiveness conditional (5) (presumably to warn Coleman he knows which way the game is heading) thus obliging Coleman to verify his sincerity (6). Coleman uses this opportunity to prove himself the bigger man by reminding Valene that he himself unconditionally forgave his brother earlier on (7), by waiving his right to a second apology (10), and then by making a further conciliatory gesture (11). The game escalates until Coleman confesses to, and apologises for, the most heinous crime, although his words and gestures suggest anything but contrition:

> (1)COLEMAN: And do you want to know something else, Valene?
> (2)I'm sorry for cutting off them dog's ears.
> (3)With all me fecking heart I'm sorry,
> (4)oh aye, because I've token a step back now,
> (5)look at me...
> (6)*He half-laughs through his nose.*
>
> (McDonagh 1997, 62)

Coleman flouts the maxim of manner and of quantity when he makes his final apology: apologising twice (2, 3) would normally be interpreted as a conversational implicature indicating sincerity, but by swearing (3) he flouts the maxim of manner and thus negates the implicature of sincerity, and therefore of contrition. (4) indicates a change in the game, 'taking a step back' is the prerogative of the victim, not the perpetrator, and this, combined with (5), indicates that the game is at an end because the rules have been violated. His laughter and transparent lack of regret are a challenge to Valene, and one which we know from past events will be answered by physical assault.

The apologising game allows the brothers to derive sport from a new form of confrontation. Throughout the play they have consistently threatened each other's positive face through their insults (e.g., 'virgin fecking gayboy', 'feck you, you tight-fisted feck'), as a prelude to physical fights (McDonagh 1997, 3, 20). Now Welsh's letter has compelled them to find new ways to provoke each other, and provided a way for their provocations to be neutralised under the guise of politeness and concern. This sequence is a source of amusement and tension: amusing because their behaviour is so childish and transparent; tense because we are aware that all such confrontations have hitherto ended in violence, and this one could well end in death (Coleman murdered their father over a petty insult). The ease with which the characters and audience can interpret what is really being communicated in this exchange exemplifies our ability to derive meaning, even when a strategy is being employed counter to its conventional function.

Talking in tongues: *Pentecost*

> It's just basic British insularity. It's suddenly the papers are full of places one had vaguely assumed to be made up.
> *Slight pause.*
> If not Slovenia, then certainly Slavonia. And then suddenly concentration camps start springing up all over pastoral Shakespearean locations.
>
> (Edgar 1995, 10–11)

This quotation is from David Edgar's *Pentecost* (1994), a play which sought to examine the break-up of Eastern Europe and to explore 'how societies work with very different groups of people' (Billingham 2007, 32). The play is set in an unspecified Eastern European country referred to as 'our country' (in the ancient region of Illyria – hence the comment about Shakespearean locations), in contemporary times, where old and new languages and ideologies compete for supremacy. It examines the importance of language as a tool for nation forming and ensuring or enforcing national solidarity, as well as the effect of English as a global second language, and as such is interesting both for the way in which language is discussed and used in the play.

Gabriella Pecs, deputy curator of the national museum, has discovered a 12th century fresco in a building which has served variously as a church (its original purpose) for the Roman Catholic, then Orthodox, faiths; a mosque; a stable; a warehouse for storing potatoes; a prison and a 'Museum of Atheism and Progressive People's Culture' (Edgar 1995, 7). The building and the fresco (which lies behind a depiction of 'the heroic revolutionary masses', stations of the cross and depictions of orthodox saints) are palimpsests of the history of the region and its colonisation. Gabriella has brought Oliver Davenport, an English art historian to look at the fresco, which, if her research is correct, predates Giotto's *Lamentation* in Padua (which it bears an uncanny resemblance to) and would therefore transform 'our country' from a typical ex-communist country into a site of international cultural importance. During the course of the play various interested parties try to claim the building, the various artworks and the prestige the fresco might bring; then a group of refugees from many different nations enter claiming sanctuary and take the art-historians hostage.

The play begins in the familiar territory of Stoppard's Eastern European plays, where non-native English speakers' grasp of colloquialisms is both humorous and poignant, and their understanding of linguistic nuance is a result of centuries of oppression and occupation. Oliver, a typically smug and condescending figure, initially finds the Babel-like effect of the country's history quaint and amusing. The nearest town to the church is Illyich, named after Lenin's father, and it has retained this name because the villagers 'cannot agree new name. Historic name for Hungarians is Cholovar, for Saxons Klozendorg, for the rest of the people Clop' (Edgar 1995, 4). Oliver finds the similarity of Clop and Clap hilarious, and Gabriella's explanation of the banning of the 'old Nagolitic language' in the 13th century tedious, not realising how crucial it will become to proving the painting's provenance. Their musings on art, nationhood and the birth of culture are rudely interrupted by the reality of the global marketplace when a prostitute enters the space with a Swedish client. Neither speaks the other's language and they settle on German to conduct their transaction (and dollars to pay for it) – reminding the audience of the recent past of 'our country' and its proximity to Germany. In the original RSC production of the play, there was no subtitling, so the audience was always reliant on the characters to translate the other languages for them (and for the characters who didn't speak that language), in this case, Gabriella acts as a human 'babelfish', translating the exchange for Oliver.[8] When it becomes clear that the prostitute is willing to have unprotected anal sex with her client for 5 dollars, Oliver interrupts, his Western sensibility unable to cope with what is obviously a common occurrence for both the prostitute and Gabriella (who reports the event utterly dispassionately).

Edgar represents the power dynamics of the different groups and different countries partly through their second language. For the representatives of 'our country', English is the second language, as it is for some of the refugees, notably Yasmin, the stateless Palestinian, whereas the Azeri, Afghan and Mozambican all speak Russian as well as English. But Edgar is also making a point about the use of ESL (English as a second language) and its power to provide a means of communication, however imperfect, among the disparate groups. English is the Pentecostal language – the common tongue – of the play. The refugees and hostages have a repertoire of incongruous phrases they pepper their exchanges with: 'Okeydoke'; 'I should coco'; 'bingo'; 'butchers'; 'merely'; 'I dare say'; and 'for love of Mike' among them. Edgar relates how he collected these 'universal' phrases during the rehearsal period:

> 'Beam me up, Scotty' was one. The word 'Okay' is obviously another, and lines such as 'Hasta la vista'. Some of them ended up in the play and a lot didn't. I ended up with some fantastic lists of things to use. It was all important because it relates to how people communicate with each other in the play.
>
> (Wu 2000, 139)

The English language is also a universal currency (in much the same way as dollars are at the beginning of the play): something which will smoothe the refugees' passage through life. Cleopatra, the young Gypsy girl, is desperate to improve her English in order to make better life in the west. Early on, she asks the hostages for help with her spelling and shows them the list of words she is compiling: 'Take good care vocabulary, grammar she will look behind' (Edgar 1995, 61). At the end of the play, in the aftermath of the rescue/raid Leo and Gabriella discover her notebook and read out the list she has compiled: roadblock; closed-circuit; permit; shrapnel; tarpaulin; checkpoint; transfer; exchanges; school; mercy mission; ambush; convoy; baggage handler; backlog; buffer; buffet; quota; flight; Chevrolet; milkshake; diaper; princess; and finally, 'huddled'; 'yearning' 'free' from the poem at the base of the Statue of Liberty which are quoted by both Leo and Oliver (Edgar 1995, 104–105).

Edgar notes that one of the consequences of the Europe breaking up into 'tiny and tinier statelets' was that 'the new nationalisms were trying to reinvent languages that were more different from each other than they needed to be – and indeed, more different than they had been before' (Billingham 2007, 33). In *Pentecost*, aspects of this nationalism also manifests itself in a hostility to using languages other than their own, for example, when Czaba the Minister for Conservation (or Preservation), in 'our language' the difference is 'too close to call' of the National Monuments, greets the assembled parties, a Catholic priest, Orthodox minister, Gabriella and Pusbas, leader of Heritage, and asks 'does anyone have a problem that we speak English?'

Pusbas: I certainly have problem
Czaba: Surely not.
Pusbas: In principle.
Czaba: But clearly not in practice. So, we can all be good Europeans, speaking in American.

(Edgar 1995, 17)

As in Stoppard, the slipperiness of language and the way in which this is exploited in politics is exposed. Czaba is asking the question from a practical point of view. If they all speak English it will make communication easier, and also mean that those with the best English can dominate the conversation and keep up much more easily. It will also serve, as Czaba says, to demonstrate their commitment to the European Union, and that their country is as forward looking and receptive as the 'old' European countries.

The divide between Oliver and Czaba is not just cultural in terms of experience of different ideologies, but also of cultural influences. In a nice twist on the difficulties of communicating in a second language, Czaba refers to the ladder as 'Babel's stairway':

Czaba: is it not Babel, where God invent all different language, to stop mankind building stairway to heaven?
Oliver: I think it's, in fact it's Babel's Tower.
Czaba: Of course. I am thinking of Led Zeppelin.
Oliver doesn't get this but acknowledges it anyway

(Edgar 1995, 20)

His assumption that Czaba has mis-translated is revealed as wide of the mark; Oliver doesn't 'get it' because he has never heard of Led Zeppelin's most famous song ['Stairway to Heaven'] – despite being of the view that 'you can't cut high art off from the culture which surrounds it' (Edgar 1995, 20). Czaba, it transpires, is quick at picking up most references, as he demonstrates when he mocks Oliver's attempts to downplay significance of fresco and the impact it could have on his career 'it isn't *merely* in my interest':

Czaba: oh sure. Interest also of truth beauty and universal European values.
Slight pause

Listen. I know. You pick it up. I don't know who your great painter is. You think – this man who has not heard of great Italian master, he is Minister of Culture, whatever fancy name they use. And you recall those past days – maybe you are visitor – and you lecture on your work at our great University and you think how nice it is that everybody speak good English and know so much more about your subject than your own students back at home. And you go on peanut costing tram and you see pretty girls with nice dress and nice hair and they are reading Tolstoy or Turgenev and you think in England they are dressed like tramp and reading garbage pail. And of course it's sad you come back and find – yes, when they have a choice, Turgenev goes in the trashcan and instead it's a video of Star Trek if not Terminator Two. And sure, I take your point. But I tell you, Doctor, it is price worth paying.

(Edgar 1995, 21)

Czaba's remark pinpoints the British Left's Romanticising of Eastern Europe and their intellectualism, and also exposes paternalism of this remark. Oliver, in fact, is shown not be as 'tight-arsed' as he first appears, as witnessed by his remark at beginning of this section when he apologises for his British insularity. The reality of life in this particular Shakespearean pastoral location is far from bucolic, and Oliver is a victim of the 'topsy-turvy' logic of events he unwittingly invokes when he quotes *Twelfth Night* to Gabriella.[9]

The talking cure: *Shopping and Fucking* and *Some Explicit Polaroids*

Find the words. Think before you speak. Don't just mouth . . . speak

This is the advice Jonathan, an aggressively capitalist businessman, gives to Nadia, a lap-dancer, with a nice line in self-affirmations towards the end of Ravenhill's *Some Explicit Polaroids*. It offers a useful starting point for this discussion of Ravenhill's work and the cynicism it conveys about the success, and desirability, of the late capitalist project to put the self at the centre of everything. It also flags up the extent to which the world was already professing to be tired of empty rhetoric and was aching to hear people 'really express' their emotions. In the play, this quotation comes at the point at which Jonathan is challenging Nadia to give up her increasingly unconvincing attempts to view everything in a positive light and 'please just be honest' (Ravenhill 2001b, 292) – a twisted echo of the New Left's call for a 'true' means of expression sounded nearly half a century before. But Nadia's generation has no 'true voice' – only a pastiche gleaned from films, television and 'trash' culture (what Richard Hoggart referred to as 'the newer mass art'). As discussed earlier in this chapter, Ravenhill's plays display great awareness of new technology, in 1997, before mobile phones and home Internet connections were an everyday fact, his characters were already using them, talking about them and speculating about the possibilities of CCTV and camcorders. The plays present a cacophony of voices, interrupting, overlapping; phones; television and music, a world in which people are never free from competing voices and discourses, in which the New Left values of communication are replaced by a society in which everyone talks and nobody listens.

Dan Rebellato has described the way in which many of Ravenhill's characters are enveloped in 'a mist of pop psychology and vacuous new agery [which] tries to validate this failure to make contact' (Rebellato 2001, xi). The protagonists of *Shopping and Fucking* and *Some Explicit Polaroids* are desperately trying not to 'mean something' in the same way that Hamm and Clov in *Endgame* are, and yet they are all obsessed with telling their story, and in being centre-stage in it.[10] Ravenhill explained the starting point for *Shopping and Fucking* as imagining 'characters whose whole vocabulary had been defined by the market, who had been brought up in a decade when all that mattered was buying and selling [...] The market had filtered into every aspect of their lives. Sex, which should have been private became a public transaction.' (quoted in Sierz 2001, 123). The play follows a trio of flatmates – Robbie, Lulu and Mark – as they struggle to survive in a world of McJobs (at one point Robbie is even working for a 'leading burger chain'), drug addiction and violent crime. Early on in the play we see Lulu auditioning for a position as a presenter on a shopping channel. Apparently a trained actress, and asked to 'do some acting' without any warning, Lulu ends up giving a topless rendition of Irina's final speech from *Three Sisters* as part of her screen test: 'One day people will know what all this was for. All this suffering. There'll be no more mysteries. But until then we have to carry on living. We must work. That's all we can do.' (Ravenhill 2001a, 13). As Rebellato notes, there is a real possibility that Lulu is not aware of the significance (and irony) of this speech, which is repeated again near the end of the play (Rebellato 2001, xix). Rather she appears to be parroting what she knows to be a weighty speech by an important writer (Chekhov), and she can gauge its success by the effect it has on Brian (who cries), yet the fact that neither she, Mark or Robbie have any intention of working if they can help it, seems lost on her.

Some Explicit Polaroids (1999) demonstrates the gap between language and feeling, and the danger of believing political slogans. The
play revolves around two groups of people: HIV positive Tim, his Russian boyfriend Victor, who he bought from the Net, and Nadia, Tim's
lap-dancing best friend; Helen, a former political activist who is now
a Labour councillor and prospective MP, Nick, her ex-boyfriend, also
an activist who has just come out of prison, and Jonathan, a global
financier and the subject of Nick's attack. Nick went to prison in 1984
and his re-emergence in 1997 means that he functions as a 'human
framing device', reminding us of the difference between the two eras
(Rebellato 2001, xviii). The exchange of an oppositional, revolutionary
discourse for a therapeutic one; the substitution of individual gain for
collective action; the move from 'what about the big targets?' to 'we're
all responsible for our own actions' (Ravenhill 2001b, 238, 269) demonstrate the shift very neatly. This is not to say that the political discourse
of the 1980s would be any less comical and pathetic if it was deployed
as relentlessly and ruthlessly as Ravenhill deploys the self-affirmations,
proclamations and explanations of the therapy culture. Indeed, Ravenhill shows us exactly how empty the revolutionary discourse appears in
the cold light of late 1990s Britain:

Nick: I did it for you.
Helen: Fuck off.
Nick: I did it because you wanted me to.
Helen: What is this bollocks? This is bollocks.
Nick: You said: 'That bastard is the scum of the earth and someone
  should kill that bastard'.
Helen: We all said that stuff. We said/rubbish like that all the time.
Nick: I'm not blaming... Listen. Your dad, when they laid off your
  dad, when that bastard buys it up and they're gonna asset-strip,
  chuck your dad away and you wanted them dead.
Helen: I was twenty. Everyone was a fascist or a scab or a class traitor.
  'Eat the rich.' We used to chant that, I mean what the fuck did that
  mean – 'eat the rich'?

(Ravenhill 2001b, 234–235)

The language of therapy is the point at which the fetishisation of communication and of the self meet and converge. This is particularly
apparent in Mark's rationalisation of his heroin habit, sexual impulses
and moral cowardice in *Shopping and Fucking*. There are examples of
this throughout the play, including the 'God squad' exchange quoted
in Chapter 1, and there is also a notable incident when Mark visits

Gary, a teenage rentboy, who is recounting his experiences of being systematically sexually abused by his stepfather, and being fobbed off by social services. With the introspection we have come to expect of him, Mark responds:

> Listen. I want you to understand because. I have this personality you see? Part of me that gets addicted. I have a tendency to define myself purely in terms of my relationship to others. I have no definition of myself you see. So I attach myself to others as a means of avoidance, of avoiding knowing the self. Which is actually potentially very desctructive. For me – destructive for me. I don't know if you're following this but you see if I don't stop myself I repeat the patterns. Get attached to people to these emotions then I'm back to where I started. Which is why, though it may seem uncaring, I'm going to have go.
> You're gonna be OK?
> I'm sorry it's just
>
> (Ravenhill 2001a, 32–33)

Mark breaks off at this point because Gary starts crying, and, as the stage direction puts it Mark '*makes a decision*' to abandon his own problems, but not before he's staked his own claim for special treatment.

There is a moment in *Some Explicit Polaroids* when Nadia, who is systematically beaten up by her ex-boyfriend, tries to brush aside Nick's misery at seeing her bruises (which he regards as yet another indication of the parlous state of the world): 'you won't be looking at the bruises. That's what make-up was invented for [...] cover up all the nasty stuff' (Ravenhill 2001b, 275). Ravenhill's characters practise a kind of linguistic maquillage: using particular phrases and mindsets to try and cover up the nasty stuff. We first meet Nadia talking to Victor at the airport while Tim is off buying food. Obviously the first time you meet your best friend's sex slave is a difficult social occasion to negotiate, particular when their grasp of English is shaky and Ravenhill's development of the scene is a sharp and witty reminder that in some situations, being 'alternative' and 'open' can have unpalatable results. Nadia's relentless positivity and determination to be non-judgemental means that she ends up condoning potentially (and, in her own case, literally) abusive behaviour:

Nadia: You've had lots of boyfriends?
Victor: Boyfriends, yes. Many boyfriends. They go crazy for my body. But also my father, yes? My father and my brother go crazy for my body.

Nadia: So... you're close as a family?

Victor: Please?

Nadia: A very loving family.

Victor: Yes I think so. Yes. My brother he likes to photograph me, you know? Polaroid? Since I was fourteen. Polaroid of my body. See? (*Offers* **Nadia** *the Polaroids.*) See? Fucking fantastic body.

Nadia: And that's you... Right. Right.

Victor: And I say to my brother when I am fourteen: I could be in porno.

Nadia: Well that's great.

Victor: Yes?

Nadia: Yes, I think it's great to have an ambition. Something you really want and go for it.

(Ravenhill 2001b, 239–240)

For every one of Victor's frank utterances, Nadia has a polite response which euphemistically repackages the unpleasant things she is being told and re-presents them as the Thatcherite dream: a close family *and* drive to succeed. The moral certainty of the state of the nation plays has gone and Ravenhill exposes the gap left behind when conviction politics gave way to spin.

Street talk: *Lift off* and *Yard Gal*

Another phenomenon of 1990s theatre was the emergence of an authentic sounding 'street style' which acknowledged the shared language of black, white and Asian youth culture. As early as 1982, linguists noted that Jamaican Patwa (the stigmatised form of Jamaican English) was being used by young white and Asian people in east London, and it is now found throughout London, the Midlands and urban areas of the UK where there is a strong Afro-Caribbean presence (Hewitt 1982, Rampton 1995). It has now become a commonplace of observational comedy, and its most famous proponent is 'Ali G', the white leader of the Staines Massive, created by Sacha Baron Cohen.[11] In Rebecca Prichard's *Yard Gal* (performed at the Royal Court Upstairs in 1998) and Roy Williams's *Lift Off* (performed at the Royal Court Upstairs in 1999) both black and white characters use lexical and grammatical features of Patwa, and, as far as can be judged from a written text (and reviews from the production), the pronunciations, as well as London English. Both plays only feature young men and women of a similar age and within their own peer group, so there is no opportunity for judging their speech in more formal situations. In both, their language choice functions as a mark of in-group behaviour and loyalty – particularly in *Lift Off* in which Tone's desire to be black is partially demonstrated by the zeal with which he uses Patwa terms, and by the mistakes he makes:

> **Young Tone**: Oh fuck me irie man
> **Young Mal** *laughs*
> **Young Tone**: Wat?
> **Young Mal**. Yu can't fuck an irie, yu fish
> **Young Tone**. Yu can
> **Young Mal**. Yu can't. Irie means yer cool, yer safe, everyting awright.
>   (*Laughs*) Fuck me irie.
>
> (Williams 2002, 165)

In the introduction to the first volume of his collected plays, Williams comments on the increased usage of Patwa-derived speech: 'I used to see white kids all around Ladbroke Grove, talking and acting like black kids. They were not being rude or disrespectful, they were absolutely genuine, reacting and responding to the world they were living in' (Williams 2002, xii). *Lift Off* explores the relationship between three childhood friends, Mal, Rich and Tone, employing the device of splitting the boys into their young and adult persona. When we first meet them, they have just started secondary school and Tone (formerly Tony, but now Tone because he thinks it sounds cooler) is doing everything in his power to prove that he is as cool as Mal: not only by adopting the same language, but also by showing off about how many times the police have stopped him, broken down his door and how many fights he's been in, even asserting at one point: 'I'm blacker than yu Mal!' (Williams 2002, 171). The first scene is dominated by physical and verbal posturing, the latter consisting largely of insults about each other and their mothers (even more insulting): 'Shut yer mum's legs'; 'yer mum' [an abbreviation of 'fuck your mum']; 'I'll fuck yer mum'; 'yer mum sucks dicks for a livin' (Williams 2002, 165–167). These insults are exchanged playfully, without any of the animosity evident in the exchange between Coleman and Valene discussed above, but it is clear that this is a fine line and could be crossed. Their friend Rich is not as privileged and does not join in this verbal sparring – a clear sign of his outsider status.

It is indicative of a change in the sensibility of reviewers and audience members that the most shocking language in the play is not the sexual swearing but the racist language used by Mal and by Hannah, a white girl who fancies Tone. In the first instance, Mal and Tone meet up in the playground (which forms the setting for most of the play) and Mal is angry because he has been sold some inferior quality 'weed' by Spencer:

Mal: Bastard! BASTARD! I swear to God Tone, it's the last time I ever do business wid a nigger.
Tone (*laughs*): Wat?
Mal: I'm serious. Nuttin but cunts man.
Tone: Yu can't say that.
Mal: Why?
Tone: Yer black ennit.
Mal: Yu know how long I was waitin' outside the tube station for Spencer to show his ugly face? An hour! Guy carries on like I got no life. Pisses me off man. When he finally shows, I ask ware he's bin, so he start givin me all de chat – 'Wa "appenin" nuh man? Ease up nuh. Wat de rass, me say me soon come, so me here. Is why yu get stress?
Come like a white man, backside!'
Tone *howls with laughter*
Mal: I goes, 'Get the fuck outta my face wid that shit Spencer, ware's my ting?' He acts like he juss come off the plane from Jamaica. Jamaica! He lives in bloody Clapham – never bin abroad in his life.
(Williams 2002, 175–176)

Although Mal's racism is shocking, it is partially neutralised by the fact of his blackness. Black civil rights campaigners have reclaimed 'nigger' in the same way that the gay rights movement has reclaimed 'queer', and although Mal's use of the word and his assertion that they are nothing but 'cunts' strongly suggests negative connotations, his use of the term in this way is more acceptable than Tone's use of it at the end of the play.[12] There is also a strong comic element in his outburst which derives from his impression of Spencer (the black drug dealer), and his parody of the wholesale adoption of Patwa by someone who has never even been to Jamaica. This in itself is an interesting demonstration of the way in which language functions as in-group marker; Tone's language is not ridiculous, because it is almost identical to Mal's. The fact that he isn't black and (probably) hasn't been to Jamaica is not important; he speaks in a way Mal considers to be authentic, whereas Spencer does not. The most shocking part of the play, however, is when Hannah reveals her racism.

She has met Mal and Tone in a club and is now waiting at the bus stop with Tone while Mal goes to get some fried chicken. Mal and Tone both think Hannah fancies Mal, so Tone is initially confused when she begins to flirt with him, having cleared up the confusion she asks:

Hannah: Wat d'you hang around with him for?

Tone: He's my mate, he's my spa.

Hannah: But you don't need him Tone. His lot ain't all that you know. I don't care what they say.

Tone: Wat you mean 'his lot'?

Hannah: You know wat I mean.

Tone: Tell me.

Hannah: They ain't all that Tone, no matter what they say and think. Blacks Tone. That's what I'm talking about.

Tone: Yu a racist.

Hannah: No.

Tone: Yu are ennit? A bloody racist.

Hannah: I jus don't hang around with blacks that's all. It's a question of taste.

Tone: Yu best fuck off then. Go get yer cab, move. Ca' if yu don't like Mal, yu don't like me right.

Hannah: You're not black though.

Tone: I might as well be right.

Hannah: Looked in the mirror lately?

Tone: Don't chat like yu know me.

Hannah: You really want to be like Mal? 'Don't fuck wid a bwai and him chicken.' There must be something seriously missing in your life if you think acting like them is going to fill it for you.

(Williams 2002, 209)

There are several interesting things about this exchange. Hannah's language becomes more standard during the course of it, while Tone's moves further from it. Both seek to assert their loyalties through their choice of language. At the beginning, Hannah is trying to avoid using the word 'black' to avoid giving offence, but also because she is trying to set up an acknowledgement that there is 'his lot' and 'our lot' black people and white people. Tone persistently refuses to be drawn into this shared code and forces her to be blatant about it. What's interesting is that in her last turn, Hannah puts her finger on the way in which in-group behaviour serves to reinforce communal bonds. There is nothing missing in Tone's life that acting like 'them' is going to fill, he is one of 'them' and he chooses to act like them in order to assert his membership of the group. The racism in this exchange is not lightened by humour (as in Mal's description of Spencer) and Williams received several complaints about the use of racist language in the play, but only about the racist language used by white people:

They thought it was racist. They were black; they though it was offensive; they couldn't believe that I, me, myself as a black man was putting these words into the mouths of these white characters.

(Williams and Sierz, 2006, 118)

Racist language has become taboo, whereas swearing, once taboo, is now accepted without question.[13] Racism was a particularly sensitive issue in when the play was first produced because it was the same month that the findings of the McPherson enquiry were released. The enquiry had examined the Metropolitan Police's handling of the murder of Steven Lawrence, a black teenager killed in 1993, and had declared the Met to be 'institutionally racist'. In the same year, the Tricycle Theatre presented *The Colour of Justice*, a documentary drama based on the McPherson enquiry. Michael Billington recalls the impact of the play:

We also heard taped extracts from conversations inside the house [of one of the suspects]. 'Every nigger', said the suspect's brother, 'should have their arms and legs chopped up and left with fucking stumps.' It was one of the most shocking utterances ever heard on the British stage.

(Billington 2007, 385)

Yard Gal was commissioned by Clean Break Theatre, a company who work with women prisoners. Prichard spent some time working with the inmates of Bulwood Hall prison in Essex, teaching creative writing and helping them to write their own pieces as well as finding out about their lives and histories. While working in the prison she discovered that the women 'created their own culture with both black and white elements in it' and ended up writing a play in which black and white members of a girl gang whose speech style is heavily influenced by Patwa. Perhaps inevitably, given the remit of the company and the 1990s emphasis on the confessional, the play takes the form of a duologue between Marie and Boo about their time as 'yard gals' in Hackney. It begins in an unusually combative and hostile style, in a way that calls attention to the language and the unconventional nature of the play. But it also rejects at the outset the story-telling compulsion which characterises other plays of the 1990s – such as *The Weir, Shopping and Fucking*, even though it will eventually settle down into the same narrative pattern.

> *Marie and Bo sit on stage staring at the floor avoiding the audience's stare.*
> *They psych each other out as to who will begin the play.*
> **Boo**: Wha' you looking at me for?
> **Marie**: Uh?
> **Boo**: Wha' you looking at me for man?
> **Marie**: Ain't you gonna start it?
> **Boo**: I ain't starting it start what?
> **Marie**: Fuck you man, the play.
> **Boo**: I ain't tellin' them shit
>
> (Prichard 1999, 5)

What is immediately obvious from this extract is the extent to which Prichard is representing speech in writing, both phonetically – glottal stops/wha/for/what/, dropped g in/telling/ – and in terms of pace, so while Boo 'drops' the comma we might expect it 'I ain't starting it start what', while Marie uses one in the next line: 'Fuck you man, the play'. In spite of their apparent hostility to each other, and to the audience, they continually draw attention to their performative function: commenting on members of the audience; insulting them ('oy you, why you sitting there like you just wet yourself?'), and flirting with them ('I wish I was the boxer shorts be hanging round your hips') (Prichard 1999, 38). They frequently refer to the fact that 'we sitting up here to tell a story innit' and end the performance on a truculent note 'Can we go now?' (Prichard 1999, 8, 55). Telling the story is both a compulsion and an obligation – and they treat it as if it were part of a community service sentence or compulsory therapy session when they comment on the performance aspect of it, but are highly energetic in their recreation of events.

Like the boys in *Lift Off* they are also aware of the power of code-switching, for example, in their recreation of the night they were all held by the police:

> **Marie** (*as Deniz as she begins speaking in unintelligible patois*) 'yeah das how dey run ting in a ghetto we jus deal wi' ting up front know what me a say then poliss 'em come an make enquiry an write it

ahn papah half hour dis half hour dat you know what me a say you want me say yes fit dis or yes fit dat cyan arks me in plain English I nah say a word. Wha? I'm speakin English wish language be dis. Yeah man y'ave to check it out 'im bring a bag a gun and dem fire 'pon yout' and yout' and yout' an ya poliss frien' come for dem gun an' I tell'em na run. Man nah stop kill man seen, man nah stop rob man seen. An' wha' gwan in de ghetto me bruddah?'

Boo: Down the station I could hear Deniz in the next room doin' her Jamaican act.

(Prichard 1999, 29)

The girls fully grasp the concept that all language use is a performance, and in Deniz's case, she presumably strengthens her accent both to show her solidarity with those in the 'ghetto' and to make life more difficult for the police. The critical reception of *Yard Gal* demonstrates the extent to which language minding in the theatre has declined. No one commented on Marie and Boo's foul-mouthed exploits in anything less than glowing terms; no one complained that they couldn't understand them or the story (in spite of the number of unfamiliar terms) and no one commented on the sad decline of the English language or English drama. Charles Spencer, who protested vehemently at the language and content of *Blasted*, describing it 'as a lazy tawdry piece of work without an idea in its head beyond an adolescent desire to shock', praised Prichard's 'wonderful ear for demotic speech and an entirely unsentimental compassion':

> The language is beguilingly rich, a mixture of cockney and Jamaican patois with even Marie adopting the inflections of a black speaker. If you met these kids on the bus, you'd pray that they didn't notice you, because they are absolutely full of lip and bad attitude. [...] Prichard writes with a wonderful ear for demotic speech and an entirely unsentimental compassion.
>
> (*Theatre Record* 1999, Vol. 18.1, 603)

A cynic might suggest that in the wake of the furore over *Blasted*, the critics had learned to be more circumspect in their reviews of plays about sex, drugs and violence written by young women and presented at the Royal Court, but by the late 1990s there seems to have been very little in the way of 'bad' language which still exercised theatrical language minders.

Coda: Lifelike-ese since 2000

Language minding and the millennium

It seems fitting, given the anxiety the threat of the millennium bug caused in the run-up to 2000, that the most recent preoccupations of language minders should be the threat to language posed by new technology, and in particular by e-mail and mobile phone messaging. In 2002, a 13-year-old Scottish provoked a furore by using 'txt' language in an exam to write an account of her holiday. The BBC news Web site, and the Children's BBC offshoot CBBC News both ran debates on the subject, and the *Guardian*'s education editor also wrote a piece on the threat of txt language, 'Txt msg surprise for examiners', citing Anne Barnes's ('a senior examiner in English') comments on the subject. Barnes commented:

> 'The thought and quality of the answer has to be balanced against the fact that it is not standard language when it should be'. She also complained of 'soap opera language' in some papers, and said 'seperate is now so common that it has almost become an official alternative for separate'.
>
> (Will Woodward, *Guardian*, 17 August 2002)

Barnes's comments show her awareness that what is at issue here (aside from 'declining' standards) is the importance of *context* in language minding. Regardless of what her own opinions on the subject might be, the point she makes is that 'txt' and 'soap opera' language are inappropriate in a classroom environment in which one of the key skills is literacy, and a knowledge of literary conventions. Some of the contributors to the BBC News debate are refreshingly open-minded compared to earlier language minders, echoing Barnes's opinion that txt language is just one aspect of linguistic competency rather than the sum: 'Text messaging is a perfect example of how people adapt and mould language to suit different contexts. Maybe schools should be studying why it happens' (Richard, UK http://news.bbc.co.uk/go/pr/fr/-/1/hi/talking_point/2815461.stm).

Other comments serve as a reminder of the tendency in language minding to proscribe first and ask questions later:

> What a disaster. The great English language, with its power to move and to anger, to frighten and perplex, to amuse and to inspire, to change the course of history, is being debased in to some moronic machine code by this mind numbing form of communication. What has happened to the passion and power of a well written letter?
>
> (Steve, UK http://news.bbc.co.uk/go/pr/fr/-/1/hi/talking_point/2815461.stm)

What indeed? Particularly when an advocate of the well-written letter is reduced to engaging with another mind-numbing form of communication to make his point. The proprieties and improprieties of standard language are back in focus thanks, in part, to the impact of these new technologies, attested to not only by the re-issuing of many of the key texts on the issues of language standardisation, such as Crowley (1st edn. 1989, 2nd edn. 2003), Milroy and Milroy (1st edn. 1985, 2nd edn. 1991, 3rd edn. 1998) and Mugglestone (1st edn. 1995, 2nd edn. 2003), but also by the simultaneous presence of issues around standard language on the AS/A2 specifications alongside a new module on Accent and Dialect. Alongside this rage the perennial debates about the inability of children to write and speak properly. In the same way that developments in lifelike-ese in British theatre 1945–2000 have been shown in this book to reflect changes in the education system and socio-cultural framework, at the present time, it seems that e-mail and txt language offer an excellent opportunity for dramatists to enact their own fetishisation of communication.

Verbatim theatre

Documentary or verbatim theatre is the ultimate in lifelike-ese because it is based on real speech. In the 1960s, Peter Cheeseman had produced documentary plays about the local area which relied on local people for their testimony. The plays ranged from the history of Methodism in Staffordshire; the experiences of men taken prisoner of war in Italy; the history of local railway service right through to the struggles to keep the local steelworks open. Cheeseman and the actors would go and interview various people, transcribe the tapes and then use extracts from them to construct the play. Other theatres, drawing inspiration from the Vic and New Vic, including the Liverpool Everyman, produced documentaries on this model in the 1970s.

In the 1990s, documentary theatre enjoyed a resurgence, but this time, the focus was national rather than local. The Tricycle, National Theatre, Royal Court (and others) have all staged verbatim plays based on current events: *The Colour of Justice* examined the McPherson enquiry into the murder of Stephen Lawrence; *The Permanent Way* scrutinised the government's failure to act to improve the safety of the British railways in the wake of numerous disasters and several public enquiries; and *My Name Is Rachel Corrie* used diary entries and letters to reconstruct the life of a woman crushed to death by Israeli bulldozers in Gaza. In each case, much of the impact came from the way in which people described their own thoughts and emotions, or, often in the case of institutional figures, their dogged repetition of the party line. Michael Billington attributes the increase in factual and factional ('faction' is the term coined by David Edgar to describe work which is a mixture of fact and fiction) drama to:

> a growing distrust with politicians, press, and the new rollingnews outlets in which an endlessly repeated 'Newsak' replaced the aural wallpaper of Muzak. Feeling that once reliable sources of information were either tainted or untrustworthy, audiences increasingly turned to theatre for raw information about public events.
>
> (Billington 2007, 384)

Alecky Blythe's company, Recorded Delivery, has advanced the techniques of verbatim drama to develop plays with a less overtly political focus. Blythe founded the company in 2003 after attending a 'Drama without Paper' workshop run at the Actors' Centre by Mark Wing-Davey. The technique he demonstrated involved interviewing people, and

> requires no transcribing but works directly from the interviews via earphones. The exact speech pattern of the interviewee – including coughs, stutters and non sequiturs – is faithfully reproduced.
>
> (Blythe 2005, 3)

The actors learn their parts by listening to the speeches of their character(s) over and over again, but also keep their earphones on during the performance in order to retain the authenticity of the interviewee's speech and to prevent them from trying to heighten their performance. As Blythe (who originally trained as an actor) observes:

> It is an actor's instinct to perform: to heighten, to try to make their lines 'more interesting' in an effort to project their character and make the person they are playing seem real. When you are recreating pre-recorded, everyday speech, this is not the best approach, because everyday speech is often more mundane and 'everyday' than anyone dares to invent. This is what gives it the ring of truth.
>
> (Blythe 2008, 81)

The idea that people will pay to sit and watch actors repeating words relayed to them through headphones would doubtless make Noel Coward and generations of actors, playwrights and language minders froth at the mouth. For the purposes of this book, however, it seems a fitting place to end. The technology that gave linguists to study naturally occurring speech is now being used to make plays out of naturally occurring speech. Lifelike-ese and speech have finally melded on stage.

Notes

Introduction

1. This methodology adapts that used by Ronald Carter's *Investigating English Discourse*. He notes that 'most of the chapters are concerned as much with accounting for the discourses within which language is debated and described as they are with analysing and interpreting the language used in relation to immediate social, cultural and pedagogic contexts' (Carter 1997, xv).
2. See also Dorney (2007), 'Hamming It Up in *Endgame*', for a reading which seeks to relocate Beckett in a theatrical context rather than a philosophical one.
3. Several of the writers examined here comment on the relative paucity of work on dramatic language (Nicoll 1968, 339; Kennedy 1975, 237).
4. The instability and 'debased' nature of speech is discussed in detail in Chapter 1, 'Language, Communication and Ideology'.
5. See, for example, Esslin's *Theatre of the Absurd* (1st edn 1962, 2nd edn 1968, 3rd edn 1980).
6. Roy Harris identifies this idea as a key part of the 'language myth', the 'telementary fallacy' by which people imagine language as a clear conduit for transferring their thoughts to another person (Harris 1981).

1 Language, Communication and Ideology

1. The transparency model of language offers a viable explanation for why people are so sensitive about their language use being explicitly 'policed' for political and social content, while accepting that their usage should be open to criticism in terms of its conformation to or deviation from the standard. The most obvious reason is that at a general level, the ideology of standardisation has been naturalised to the extent that it is regarded as common-sense: most people believe that the standard English is 'proper' English. This is why people tend to devalue their own language variety (see Trudgill 1983). Even if they do nothing to change it to be nearer the standard, they still acknowledge that there is a 'correct' way of doing it (rather like acknowledging that 'feeding the wheel' through your hands is correct when driving, when in fact, as soon as you passed your test, you started to cross your hands instead).
2. The term 'language maven' is also used to describe language guardians/ maintainers, especially in the US (see Pinker 1994, Cameron 1995).
3. Althusser's footnote reads: 'Linguists and those who appeal to linguistics for various purposes often run up against difficulties which arise because they ignore the action of ideological effects in all discourses – including even scientific discourses' (Althusser in Rivkin and Ryan 1999, 300).

4. As I will discuss later in this chapter, the need for uniformity in language is usually associated with the standardisation process undergone by written language, and the same criteria are then projected onto spoken language, more often than not with far less overt success, but nevertheless shoring up certain expectations regarding articulacy, class origin and level of education.

5. For a fuller discussion of Orwell's writing on language see Chapter 3, 'Orwell on language and politics', of *Landmarks in Linguistic Thought II*, ed. Joseph, Love and Taylor.

6. In *Language as Ideology* (1979) Kress and Hodge refer to Chomsky's 'The Back-room Boys at Dow', a piece in which a soldier describes the improvements made to napalm to make it a more effective killer. The soldier's language illustrates this point perfectly. By using a mix of technical terms and army jargon the impact on human life is sidelined (Kress and Hodge 1979, 71).

7. See Cameron and Bourne 1989; Cameron 1995, 2000.

8. An interesting counter example to this equation of the prestige with power is recent media interest in the fact that the Queen's style of speech is apparently becoming closer to Estuary English in an effort to appear more populist and thus more popular, following Tony Blair's example (see Mugglestone 2003, 277–285).

9. The origin of standard English and its subsequent naturalisation can be interpreted in terms of Fiske's commentary on Althusser's theory of overde-termination. Fiske states that:

> For Althusser, ideology is not a static set of ideas imposed upon the subor-dinate by the dominant classes but rather a dynamic process constantly reproduced and reconstituted in practice – that is, in the way that people think, act and understand themselves and their relationship to society. He rejects the old idea that the economic base of society determines the entire cultural superstructure. He replaces this base/superstructure model with his theory of overdetermination, which not only allows the superstructure to influence the base but also produces a model of the relationship between ideology and culture that isn't determined solely by economic relations.
>
> (Fiske in Rivkin and Ryan 1998, 306)

The origins, development and maintenance of standard English are explica-ble in precisely these terms, the standard variety being chosen because it was the language variety used first by the Chancery, which then incorporated features from the central Midlands used by the wealthy and influential mer-chants, the variety used for record keeping became the variety to be taught, which became the variety associated with education, and so on. What began as a regional variety became the standard to be emulated and against which all other varieties must be judged, because of the dynamic interaction of economics, politics and culture.

10. As discussed later in this chapter, spoken language is very often and very conveniently conflated with literacy.

11. David Crystal talks about this at some length in both *The Fight for English* (2006) and *The Stories of English* (2004).

12. 'The great grammar crusade illustrates a paradox to which this book repeatedly draws attention. It is a classic case where a bad argument, put forward by people who know little or nothing about language, nevertheless succeeds, because although much of its substance is nonsensical it engages with the underlying assumptions of its audience and therefore makes a kind of sense; whereas the opposing argument put forward by experts fails, because it is at odds with the audience's underlying assumptions and is therefore apprehended as nonsensical. [...] we have to acknowledge people's deep-rooted *belief* that it is possible and indeed proper to make value judgements on language' (Cameron 1995, 81).

13. '*Gemeinschaft*-relationships are characterised by affectivity, mutuality and naturalness' (*Penguin Dictionary of Sociology* 1984, 94).

14. Cameron expands on the 'fetish of communication' in *Good to Talk? Living and Working in a Communication Culture* (London: Sage, 2002), exploring the way in which 'communication' as an unmarked term has become synonymous with 'talk', that is, spoken, usually spontaneous discourse, and how it has been constructed as a highly necessary skill for the workplace, casual encounters and relationships, and particularly how it has been reconfigured as a skill which must be taught and worked upon, rather than as something everyone can do.

15. Whenever years in parenthesis after a play's name does not match with their respective years present in the bibliography, note that years in parentheses refer to the date of first performance, not date of publication.

2   Fetishising Communication on Stage

1. As early as 1977, drama critic Oleg Kerensky observed that audiences 'are now more accustomed to watching drama on television than in the theatre. New audiences start watching the box in their infancy, long before they could possibly go to a theatre' (Kerensky 1977, xv).

2. Stephen Fay recounts the following anecdote in his biography of Peter Hall, *Power Play*:

> Daneman [the actor playing Vladimir] recalls that in rehearsal the humanity of the characters began to emerge. They had been played in the Paris production as clowns, but now the cast began to think of Vladimir and Estragon as tramps. It was partly because of their costumes; they were dressed out of second-hand shops.
>
> (Fay 1995, 100)

3. The principles of Speech Act Theory I outline here are in accordance with those laid out by Austin, rather than Searle. For the difference between Austin and Searle's methodology see Petrey 1990, 63–69.

4. In 'Prose and the Playwright' (1954), Tynan pre-empts Nicoll's view of the prose/verse debate: 'On naturalism I shrink from pronouncing, because I have never (has anyone?) seen a completely naturalistic play – I doubt if one exists. What bothers me is the way in which higher criticism equates prose with poverty of dramatic expression...Nobody wants to banish luxury

of language from the theatre; what needs banishing is the notion that it is incompatible with prose, the most flexible weapon the stage has ever had' (Tynan 1961, 70).

5. 'The first problem clearly is to find a form of language which may have such a connexion with our debased common speech as the standard Elizabethan blank verse measure had with the richer, less stereotyped, and more expressively familiar utterance of the term' (Nicoll 1968, 362).

6. Note Nicoll's use of 'disfigure' to refer to a non-standard method of punctuation merely serves to reinforce his prescriptive attitude.

7. Gareth Lloyd Evans's *The Language of Modern Drama* is similarly fascinated by, yet fearful of, linguistics, and its forays into literature and drama.

8. Barthes, 'Style and Its Images', in *Literary Style, A Symposium* (ed. Seymour Chatman), Oxford University Press: London and New York, 1971 (quoted from p. 7).

9. It is quite possible that Kennedy was familiar with Derrida's writings on this subject. As Peggy Kamuf notes in her introduction to 'Signature Event Context' (first published 1972), 'The necessary iterability or citationality of the sign has had an important place in Derrida's thinking since *Speech and Phenomena* [published in French 1967, translated 1973]' (Kamuf 1991, 80).

10. Kennedy makes several references to this new practice of analysing taped conversation, but comments in his Preface that he feels it is too detailed a method to be of much help in the study of dramatic dialogue: 'the description of tape-recorded samples of everyday conversation made by two linguists, Crystal and Davy – and which I was eager to test in my study of Pinter – turned out to be too space-consuming and microscopic for my purposes' (Kennedy 1975, xii).

3 1945–1955: The 'Dissociation of Sensibility' and 'the Jewelled Epigram'

1. The play's first director. As Priestley's letter explains, *An Inspector Calls* had its world premier in Moscow because of the lack of a suitable English venue in 1945.

2. See the description of Arthur Birling quoted above: 'fairly easy manners *but* provincial in speech' – my emphasis. Why it should be 'but' provincial in speech rather than 'and' is further proof of the lack of provincial accents on stage during this period.

3. *When the curtain rises it is just after dinner on the Sunday of the week-end party – the gramophone is going, and there is a continual buzz of conversation.*
   [. . .]
   There must be a feeling of hectic amusement and noise and the air black with cigarette smoke and superlatives. During the first part of the scene everyone must appear to be talking at once, but the actual lines spoken while dancing must be timed to reach the audience as the speakers pass near the footlights (Coward 1979, 129).

4. Lahr 1982, 140.

5. The focus on the 'contemporary' in the reviews of *Look Back in Anger* is testimony to its structured absence from the theatre of the time. 'The

contemporary' frequently functions as a synonym for social criticism, and against an unengaged, reactionary culture, the contemporary became a banner, behind which the oppositional forces in the theatre could (temporarily) gather.

The lack of the contemporary was not confined to theatre but was a feature of intellectual culture generally, and is related to the absence of sustained social criticism in the period. It is not so much that there were no oppositional or counter-hegemonic ideas in circulation, but rather there were relatively few forums outside the main institutions of political power for initiation into political practice (Lacey 1995, 20).

6. George Devine, the founder of the English Stage Company (ESC), was comparing Coward to 'a well-paid chorus girl' as early as 1943. Wardle's *Theatres of George Devine* (London: Johnathan Cape, 1978), p. 91, quoted in Lahr 1982.

7. The information on Coward's earnings comes from Hoare 1995, 231.

8. Rattigan is also praised for the 'craftsmanship': 'Whatever his shortcomings as a theorist, nobody can deny Rattigan's supreme agility as a craftsman. His mastery of exposition is complete: give one of his characters a telephone, and within a minute, imperceptibly, the essentials of the situation will have been clearly sketched in' (Tynan 1961, 75).

9. The issue of other kinds of theatre that were underway during this period will be discussed in the next chapter. Specifically the work of Unity Theatre and the Theatre Workshop, once again, the New Wave is perceived as the turning point – in this case for discovering Brecht, agit-prop and non-naturalistic staging techniques – when in fact, work had started in these areas decades previous to 1956.

10. 'The Scratch and Mumble School' was Coward's second critique of the New Wave published in the *Sunday Times*, 22 January 1961.

11. So aspiring playwright Roland Maule tells Garry Essendine in Coward's *Present Laughter* (Coward 1979, 172).

12. 'Face Threatening Act' (FTA) – a term used in studies of linguistic politeness to describe an utterance which challenges the individual's desire not to be coerced or insulted. 'Face' describes the individual's sense of self-worth and their desire for respect and consideration.

13. Hobson describing *The Browning Version*, Hobson 1984, 148.

14. In his 'advice' to the 'new movement' titled 'These Old Fashioned Revolutionaries' which appeared in the *Sunday Times*, 15 January 1961, Coward admonished: 'Consider the Public ... To better it with propaganda, bewilder it with political ideologies, bore it with class prejudice [...] is a policy that can only end in dismal frustration and certain failure' (quoted in Russell 1987, 91). Rattigan was more specific in his attack: 'It's only Aunt Edna's *emotions* that a playwright can hope to excite ... She is bored by propaganda, enraged at being "alienated", loathes placards coming down and telling her what is going to happen next, hates a lot of philosophical talk on the stage with nothing happening at all' (quoted in Innes 1992, 94).

15. Although Ronnie's hearty elder brother Dickie has a nice line in school-boy slang, greeting the news of his sister's impending nuptials with 'Dickie: Oh, is that all finally spliced up now? Kate definitely being entered for the marriage stakes. Good egg!' (Rattigan 1981, 104).

16. Hoare notes Pinter's acknowledgement of this similarity: 'What he liked was a kind of objectivity of the stage', said Pinter, who saw a shared desire not 'in expressing ourselves, but in expressing objectively and as lucidly as possible what was actually taking place in any given context' (Hoare 1995, 458).

4 1956–1964: Moribund and Vital; Demotic and Epic

1. I prefer the term 'kitchen-sink' to New Wave for its more expressive quality and because New Wave is more commonly associated with film. However, where authors have spoken of the new wave, I have followed their usage, although, certainly in Rebellato's case, New Wave can be read as a much wider movement than theatre alone.
2. As discussed above, Leavis was firmly of the opinion that great literature – and great literary artists – was characterised by its attention to life and experience.
3. Anderson in Marowitz, Milne and Hale *The Encore Reader* 1970, 41–51.
4. This is certainly the impression of working-class life that Coward depicts in *This Happy Breed* (1942). The Gibbons' neighbour, Bob, is always popping in and out of their house (usually through the French windows), staying for tea and involving himself in their lives. Eventually Bob's son marries the Gibbons' daughter intensifying these bonds still further.
5. *Joan's Book. Joan's Peculiar History as She Tells It*, London: Minerva, 1995.
6. As explained in Chapter 2, in the section on 'Performativity, Performatives and Cliché'.
7. Beckett *The Complete Dramatic Works* 1990a, 58, 70; Stoppard *Rosencrantz and Guildenstern* 1967, 32.
8. Samuel Beckett and George Duthuit, 'Three Dialogues', *Samuel Beckett: A Collection of Critcal Essays*, Esslin (ed.) 1965, 17.
9. Levinson describes implicature as a means of providing 'some explicit account of how it is possible to mean (in some more general sense) more than what is actually "said" (i.e. more than what is literally expresses by the conventional sense of the linguistics impressions uttered)' (1983, 97).
10. In his habitually grandiose manner, Tynan proclaimed thus: 'He [Brecht] wrote morality plays and directed them as such, and if we of the West End and Broadaway find them as tiresome as religion, we are in a shrinking minority. [...] I was bored to death, said a bright Chelsea type after *Mother Courage*. "Bored to life" would have been apter' (Tynan, 1984, 196).
11. Robert Stephens's account of rehearsing *The Good Woman of Setzuan*:

> You always got a long lecture before rehearsals about alienation and Brecht, but once you got started you never heard another word about it. You went on and did it in the same way as you did everything else. We had all this ghastly Chinesey music.
>
> Peggy Ashcroft as Shen The had a song to sing about the need for a big blanket to cover the people of the city. She was wearing a half mask and a moustache, and old Teo Otto who had done the music for the Berliner Ensemble, bellowed from the back of the stalls: 'No. no. no, no, this is

Ashcroft, not Shen The.' She was terribly upset because she didn't know –
none of us did – how to do alienation acting. There is, of course, no such
thing.

(Stephens 1995)

12. Gray (1987) notes:

the kind of delivery Coward expects can be clearly seen in the songs by
the way in which he distributes rhyme. It will strike, not just the end
of the line where the singer can take a breath, but in the middle, where
he can only take the briefest break [...] In fact, most of Coward's verbal
strategies are designed to promote speed of delivery.

(Gray 1987, 132–133)

13. Innes 1992, 122.
14. Shellard 1999, 75–76.
15. Lacey 1995, 154–161.

5   1964–1975: Revolution On and Off Stage

1. Literally as well as figuratively. The April 1966 issue of American magazine
   Time focused on 'London: The Swinging City' and included a tourist map of
   'the Scene'. There is also a map of the England inset in the right hand corner
   which shows Liverpool '(home of the Beatles)', Manchester, Yorkshire and
   Birmingham all with arrows pointing towards London.
2. MacCabe. C., *The Eloquence of the Vulgar. Language, Cinema and the Politics of
   Culture*, London, 1999, quoted in Mugglestone 2003.
3. This generalisation should not obscure the fact that certain accents still have
   negative connotations for certain people: a 1993 survey by the Institute of
   Personnel found that employers 'tend to look down their noses at those who
   speak in the accents of Liverpool, Glasgow and Birmingham' (*Guardian*, 3
   January 1993).
4. Olivier in a letter to Hall about the formation of the National Theatre:

The Nat. Th seems to be at a complete impasse, *tout laisse, tout casse* and
fuck me all dandy. I am in a bad way. I can't get a National Theatre. I can't
get a cast or repertoire for Chichester. I can't get into my own home, and
Joanie's baby is *bursting* out. I can't wake up in the morning or go to sleep
at night. I'm absolutely fucked. How are you cock?

(quoted in Fay 1995, 177)

5. Orton himself got a local authority grant to RADA (Interview with Barry
   Hanson, published in the *Crimes of Passion* double-bill at the Royal Court
   programme 6 June 1967.) He also had elocution lessons as part of his
   preparation for getting into RADA.
6. When McKellen was on *Desert Island Discs* in 2003 he spoke of his regret
   at losing his accent, and noted his difficulty in portraying a 'convincing'
   Lancashire accent.

7. The shift in attitudes is so marked that former Prime Minister Tony Blair (1997–2007), educated at a prestigious Scottish public school, was frequently mocked for affecting an Estuary accent and his deployment of the odd non-standard usage in order to convey his common touch (see Mugglestone 2007 for further discussion).

8. Reviews and accounts of this production abound; for further elucidation see Elsom 1981, 28–30; Fay 1995, 37; and Brook 1999, 36.

9. In *Women, Crime and Language* (2003), Gray notes that *Daily Telegraph* journalist Pamela Hansford Johnson makes an explicit link between education, articulacy and crime in her meditations on the Moors Murderers' Trials, *On Iniquity* (1968), suggesting that 'the early school leaver in his dead-end job' should have restricted access to certain texts (e.g., the works of de Sade, which Ian Brady had read):

> Not unnaturally he wants to 'know' … the trouble is that they are entirely without instinct for selection and unfitted by their meagre schooling to take a serious work of sexology, for example, in the spirit in which it was written.
>
> (Hansford Johnson, quoted in Gray 2003, 112)

10. I am referring here to the widely quoted examples of Pinter's dialogue. Namely, the interrogation scene in *The Birthday Party*, and the 'light the kettle, light the gas' argument in *The Dumb Waiter* (Pinter 1990, 41–47, 125–126).

11. Orton knew very well the value of appearing to be richer, posher and/or more educated. He had elocution lessons because he thought it would help him get into/get on at RADA, and worked hard to erase his Leicester accent (interview with Barry Hanson in the *Crimes of Passion* double-bill at the Royal Court programme 6 June 1967).

12. Cheeseman, interview with the author, June 2005.

13. One of the things that help up the repeal of the censorship laws was the reluctance of the theatre industry to arbitrate for itself what was and wasn't permissible. The Society of West End Managers and other bodies were fearful of producing plays which might be prosecuted for libel or sexual indecency, and preferred the safety blanket of censorship to the risk of legal proceedings. Producers are even more mindful of this in the wake of Mary Whitehouse's attempts to bring a case against Brenton's *The Romans in Britain* (1980) because of an act of simulated buggery: the play has only been revived once since the original production (Sheffield Crucible 2005).

14. Cheeseman, for example, had a policy of producing documentary plays focused on the local area (Stoke-on-Trent) and dealing with local issues, so the audience were not surprised to hear the actors using their local accent or other regional accents. Similarly, the Liverpool Everyman produced shows by local writers and about the local area, and so the audience expected to hear Liverpudlian accents and dialect words as well as a variety of other accents.

6   1976–1989: Staging the Nation

1. See David Eldridge's *Market Boy* (2006) for a brief account of this. There is also an amusing episode in David Lodge's *Nice Work* when Robyn, an academic, assumes that her brother's 'decidedly lower class' girlfriend Debbie must be a secretary when in fact she is a foreign exchange dealer and earns three times as much as Robyn (Lodge 1988).
2. 'Selsdon Man' was the phrase (briefly) coined to designate the new breed of free enterprise Conservative, so named because of the Conservative Party meeting held in a hotel at Selsdon in Croydon.
3. Derby Day also makes an appearance in Eliot's *Notes Towards the Definition of Culture* (1948) as one of the things which defines culture.
4. See Ronald Carter's *Language and Creativity: The Art of Common Talk* (Routledge: 2004).

7   1990–2000: Talk Is Cheap

1. Although it is beyond the chronological remit of this chapter, Complicité's *A Disappearing Number* (2007) uses the device of a character in an endless series of phone calls to a call centre based in India.
2. Deborah Tannen is a noticeable exception to this, and is David Crystal, writing academic books and articles as well as more populist ones on language use and communication.
3. In fact, the positive effects of the government's economic policy after leaving the Exchange Rate Mechanism (ERM) were not really palpable until Blair took office.
4. See David Hare's *Asking Around* (1993) which details the research he did for his 'State of the Nation' trilogy into the Church, the criminal justice system and the Labour party, culminating with his account of being on the campaign trail with Labour in 1992.
5. For more information see Carter's account: 'Politics and Knowledge about Language: the LINC Project', in Carter 1997, 36–53. Given the circumstances, it is a remarkably even-handed piece.
6. See Chapter 5 for an in-depth discussion of this.
7. The original poster had a fork covering the 'uck'.
8. A babelfish is a device featured in Douglas Adams's sci-fi series *A Hitch-hiker's Guide to the Galaxy*. It's a small fish the hitch-hikers insert into their ear and it allows them to understand and speak any language in the galaxy. It is obviously not a technical term, but it is a useful one.
9. After Oliver's derision, Gabriella is surprised at his willingness to help her, when she asks for a reason, he replies 'Because…because…this is Illyria, lady' (Edgar 1995, 13) – which is exactly what is said to Olivia at the beginning of *Twelfth Night* (Act 1, Sc. ii).
10. For a further discussion of 'meaning something' in *Endgame*, see Dorney, 'Hamming It Up in *Endgame*: A Theatrical Reading' in *Endgame: A Collection of Critical Essays*, ed. Mark Byron (Rodopi, 2007).

11. One of Ali G's catchphrases was 'Is it cos I is black?' – which invariably caused either consternation, embarrassment or incredulity, or sometimes a mixture of all three.
12. Mal has an affair with Tone's younger sister Carol, gets her pregnant and, when confronted by Tone, insults him and Carol. Tone retaliates, calling him a 'black bastard' and a 'nigger' (Williams 2002, 232).
13. Although Williams shows a double standard at work in Tone's treatment of his sister, whom he condemns for having a 'nasty mout' when she comments on penis size in a pornographic film she finds him watching (Williams 2002, 180).

Bibliography

Plays

Arden, J., 1961 *Live Like Pigs, New English Dramatists Vol. 3*. Harmondsworth: Penguin.

Arden, J., 1977 *Serjeant Musgrave's Dance, Plays One*. London: Eyre Methuen.

Ayckbourn, A., 1991 *The Revengers' Comedies*. London: Faber and Faber.

Beckett, S., 1990a *Waiting for Godot, The Complete Dramatic Works*. London: Faber and Faber.

Beckett, S., 1990b *Endgame, The Complete Dramatic Works*. London: Faber and Faber.

Beckett, S., 1990c *Happy Days, The Complete Dramatic Works*. London: Faber and Faber

Beckett, S., 1995 *Eleutheria*. New York: Foxrock.

Bond, E., 1977a *The Pope's Wedding, Plays One*. London: Eyre Methuen.

Bond, E., 1977b *Saved, Plays One*. London: Eyre Methuen.

Brenton, H., 1986 *Epsom Downs, Plays One*. London: Methuen.

Brenton, H., 1989 *The Romans in Britain, Plays Two*. London: Methuen.

Blythe, A., 2005 *Cruising*. London: Nick Hern Books.

Blythe, A., 2008 *The Girlfriend Experience*. Nick Hern Books.

Cartwright, J., 1989 *Road*. London: Methuen.

Churchill, C., 1985a *Cloud Nine, Plays One*. London: Methuen.

Churchill, C., 1985b *Light Shining in Buckinghamshire, Plays One*. London: Methuen.

Churchill, C., 1985c *Vinegar Tom, Plays One*. London: Methuen.

Churchill, C., 1990a *Top Girls, Plays Two*. London: Methuen.

Churchill, C., 1990b *Serious Money, Plays Two*. London: Methuen.

Coward, N., 1950 *Ace of Clubs*. London: Chappell & Co.

Coward, N., 1979a *The Vortex, Plays One*. London: Eyre Methuen.

Coward, N., 1979b *Private Lives, Plays Two*. London: Eyre Methuen.

Coward, N., 1979c *Present Laughter, Plays Four*. London: Eyre Methuen.

Coward, N., 1979d *Design for Living, Plays Three*. London: Eyre Methuen.

Coward, N., 1979e *This Happy Breed, Plays Four*. London: Eyre Methuen.

Coward, N., 1983a *Look After Lulu, Plays Five*. London: Methuen.

Coward, N., 1983b *A Song at Twilight* (from *Suite in Three Keys*), *Plays Five*. London: Methuen.

Coward, N., 1983c *Relative Values, Plays Five*. London: Methuen.

Coward, N., 1999a *Nude with Violin, Plays Six*. London: Methuen.

Coward, N., 1999b *Cavalcade, Plays Three*. London: Methuen.

Coward, N., 1999c *Shadow Play, Plays Seven*. London: Methuen.

Coward, N., 1999d *Semi-Monde, Plays Six*. London: Methuen.

Coward, N., 1999e *Peace in Our Time, Plays Seven*. London: Methuen.

Coward, N., 1999f *Quadrille, Plays Seven*. London: Methuen.

Coward, N., 2000a *I'll Leave It to You, Plays Eight*. London: Methuen.

Coward, N., 2000b *The Young Idea, Plays Eight*. London: Methuen.

Coward, N., 2002c *After the Ball*. London: Samuel French.

Delaney, S., 1959 *A Taste of Honey*. London: Methuen.

Delaney, S., 1961 *The Lion in Love*. London: Methuen.

Dunbar, A., 1980 *The Arbor*. London: Pluto Press/Royal Court Society.

Edgar, D., 1987 *Destiny, Plays One*. London: Methuen.

Edgar, D., 1995 *Pentecost*. London: Nick Hern Books.

Frayn, M., 1998 *Copenhagen*. London: Methuen.

Hare, D., 1984 *Plenty, The History Plays*. London: Faber and Faber.

Hare, D. 1992a 'Introduction: On Political Theatre', *The Early Plays*. London: Faber and Faber.

Hare, D., 1992b *Slag, The Early Plays*. London: Faber and Faber.

Hare, D., 1992c *The Great Exhibition, The Early Plays*. London: Faber and Faber.

Ionesco, E., 1958 *The Bald Prima Donna, Plays One*. London: John Calder.

Ionesco, E., 1958 (1962) *The Lesson, Eugene Ionesco*. Harmondsworth: Penguin.

Ionesco, E., 1997 *The Chairs*. London: Faber and Faber, trans. Martin Crimp.

Jellicoe, A., 1958 *The Sport of My Mad Mother*. London: Faber and Faber.

Jellicoe, A., 1962 *The Knack*. London: Faber and Faber.

Kane, S., 2001 *Blasted, Complete Plays*. London: Methuen.

Marber, P., 2000 *Closer*. New York: Dramatists Play Service.

McDonagh, M., 1997 *The Lonesome West*. London: Methuen.

Norman, F., 1960 *Fings Ain't Wot They Used T'be*. London: Secker and Warburg.

Orton, J., 1995a *Entertaining Mr Sloane, Complete Plays*. London: Methuen.

Orton, J., 1995b *What the Butler Saw, Complete Plays*. London: Methuen.

Orton, J., 1995c *Loot, Complete Plays*. London: Methuen.

Orton, J., 1995d *The Ruffian on the Stair, Complete Plays*. London: Methuen.

Osborne, J., 1957 *Look Back in Anger*. London: Faber and Faber.

Osborne, J., 1961a *The Entertainer*. London: Faber and Faber.

Osborne, J., 1961b *Luther*. London: Faber and Faber.

Osborne, J., 1966 *A Patriot for Me*. London: Faber and Faber.

Osborne, J., 1993 'Introduction' to *Look Back in Anger and Other Plays* (Collected Plays. Vol. 1). London: Faber and Faber, pp. vii–xiv.

Pinter, H., 1978 *The Homecoming, Plays Three*. London: Eyre Methuen.

Pinter, H., 1990a 'Writing for the Theatre', *Plays One*. London: Faber and Faber.

Pinter, H., 1990b *The Room, Plays One*. London: Faber and Faber.

Pinter, H., 1990c *The Dumb Waiter, Plays One*. London: Faber and Faber.

Pinter, H., 1990d *The Birthday Party, Plays One*. London: Faber and Faber.

Pinter, H., 1965 *The Homecoming*. London Methuen.

Pinter, H., 1991a *The Caretaker, Plays Two*. London: Faber and Faber.

Pinter, H., 1991b *Last to Go, Plays Two*. London: Faber and Faber.

Pinter, H., 1994a *No Man's Land, Plays Four*. London: Faber and Faber.

Pinter, H., 1994b *Old Times, Plays Four*. London: Faber and Faber.

Prichard, R., 1999 *Yard Gal*. London: Faber and Faber.

Priestley, J.B., 1947 *An Inspector Calls*. London: Heineman.

Priestley, J.B., 1948 *The Linden Tree*. London: Heineman.

Rattigan, T., 1953 *Collected Plays*, Vol. 2. London: Hamish Hamilton.

Rattigan, T., 1981a *The Browning Version, Plays One*. London: Methuen.

Rattigan, T., 1981b *French Without Tears, Plays One*. London: Methuen.

Rattigan, T., 1981c *Harlequinade, Plays One*. London: Methuen.
Rattigan, T., 1981d *The Winslow Boy, Plays One*. London: Methuen.
Rattigan, T., 1985a *The Deep Blue Sea, Plays Two*. London: Methuen.
Rattigan, T., 1985b *Separate Tables, Plays Two*. London: Methuen.
Rattigan, T., 1985c *In Praise of Love, Plays Two*. London: Methuen.
Ravenhill, M., 2001a *Shopping and Fucking, Plays One*. London: Methuen.
Ravenhill, M., 2001b *Some Explicit Polaroids, Plays One*. London: Methuen.
Russell, W., 1986 *Educating Rita, Stags & Hens and Blood Brothers*. London: Methuen.
Shaffer, P., 1966 *The Royal Hunt of the Sun*. London: Longman.
Stoppard, T., 1968 *Rosencrantz and Guildenstern Are Dead*. London: Faber and Faber.
Stoppard, T., 1972 *Jumpers*. London: Faber and Faber.
Stoppard, T., 1975 *Travesties*. London: Faber and Faber.
Stoppard, T., 1978a *Every Good Boy Deserves Favour*. London: Faber and Faber.
Stoppard, T., 1978b *Professional Foul*. London: Faber and Faber.
Stoppard, T., 1993a *The Real Inspector Hound, The Real Inspector Hound and Other Entertainments*. London: Faber and Faber.
Stoppard, T., 1993b *Dogg's Hamlet, The Real Inspector Hound and Other Entertainments*. London: Faber and Faber.
Stoppard, T., 1993c *Cahoot's Macbeth, The Real Inspector Hound and Other Entertainments*. London: Faber and Faber.
Storey, D., 1978 *The Changing Room*. Harmondsworth: Penguin.
Theatre Workshop, 1981 *Oh What A Lovely War!* London: Eyre Methuen.
Weiss, P., 1965 *The Persecution and Assassination of Marat as Performed by the Inmates of Charenton under the Direction of the Marquis de Sade*. London: Calder and Boyars, trans. Geoffrey Skelton, verse adaptation by Adrian Mitchell.
Wesker, A., 1963 *Chips with Everything*, in *New Penguin Dramatists. Vol. 7*. Harmondsworth: Penguin.
Wesker, A., 1995a *Chicken Soup with Barley, The Wesker Trilogy*. Harmondsworth: Penguin.
Wesker, A., 1995b *Roots, The Wesker Trilogy*. Harmondsworth: Penguin.
Wesker, A., 1995c *I'm Talking About Jerusalem, The Wesker Trilogy*. Harmondsworth: Penguin.
Williams, R., 2002 *Lift Off, Plays One*. London: Methuen.

Critical Texts

Abercrombie, N., Hill, S. and Turner, B.S., 1984 *The Penguin Dictionary of Sociology*. Harmondsworth: Penguin.
Acheson, J., ed., 1993 *British and Irish Drama Since 1960*. London: Macmillan.
Allen, P., 2004 *A Pocket Guide to Alan Ayckbourn's Plays*. London: Faber and Faber.
Althusser, L., 1999 'Ideology and Ideological State Apparatuses' in Rivkin and Ryan eds., pp. 294–304.
Anderson, L., 1958 'Vital Theatre?' in Marowitz et al eds., 1970, pp. 41–51.
Artaud, A., 1970 *The Theatre and Its Double*. London: Calder.
Ascherson, N., 2003 'What Made Gunther grass?', The *Observer Review*, 7 September 2003, p. 6.

Aston, E. and Savona, G., 1991 *Theatre as Sign-System: A Semiotics of Text and Performance*. London: Routledge.

Atkinson, P., 1985 *Language, Structure and Reproduction. An Introduction to the Sociology of Basil Bernstein*. London: Methuen.

Austin, J.L., 1962, repr. 1980 *How to Do Things with Words*. Oxford: Oxford University Press.

Barthes, R., 1971 'Style and Its Images' in Chatman ed., 1971, pp. 3–10.

Beckett, S. and Duthuit, G., 1965 'Three Dialogues', in Esslin ed., 1965, pp. 16–20.

Bernstein, B., 1971 *Class, Codes and Control* (Vol. I). London: Routledge and Kegan Paul.

Bex, T. and Watts, R.J., eds., 1999 *Standard English: The Widening Debate*. London: Routledge.

Bignell, J., Kavanagh, M. and Lacey, S., eds. 2000 *British Television Drama. Past, Present and Future*. London: Palgrave.

Bigsby, C.W.E., ed. 1981 *Contemporary English Drama*. London: Edward Arnold.

Bigsby, C.W.E., 1981 'The Language of Crisis in British Theatre: The Drama of Cultural Pathology' in Bigsby ed., 1981, pp. 11–52.

Billingham, P., 2007 *At the Sharp End: Uncovering the Work of Five Leading Dramatists*. London: Methuen.

Billington, M., 1992, repr. 2001 *One Night Stands: A Critic's View of Modern British Theatre*. London: Nick Hern Books.

Billington, M., 2007 *The State of the Nation*. London: Faber and Faber.

Birch, D., 1991 *The Language of Drama*. London: Macmillan.

Bloom, H., ed. 1987 *Harold Pinter*. New York: Chelsea House.

Blythe, A., 2008 'Alecky Blythe' in Hammond and Steward eds., pp. 78–102.

Bock, H. and Wertheim, A., eds., 1981 *Essays in Contemporary British Drama*. Munich: Max Hueber.

Bolinger, D., 1980 *Language – The Loaded Weapon. The Use and Abuse of Language Today*. London: Longman.

Bond, E., 1977 'First Author's Note to *Saved, Plays One*'. London: Eyre Methuen.

Bourdieu, P., 1991 *Language and Symbolic Power*. Cambridge: Polity Press, edited and introduced by John B. Thompson, trans. Gino Raymond and Matthew Adamson.

Bradbrook, M., 1972 *Literature in Action*. London: Chatto and Windus.

Brenton, H., 1986 'Preface', *Plays One*. London: Methuen.

Brook, P., 1959 'Oh for Empty Seats' in Marowitz et al, 1970, pp. 68–74.

Brook, P., 1968 *The Empty Space*. Harmondsworth: Penguin.

Brook, P., 1999 *Threads of Time*. London: Methuen.

Brown, J. Russell, ed., 1968 *Modern British Dramatists. A Collection of Critical Essays*. New Jersey: Prentice Hall.

Brown, J. Russell, 1972 *Theatre Language*. London: Allen Lane.

Browne, T., 1975 *Playwright's Theatre*. London: Pitman.

Bull, J., 1984 *New British Political Dramatists*. Basingstoke: Palgrave Macmillan.

Bull, J., 1994 *Stage Right: Crisis and Recovery in British Contemporary Mainstream Theatre*. Basingstoke: Palgrave Macmillan.

Bull, J. and Gray, F., 1981 'Joe Orton' in Bock and Wertheim eds., 1981, pp. 71–96.

Burke, L., Crowley, T. and Girvin, A., eds., 2000 *The Language and Cultural Theory Reader*. London: Routledge.

240 *Bibliography*

Burke, L., Crowley, T. and Girvin, A., 2000 'Theorising the Sign' in Burke, Crowley and Girvin eds., 2000, pp. 13–20.

Burton, D., 1980 *Dialogue and Discourse: A Sociolinguistic Approach to Modern Drama Dialogue and Naturally Occurring Conversation*. London: Routledge.

Burton, D., 1982 'Through Glass Darkly, Through Dark Glasses', in Carter ed., 1982, pp. 195–214.

Butler, J., 1990 *Gender Trouble: Feminism and the Subversion of Identity.* London: Routledge.

Byron, M.S., ed., 2007 *Samuel Beckett's Endgame: A Collection of Critical Essays*. Amsterdam: Rodopi.

Calderwood, J.L. and Tolliver, H.E., eds., 1968 *Perspectives in Drama*. Oxford: Oxford University Press.

Cameron, D., 1995 *Verbal Hygiene*. London: Routledge.

Cameron, D., 2002 *Good to Talk? Living and Working in a Communication Culture*. London: Sage.

Cameron, D. and Bourne, J., 1989 'No Common Ground: Kingman, Grammar and the Nation', *Language in Education* 2.3, 147–160.

Carey, J., 1992 *The Intellectuals and the Masses: Pride and Prejudice Among the Literary Intelligentsia, 1880–1939*. London: Faber and Faber.

Carter, R., ed., 1982 *Language and Literature: An Introductory Reader in Stylistics*. London: Allen and Unwin.

Carter, R., 1997 *Investigating English Discourse: Language, Literacy and Literature*. London: Routledge.

Carter, R., 2004 *Language and Creativity: The Art of Common Talk*. London: Routledge.

Carter, R. and Nash, W., 1990 *Seeing Through Language: Guide to Styles of English Writing*. Oxford: Blackwell.

Carter, R. and Simpson, P., eds., 1989 *Language, Discourse and Literature: An Introductory Reader in Discourse Stylistics*. London: Unwin Hyman.

Carter, R. and Simpson, P., 1989 'Introduction', in Carter and Simpson eds., 1989, pp. 1–20.

Castle, C., 1972 *Noël. A Narrative on Charles Castle's Documentary Film, This is Noël Coward*. London: W.H. Allen.

Cavell, S., 1976 'Ending the Waiting Game. A Reading of Samuel Beckett's *Endgame*' in *Must We Mean What We Say?*, Cambridge: Cambridge University Press, pp. 115–162.

Chatman, S., ed., 1971 *Literary Style, A Symposium*. Oxford: Oxford University Press.

Coupland, N., Wiemann, J. and Giles, H., 1991 'Talk as "Problem" and Communication as "Miscommunicative": An Integrative Analysis' in Coupland, Giles and Wiemann eds., pp. 1–17.

Coupland, N., Giles, H. and Wiemann, J., eds., 1991 *'Miscommunication' and Problematic Talk*. London: Sage.

Coward, N., 1961 'These Old Fashioned Revolutionaries', *The Sunday Times*, 15 January.

Coward, N., 1961 'The Scratch and Mumble School', *The Sunday Times*, 22 January.

Crowley, T., 1991 *Proper English? Readings in Language, History and Cultural Identity*. London: Routledge.

Crowley, T., 2003 *Standard English and the Politics of Language*. London: Palgrave (formerly, *The Politics of Discourse*, 1989).

Crystal, D., 1995 *Cambridge Encyclopedia of Language*. Cambridge: Cambridge University Press.

Crystal, D., 2004 *The Stories of English*. Harmondsworth: Penguin.

Crystal, D., 2006 *The Fight for English: How the Language Pundits Ate, Shot and Left*. Oxford: Oxford University Press.

Crystal, D. and Davy, D., 1969 *Investigating English Style*. London: Longman.

Culler, J., 1976 *Saussure*. London: Fontana/Collins.

Culpeper, J., Short, M. and Verdonk, P., eds., 1998 *Exploring the Language of Drama*. London; Routledge.

Culpeper, J., Short, M. and Verdonk, P., 1998 'Introduction' in Culpeper, Short and Verdonk eds., 1998, pp. 1–6.

D'Monté, R. and Saunders, G., 2008 *Cool Britannia? British Political Theatre in the 1990s*. Basingstoke: Palgrave Macmillan.

Davies, A. and Saunders, P., 1983 'Literature, Politics and Society', in Sinfield ed., 1983, pp. 14–50.

Devine, H., 2006 *Looking Back. Playwrights at the Royal Court 1956–2006*. London: Faber and Faber.

Derrida, J., 1972 'Signature, Event, Context' in Derrida ed., 1988, pp. 1–23.

Derrida, J., 1988 *Limited Inc*. Evanston: Northwestern University Press.

Dorney, K., 2007 'Hamming It Up in *Endgame*: A Theatrical Reading', in Byron ed., pp. 227–252.

Dukore, B., 1982 *Harold Pinter*. New York: Grove Press.

Eagleton, T., 1983 *Literary Theory*. Oxford: Blackwell.

Edgar, D., 1981 'A Drama of Dynamic Ambiguities' in Trussler ed., 1981, pp. 157–171.

Elam, K., 1980 *The Semiotics of Theatre and Drama*. London: Methuen.

Eliot, T.S., 1932 'The Metaphysical Poets' (1921) in *Selected Prose Essays*. London: Faber and Faber, pp. 281–291.

Eliot, T.S., 1939 *The Idea of Christian Society*. London: Faber and Faber.

Eliot, T.S., 1948 *Notes Toward the Definition of Culture*. London: Faber and Faber.

Elsom, J., 1981 *Post-war British Theatre Criticism*. London: Routledge.

Elsom, J., 1992 *Cold War Theatre*. London: Routledge.

Esslin, M., ed., 1965 *Samuel Beckett: A Collection of Critical Essays*. New Jersey: Prentice Hall.

Esslin, M., 1977 *Pinter: A Study of His Plays*. London: Eyre Methuen.

Esslin, M., 1980 *Theatre of the Absurd*. Harmondsworth: Penguin.

Esslin, M., 1987a 'Language of Silence', in Bloom ed., 1987, pp. 139–163.

Esslin, M., 1987b *The Field of Drama, How the Signs of Drama Create Meaning on Stage and Screen*. Harmondsworth: Penguin.

Evans, G.L., 1977 *The Language of Modern Drama*. London: Longman.

Eyre, R., 2003 *National Service. Diary of a Decade at the National Theatre*. London: Bloomsbury.

Eyre, R. and Wright, N., 2000 *Changing Stages: A View of British Theatre in the Twentieth Century*. London: Bloomsbury.

Fairclough, N., 1989 *Language and Power*. London: Longman.

Fairclough, N., 1991 *Discourse and Social Change*. Cambridge: Polity Press.

Fairclough, N., 1995 *Critical Discourse Analysis: The Critical Study of Language*. London: Longman.

Fairclough, N., 2000 *New Labour, New Language?*, London: Routledge.

Fasold, R., 1990 *Sociolinguistics of Language*. Oxford: Blackwell.

Fay, S., 1995 *Power Play: The Life and Times of Peter Hall*. London: Hodder and Stoughton.

Findlater, R., ed., 1981 *At the Royal Court*. London: Amber Lane Press.

Fiske, J., 1999 'Culture, Ideology, Interpellation' in Rivkin and Ryan eds., 1998, pp. 305–311.

Flew, A.G.N., ed., 1951 *Essays on Logic and Language* (1st Series). Oxford: Blackwell.

Fowler, R., 1991 *Language in the News: Discourse and Ideology in the Press*. London: Routledge.

Fowler, R., Hodge, R., Kress, G. and Trew, T., eds., 1979 *Language and Control*. London: Routledge and Kegan Paul.

Gaskill, W., 1988 *A Sense of Direction*. London: Faber and Faber.

Giglioli, P., ed., 1972 *Language and Social Context*. Harmondsworth: Penguin.

Gottlieb, V. and Chambers, C., eds., 1999 *Theatre in a Cool Climate*. Oxford: Amber Lane.

Gramsci, A., 1998 ' "Hegemony" (from 'The Formation of the Intellectuals')' in Rivkin and Ryan eds., pp. 277–278.

Gray, F., 1987 *Noel Coward*. London: Macmillan.

Gray, F., 1993 'Mirrors of Utopia: Caryl Churchill and Joint Stock' in Acheson ed., pp. 47–59.

Gray, F., 2003 *Women, Crime and Language*. London: Palgrave Macmillan.

Green, J., 1999 *All Dressed Up. The Sixties and the Counterculture*. London: Pimlico.

Griffin, G., 2003 *Contemporary Black and Asian Women Playwrights in Britain*. Cambridge: Cambridge University Press.

Gussow, M., 1995 *Conversations with Stoppard*. London: Nick Hern Books.

Hare, D., 1992 'On Political Theatre', *The Early Plays*. London: Faber and Faber.

Hall, P., 1983 *Peter Hall's Diaries*. London: Hamish Hamilton.

Hall, S., 1961 'Beyond Naturalism Pure. The First Five Years' in Marowitz et al eds., 1970, pp. 212–220.

Hammond, W. and Steward, D., eds., 2008 *Verbatim Verbatim: Contemporary Documentary Theatre*. London: Oberon Books.

Harris, R., 1980 *The Language Makers*. London: Duckworth.

Harris, R., 1981 *The Language Myth*. London: Duckworth.

Harris, R., 1987 *The Language Machine*. London: Duckworth.

Harris, R. and Taylor, T.J., eds., 1989 *Landmarks in Linguistic Thought: The Western Tradition from Socrates to Saussure*. London: Routledge.

Herman, V., 1995 *Dramatic Discourse: Dialogue as Interaction in Plays*. London: Routledge.

Herman, V., 1998 'Turn Management in Drama' in Culpeper, Short and Verdonk eds., 1998, pp. 19–33.

Hewison, R., 1986 *Too Much: Art and Society in the Sixties*. London: Methuen.

Hewitt, R., 1982 'White Adolescent Creole Users and the Politics of Friendship', *Journal of Multilingual and Multicultural Development*, 3.3, 217–232.

Hoare, P., 1995 *Noel Coward. A Biography*. London: Sinclair Stevenson.

Hobson, H., 1984 *Theatre in Britain. A Personal View*. Oxford: Phaidon.

Hoggart, R., 1957 (1971) *The Uses of Literacy*. Harmondsworth: Penguin.

Honey, J., 1989 *Does Accent Matter? The Pygmalion Factor*. London: Faber and Faber.

Honey, J., 1998 *Language Is Power: The Story of Standard Language and Its Enemies*. London: Faber and Faber.

Honey, J., 1983 *The Language Trap. Race, Class and the Standard English Issue in British Schools*. London: National Council for Educational Standards.

Hope–Wallace, P., 1958 'A Double Beckett Bill: Subtler "Endgame"', *Manchester Guardian*, 30 October.

Howard, P., 1990 *The State of the Language*. Harmondsworth: Penguin.

Humphrys, J., 2004 *Lost for Words: The Mangling and Manipulating of the English Language*. London: Hodder.

Hymes, D., 1996 *Ethnography, Linguistics, Narrative Inequality*. London: Taylor and Francis.

Ionesco, E., 1958 'The Playwright's Role', *Observer*, 29 June.

Innes, C., 1992 *Modern British Drama*. Cambridge: Cambridge University Press.

Jefferson, A. and Robey, D., eds., 1993 *Modern Literary Theory*. London: Batsford.

Joseph, J.E., Love, N. and Taylor, T.J., eds., 2001 *Landmarks in Linguistic Thought II. The Western Tradition in the Twentieth Century*. London: Routledge.

Kane, L., 1984 *The Language of Silence*. London: Associated University Presses.

Kamuf, P., 1991 *A Derrida Reader. Between the Blinds*. Hemel Hempstead: Harvester Wheatsheaf.

Kennedy, A., 1975 *Six Dramatists in Search of a Language: Studies in Dramatic Language*. Cambridge: Cambridge University Press.

Kerensky, O., 1977 *The New British Drama: Fourteen Playwrights since Osborne and Pinter*. London: Hamish Hamilton.

Kidd, K.S., 2001 'Educating the Audience: The Idea of the Audience in Post-war English Theatre and Culture, 1945–1965, with Particular Reference to the English Stage Company at the Royal Court', unpublished doctoral thesis, University of Sheffield.

Kress, G. and Hodge, R., 1979 *Language as Ideology*. London: Routledge and Kegan Paul.

Labov, W., 1969 'The Logic of Non-standard English' in Giglioli ed., 1972, pp. 179–215.

Lacey, S., 1995 *British Realist Theatre: The New Wave in Its Context 1956–1965*. London: Routledge.

Lahr, J., 1980 *Prick Up Your Ears: The Biography of Joe Orton*. Harmondsworth: Penguin.

Lahr, J., 1982 *Coward the Playwright*. London: Methuen.

Lahr, J., 1986 *The Orton Diaries*. London: Methuen.

Lahr, J., ed., 1995 'Introduction', *Orton: The Complete Plays*. London: Methuen.

Lambert, J.W., 1974 *Drama in Britain 1964–1973*. Harlow: Longman.

Leavis, F.R., 1972 *Revaluation*. Harmondsworth: Penguin.

Leavis, F.R., 1962 (1974) *The Great Tradition*. Harmondsworth: Penguin.

Leavis, F.R. and Thompson, D., 1933 *Culture and Environment: The Training of Critical Awareness*. London: Chatto and Windus.

Leavis, Q.D., 2000 *Fiction and the Reading Public*. London: Pimlico.

Levinson, S., 1983 *Pragmatics*. Cambridge: Cambridge University Press.

Little, R. and McLaughlin, E., 2007 *The Royal Court Theatre Inside Out*. London: Oberon.

Littlewood, J., 1994 *Joan's Book. Joan's Peculiar History as She Tells It*. London: Minerva.

Lodge, D., 1988 *Nice Work*. Harmondsworth: Penguin.

Mandala, S., 2007 *Twentieth Century Drama Dialogue as Ordinary Talk*. Edinburgh: Ashgate.

Marowitz, C., Milne, T. and Hale, O., eds., 1970 *The Encore Reader: A Chronicle of the New Drama*. London: Methuen.

Marr, A., 2007 *A History of Modern Britain*. Basingstoke: Palgrave Macmillan.

Miller, J., 1995 *Ralph Richardson: The Authorised Biography*. London: Sidgwick and Jackson.

Milroy, L., 1973 'Codes Theory and Language Standardisation', Ulster Polytechnic: Mimeo.

Milroy, L., 1980 *Language and Social Networks*. Oxford: Basil Blackwell.

Milroy, L., 1984 'Comprehension and Context: Successful Communication and Communication Breakdown', in Trudgill ed., pp. 7–31.

Milroy, J. and Milroy, L., 1991 (2nd edn) *Authority in Language: Investigating Language Prescription and Standardisation*. London: Routledge.

Mitford, N., ed., 1956 *Noblesse Oblige: An Enquiry into the Identifiable Characteristics of the English Aristocracy*. London: Hamish Hamilton.

Moore-Gilbert, B. and Seed, J., eds., 1992 *Cultural Revolution? The Challenge of the Arts in the 1960s*. London: Routledge.

Morley, S., 1983 *Shooting Stars: Plays and Players 1975–1983*. London: Quartet.

Mugglestone, L., 2003 *'Talking Proper?' The Rise of Accent as Social Symbol*. Oxford: Oxford University Press.

Newbolt, H., 1926 *The Teaching of English in England*, HMSO: London.

Nicholson, S., 2003 *The Censorship of British Drama, 1900–1968/Vol. 1: 1900–1932*. Exeter: University of Exeter Press.

Nicoll, A., 1968 'Dramatic Dialogue' in Calderwood and Tolliver eds., pp. 337–377.

Ochs, E., 1979 'Planned and Unplanned Discourse' in *Syntax & Semantics 12: Discourse and Syntax*. New York: Academic Press.

Orton, J., 1967 'Interview with Barry Hanson', *Crimes of Passion* double-bill at the Royal Court programme, 6 June.

Ortony, A., ed., 1979 *Metaphor and Thought*. Cambridge: Cambridge University Press.

Orwell, G., 1946 'Politics and the English Language' in *Collected Essays*. London: Mercury, pp. 337–351.

Osborne, D., 2007 'Know Whence You Came': Dramatic Art and Black British Identity. Kwame Kwei-Armah in conversation with Deirdre Osborne. *New Theatre Quarterly*, 23.1 (Cambridge: Cambridge University Press).

Partridge, E., 1942, rev. 1994 *Usage and Abusage: A Guide to Good English*. London: Hamish Hamilton.

Peacock, D.K., 1999 *Thatcher's Theatre: British Theatre and Drama in the Eighties*. Connecticut: Greenwood Press.

Petrey, S., 1990 *Speech Acts and Literary Theory*. London: Routledge.

Pinker, S., 1994 *The Language Instinct*. Harmondsworth: Penguin.

Rabey, D.I., 2003 *English Drama since 1940*. London: Longman.

Rampton, B., 1995 *Crossing: Language and Ethnicity Among Adolescents*. London: Longman.

Rankema, J., 1993 *Discourse Studies*. Amsterdam and Philadelphia: John Benjamins.

Rebellato, D., 1999 *1956 and All That*. London: Routledge.

Rebellato, D., 2001 'Introduction to *Mark Ravenhill, Plays One*. London: Methuen.

Ricks, C. and Michaelis, L., eds., 1980 *The State of the Language*. London: Faber and Faber.

Ricks, C. and Michaelis, L., eds., 1990 *The State of the Language II*. London: Faber and Faber.

Rivkin, J. and Ryan, M., eds., 1999 *Literary Theory: An Anthology*. Oxford: Blackwell.

Roberts, P., 1986 *The Royal Court Theatre 1965–1972*. London: Routledge.

Roberts, P., 1999 *The Royal Court and the Modern Stage*. Cambridge: Cambridge University Press.

Roberts, P. and Stafford-Clark, M., 2007 *Taking Stock: The Theatre of Max Stafford-Clark*. London: Nick Hern Books.

Robey, D., 1993 'Modern Linguistics and the Language of Literature' in Jefferson and Robey eds., 1993, pp. 46–72.

Ross, A.S.C., 1956 'U and Non U: An Essay in Sociological Linguistics' in Mitford ed., 1956, pp. 11–36 (Originally published as 'Linguistic Class-Indicators in Present-Day English' in *Neuphilologische Mitteilung*, 55 (1954)).

Russell, J., 1987 *File on Coward*. London: Methuen.

Ryle, G., 1951 'Systematically Misleading Expressions' in Flew ed., pp. 85–100.

Sandbrook, D., 2005 *Never Had It So Good? A History of Britain from Suez to the Beatles*. London. Little Brown.

Sandbrook, D., 2006 *White Heat. A History of Britain in the Swinging Sixties*. London: Little Brown.

Sanger, K., 2001 *The Language of Drama*. London: Routledge.

Saussure, F de, 1983 *Course in General Linguistics*. London: Duckworth, trans. R. Harris.

Seed, J., 1992 'Hegemony Postponed: The Unravelling of the Culture of Consensus in Britain in the 1960s', in Moore-Gilbert and Seed eds., 1992, pp. 15–40.

Shellard, D., 1999 *British Theatre since the War*. New Haven and London: Yale University Press.

Shellard, D., ed., 2000 *British Theatre in the 1950s*, Sheffield: Sheffield Academic Press.

Short, M., 1989, 'Discourse Analysis and the Analysis of Drama' in Carter and Simpson eds., pp. 139–170.

Short, M., 1998 'From Dramatic Text to Dramatic Performance' in Culpeper, Short and Verdonk eds., pp. 6–18.

Sierz, A., 2001 *In-Yer-Face Theatre: British Drama Today*. London: Faber and Faber.

Simpson, P., 1989 'Politeness Phenomena in Ionesco's *The Lesson*' in Carter and Simpson eds., pp. 171–193.

Sinfield, A., ed., 1983 *Society and Literature 1945–70*. London: Methuen.

Steiner, G., 1969 *Language and Silence*. Harmondsworth: Penguin.

Steiner, G., 1972 *Extra-Territorial: Papers on Literature and the Language Revolution*. London: Faber and Faber.

246   *Bibliography*

Steiner, G., 1976 *After Babel*. Oxford: Oxford University Press.
Stephens, R., 1995 *Knight Errant. Memoirs of a Vagabond Actor*. London: Hodder and Stoughton.
Stockwell, P., 2002 *Sociolinguistics*. London: Routledge.
Stubbs, M., 1980 *Language and Literacy: The Sociolinguistics of Reading and Writing*. London: Routledge.
'Strix' 1956 'Posh Lingo' in Mitford ed., pp. 85–93.
Styan, J.L., 1981 *Modern Drama in Theory and Practice. Volume One: Realism and Naturalism*. Cambridge: Cambridge University Press.
Taylor, J.R., 1963 *Anger and After*. Harmondsworth: Penguin.
Theatre Record 1995 Vol. 14.1.
Theatre Record 1999 Vol. 18.1.
Trudgill, P., 1983 *Sociolinguistics*. Harmondsworth: Penguin.
Trudgill, P., ed., 1984 *Applied Sociolinguistics*. London: London Academic Press.
Truss, L., 2003 *Eats, Shoots and Leaves*. London: Profile Books.
Trussler, S., ed., 1981 *New Theatre Voices of the Seventies*. London: Eyre Methuen.
Tynan, K., 1958a 'Ionesco: Man of Destiny?', *Observer*, 22 June.
Tynan, K., 1958b 'Ionesco and the Phantom', *Observer*, 6 July.
Tynan, K., 1958c 'Slamm's Last Knock', *Observer*, 2 November.
Tynan, K., 1961 *Curtains*. London: Longman.
Tynan, K., 1981 'On the Moral Neutrality of Peter Brook', in Trussler ed., 1981, pp. 134–144.
Tynan, K., 1984 *A View of the English Stage 1944–1963*. London: Methuen.
Tynan, K., 1988 *The Life of Kenneth Tynan*. London: Methuen.
Urmson, J. and Ree, J., eds., 1992 *The Concise Encyclopedia of Western Philosophy and Philosophers*. London: Routledge.
Wardle, I., 1978 *The Theatres of George Devine*. London: Johnathan Cape.
Williams, R., 1954 *Drama from Ibsen to Eliot*. London: Chatto and Windus.
Williams, R., 1961 *The Long Revolution*. London: Chatto and Windus.
Williams, R., 1968a 'New English Drama' in Russell Brown ed., 1968, pp. 26–37.
Williams, R., 1968b *Drama from Ibsen to Brecht*. London: Chatto and Windus.
Williams, R., 1972 *Drama in Performance*. Harmondsworth: Penguin.
Williams, R., 1976, rev. 1983 *Keywords: A Vocabulary of Culture and Society*. London: Fontana.
Williams, R., 1977 *Marxism and Literature*. Oxford: Oxford University Press.
Williams, R., 1982 *Culture and Society 1780–1950*. Harmondsworth: Penguin.
Williams, R. and Sierz, A., 2006 'What Kind of England Do We Want? Roy Williams in conversation with Aleks Sierz'. *New Theatre Quarterly* 22.2 (Cambridge: Cambridge University Press).
Wittgenstein, L., 1981 *Tractatus Logico-Philosophicus*. London: Routledge & Kegan Paul, trans. C.K. Ogden.
Willet, J., ed., 1981 *Brecht on Theatre*. London: Eyre Methuen.
Wodak, R., ed., 1990 *Language, Power and Ideology: Studies in Political Discourse*. Amsterdam and Philadelphia: John Benjamins.
Wu, D., 2000 *Making Plays: Interviews with Contemporary British Dramatists and Their Directors*. London: Palgrave Macmillan.
Žižek, S., 1989 *The Sublime Object of Ideology*. London: Verso.

Archival Sources

Production file for *You Won't Always Be on Top*, Theatre Royal, Stratford, 1957, V&A Theatre & Performance collection.

Production file for *Fings Ain't Wot They Used T'be*, Theatre Royal, Stratford, 1959, V&A Theatre & Performance collection.

Production file for *Sparrers Can't Sing*, Theatre Royal, Stratford, 1960, V&A Theatre & Performance collection.

Lord Chamberlain's Correspondence for *Fings Ain't Wot They Used T'be*, LCP Corr. 1958/1359, British Library.

Lord Chamberlain's Correspondence for *A Night to Make the Angels Weep*, LCP Corr. 1964/4247, British Library.

Lord Chamberlain's Correspondence for *The Mighty Reservoy*, LCP Corr. 1964/4421, British Library.

Production file for *The Mighty Reservoy*, Victoria Theatre, Newcastle Under Lyme, 1964, V&A Theatre & Performance collection.

Production file for *The Arbor*, Royal Court Theatre, 1980, V&A Theatre & Performance collection.

Production file for *The Changing Room*, Royal Court Theatre, London, 1971, V&A Theatre & Performance collection.

Production file for *Educating Rita*, [Donmar] Warehouse Theatre, London, 1980, V&A Theatre & Performance collection.

Biographical File, Caryl Churchill, V&A Theatre & Performance collection.

Index